10⁻
236

DANGEROUS DAN TUCKER

DANGEROUS DAN TUCKER

NEW MEXICO'S DEADLY LAWMAN

By

BOB ALEXANDER

High-Lonesome Books
Silver City, New Mexico

ISBN #0-944383-52-1 softcover
ISBN #0-944383-53-X hardcover

Library of Congress Control Number: 2001088287

First Edition May 2001

High-Lonesome Books
P.O. Box 878
Silver City, NM 88062

Respectfully dedicated to the memory

of

Lou Blachly, Pat Humble, Dan Rose

and

their passion for preserving the past.

TABLE OF CONTENTS

Preface & Acknowledgments 1

Introduction 4

Chapter 1   "fearless as a man ever gets to be" 6

Chapter 2   "stopped by a ball from Tucker's pistol" 21

Chapter 3   "hard faced and battle scarred" 35

Chapter 4   "I guess he done a good job killin' him" 47

Chapter 5   "keeps that town free of rough characters" 70

Chapter 6   "peacefully sleeps beneath the daisies" 83

Chapter 7   "put the clamps on Deming" 92

Chapter 8   "even such a determined officer as Tucker" 114

Chapter 9   "jerked to Jesus" 124

Chapter 10   "no arms except six-shooters" 136

Chapter 11   "the two greatest civilizers: Dan Tucker and his shotgun" ..149

Chapter 12   "in every village and on every train" 160

Appendix A   Photographs and Map 170

Bibliography 178

Index 186

PREFACE & ACKNOWLEDGMENTS

Whether this volume qualifies as biography the author is not certain. Although a great deal was learned about Dan Tucker during the research phase of the investigation, there still remain many unanswered questions, especially pertaining to his life prior to the sojourn in the New Mexico Territory. However, of the thirteen years the intractable Dan Tucker spent as a New Mexico territorial lawman and man-killer there is no shortage of soundly authenticated materials. And that is exactly what this discourse purports to be—the story of Dan Tucker's life in New Mexico. For anyone interested in frontier law enforcement or straightforward portrayals of southwestern gunmen it is a story deserving consideration.

Nothing extensive has been written of Dan Tucker prior to this volume. However, few would be the number of Western history professionals, aficionados, or gunfighter buffs who have not already seen his name in print, for he is favorably mentioned in a number of the frontier classics. Predictably, many readers will discover that while they already possess a reasonable understanding of a particular historic event, they have little knowledge of the significant role sometimes played by Dan Tucker. Hopefully the reader will be pleasantly surprised to discover another nineteenth-century personality worthy of recognition. Even from the lofty perspective of historic overview it is readily determinable that Dan Tucker made a noteworthy contribution to taming a portion of the frontier Southwest. And from the somewhat less scholarly approach, its just plain fascinating to explore from afar the hair-raising escapades of early gunmen—outlaw or lawman. Dan Tucker, during the time he lived, was in fact a southwestern legend and much feared peace officer, and that may offer a degree of prodding intrigue to readers chiefly familiar with gunfighters who owe their reputations to twentieth century television script-writers and movie producers. Dan Tucker was the *genuine* article!

Dan Tucker lived at the time and at a place which would become the focal point for numerous historians and journalists, and their body of work is remarkable indeed. In telling the story of Dan Tucker it will not be necessary to repeat renditions of significant and thrilling happenings which swirled about the formidable deputy, but which cannot be either directly or indirectly tied to his remarkable narrative. As an example, it would be ludicrous to stray from the Dan Tucker story and recount the history of the Mimbres Apaches and Victorio's New Mexico raids into Dan Tucker's bailiwick, the subsequent cat and mouse martial strategy, eventually ending the treatise with a description of the renowned warrior's death at the hands of beleaguered Mexican soldiers. Suffice to say, portions of southwestern history have already been more than

1

competently recorded and Dan Tucker's story can be faithfully reviewed without trampling over well-worn historic ground. In other cases, however, it will be necessary to briefly mention background material relating to a particular crime, set the geographical stage, or quickly elaborate with a few details regarding particular personalities which comprise this cast of border-country players. Simply stated, this is Dan Tucker's story, nothing more.

The law enforcement life of dangerous Dan Tucker warrants inclusion on the list reserved for frontier figures of the man-killing variety, but it is a story that would never have materialized without the work and assistance of others, and they must be properly recognized.

The twenty-first century reader is fortunate to have readily accessible primary source volumes actually penned by those who were present on the Western scene, and as such, eye-witnesses to a plethora of thrilling historic episodes. Correspondingly, interested students of the frontier Southwest are privy to journalistic riches written from the secondary perspective. Those frontier spirits who actually lived the life and "walked the walk," as well as journalists and historians who later offered requisite organization, methodical analysis, and carefully crafted conclusions have my utmost admiration and respect.

Three of those individuals merit particular mention, especially in the context of telling Dan Tucker's story. From the secondary viewpoint Dan Rose would be labeled an "old-timer." During Rose's childhood he actually knew Dan Tucker, made personal observations, and on at least one well-documented occasion watched the deputy in action. Thankfully, in the early part of the twentieth-century Dan Rose put to paper many of his remembrances of life in frontier New Mexico. At some point, Lou Blachly recognized a wealth of historic information was quickly becoming forever lost, and by the middle of the twentieth-century was tirelessly hammering out interviews with surviving members of generations past. His transcripts and recordings number into the hundreds, several of which make particular reference to the subject of this story, and we should be truly thankful for his foresight in permanently securing these gems of historic wealth. Lastly, Pat Humble, through public speaking engagements to civic groups, Westerners affiliates, archeological societies, and other enthralled audiences in the 1980's, breathed life into a generally overlooked Dan Tucker. Pat Humble resurrected Tucker from musty and forgotten pages and made him once again real.

As well, Dan Tucker's story could not have been narrated absent the outstanding contributions made by Terry Humble of Bayard, New Mexico. He graciously shared invaluable historic intelligence from his late father's collection, but more importantly Terry accepted the challenge to delve deep into the jumble of courthouse records and newspaper archives when a question arose that demanded a factual answer. Tapping into his expertise and knowledge of Grant County history is the lifeline that sustained the Dan Tucker project. Terry's commitment to search for unvarnished truth is exceptional. The quality of his research is matchless and the value of his friendship is irreplaceable

Susan Berry, Director, Silver City Museum gave of her time during several personal interviews. A multitude of writers are beneficiaries of Susan's encyclopedic reservoir of historic treasures. This story remains in debt to her charitable assistance and cordial encouragement.

A special thanks must also be extended to Cookie Stolpe, Miller Library, Western New Mexico University at Silver City. It was always a pleasant surprise to open the mail and receive an unexpected historic tidbit, accompanied by the casual notation, "Thought this may be of interest." Her enthusiastic professionalism is worthy of especial commendation.

The following persons either individually or collectively made significant contribution to telling the Dan Tucker story, and their efforts are sincerely appreciated.

Pete Crum, Silver City Library, Silver City; Carolyn Autry, Indiana Historical Society, Indianapolis; Shelly Kelly, Rosenberg Library, Galveston; Barbara Dey, Colorado Historical Society, Denver; Donaly Brice, Texas State Library and Archives Commission, Austin; Nancy Brown, Zimmerman Library—Center for Southwest Research, University of New Mexico, Albuquerque; Robert J. Torrez, New Mexico State Records Center and Archives, Santa Fe; Rose Byrne and Scott Denlinger, Arizona Historical Society, Tucson; Dee Harris, Wichita Public Library, Wichita; Christine Rhodes, Cochise County Recorder, Bisbee; Colleen Crowlie, Cochise County Library District, Bisbee; Judy Harris, Benson Public Library, Benson; Art Roman, Deming Luna Mimbres Museum, Deming; Claudia Rivers, Texas Western—University of Texas at El Paso, El Paso; Dick Staley El Paso Public Library, El Paso; Wayne B. Humphrey, Deming; Nannette Bricker-Barrett, San Bernardino County Library, San Bernardino; Sue Payne, California Room, San Bernardino Public Library, San Bernardino; The Center for American History, University of Texas, Austin; and the entire staff of the Hillsboro Public Library, Hillsboro, Texas.

Lastly, much thanks must go to Lenora Jill Adams at Navarro College. Her extraordinary computer skills and patience made this project a technical reality.

Just when historians and readers believe there is nothing left of significance to inquire into or say about gunmen, lawmen, and outlaws in the American West, along comes a writer with a magnitude of competence and research ability such as Bob Alexander. Alexander is extraordinary in part because he never takes anything for granted. He never stops looking and evaluating until the last page is turned, until the last fact has been examined.

To substantiate the Tucker biography and build his case, Alexander visited the gunfighter proving ground of the Southwest, specifically the remote deserts and mountains of New Mexico, the blistering cauldron where so many Wild West gunmen made their reputations. Alexander went there specifically in pursuit of knowledge concerning a remarkable individual, a one David Tucker, born in Canada, raised in Indiana, and who by way of Colorado reached his zenith in the New Mexico highlands. There he became Dan Tucker, a lawman whose bravery and exploits set the standards for law enforcement officers ever-after.

Tucker was not a showman gunfighter. Unlike most Hollywood gunmen, Tucker was as handy and deadly with a shotgun as with a six-shooter. He used whatever the situation demanded, and in doing so he never stepped backwards. In Silver City, New Mexico, Tucker initially became a deputy serving under Harvey Whitehill, a sheriff whose fame rests in part on being the first lawman to arrest Billy the Kid. And Billy the Kid was fortunate that he never encountered Dan Tucker.

After a few shooting episodes in New Mexico, Tucker in 1877 led what became known as the Silver City Volunteers (often called the Silver City Rangers) into West Texas for suppression of the El Paso Salt War. It seems strange that desperate men would die over salt, but salt had its value not only on the table, but in the mines.

Most of the Salt War action occurred fifteen to thirty miles southeast of El Paso, Texas, in obscure adobe villages called San Elizario, Socorro and Ysleta. This rangy group of Silver City mercenaries stopped the War practically in its tracks, primarily by shedding copious amounts of unnecessary blood. Tucker, who was ostensibly in charge, seems on occasion to have lost control of processes he helped set in motion. Alexander states that Tucker should "not escape historic admonishment" for his role in the Salt War bloodshed.

Tucker returned to Silver City to become a city marshal as well as a deputy Sheriff, and over the next few years he held several other law enforcement offices, including deputy United States Marshal. While Tucker was ordinarily not the killer type, and doesn't seem to have envied others who were, nevertheless his long New Mexico tenure suggests that at least eight men fell before his flaming six-shooter or deadly shotgun. Still, in making evaluations of his blood-letting ability, one can build a good case for an even higher body count, especially if one figures in the fact that certain individuals seemed to drop off the face of the earth when Tucker set out in pursuit. All of this leads to speculation regarding what really might have happened to them. Tucker himself rarely commented.

Overall, Tucker was a better lawman, and more dangerous, than such redoubtable, high-profile figures as Wyatt Earp and Wild Bill Hickok. Yet he is practically unheard of today largely because he lacked the ability or the need to exploit himself. Somehow Tucker slipped between the pages of Wild West history, a deserving lawman but having no literary champion such as Ash Upson and Walter Noble Burns, who brought fame to Pat Garrett and Billy the Kid, or Stuart Lake, who lionized Wyatt Earp, or Ned Buntline with Buffalo Bill, or *Harpers New Monthly Magazine* with Wild Bill Hickok. And unlike John Wesley Hardin, Tucker never considered writing his own autobiography.

Dangerous Dan Tucker therefore is a story that needed to be told by an author who needed to tell it. Bob Alexander himself toted a badge for thirty-five years as an agent for the U.S. Treasury Department and as a city detective in Garland, Texas. As a sleuth himself he understood the processes of investigation, arrest, trial and punishment. He knew what it was like to lay his life on the line. His own background prepared him not only for tedious research, but for recognizing in Dangerous Dan Tucker the qualities that make up a good lawman: courage, perseverance, diligence, dedication, and the ability to make the right decision when the right decision had to be made.

Alexander spent months in New Mexico reading old letters, digging through old newspaper files, carefully checking court and census records, talking with the descendants of people who might have known Tucker, comparing each account against other chronicles, and then going back over everything again, in the process piecing together a compelling story.

If Bob Alexander is anything, he is a tough, diligent researcher. And with this biography, he has also proven himself an admirable writer.

With luck we will see more of his work.

Leon C. Metz
El Paso, Texas

1

"FEARLESS AS A MAN EVER GETS TO BE"

John Wesley Hardin, admired "pluck, push and virtue" wherever he found it.[1] Hardin would have liked Dan Tucker. Tucker had "pluck!" Unfortunately, at least for later day writers who might wish to pair the two shootist in a sensational but imaginary duel, the gunmen probably never met. It is, however, permissible to presume they knew of each other's exploits. Hardin, contemplating his autobiography, was already doing hard time at Huntsville with the Texas prison system while Tucker was repeatedly making news in the raw and blustery Southwest.[2]

Both Hardin and Tucker killed men. Why then is John Wesley Hardin considered an implicit icon—one of the premier examples of the western gunfighter—while Dan Tucker remains virtually unknown in general twentieth-century histories of the era? Perhaps the phenomena can be explained by Tucker's reluctance to engage in self-promotion, coupled with the fact many of his sizzling escapades were geographically confined, and additionally by a realization that America's fascination with frontier gunmen had not yet reached zenith during the time he lived.

Today, relatively few are aware of Tucker's exciting life and dangerous encounters. However, his contemporaries and many wanna-be badmen, either stood in awe of Tucker's presence, or avoided his heavy-handed law enforcement approach. Some who failed to take note suffered fatal consequences. Tucker's skill with firearms and his willingness to resort to their use was lauded *back in the states*.[3] One who knew Tucker intimately and watched him in action remarked, "he wasn't afraid of nothing."[4] Another characterized Tucker as "fearless as a man ever gets to be."[5] At least one early resident thought Tucker, "the deadliest of all the deputy sheriffs who had ever served Grant County."[6] And yet another report summed up Tucker's enforcement ability and style: "He was the one 'dead game hombre' that was needed at that time, for he was not afraid to kill."[7] Although generally overlooked by modern historians, noted author Robert DeArment did strive to rescue Dan from obscurity in a 1991 article in which he credited Tucker as a man of "demonstrated leather-slapping ability...the top gun in a very tough district."[8]

A general theme becomes apparent as the Tucker chronology uncoils. Dan Tucker, usually working alone, becomes embroiled time and time again in desperate situations, some possibly of his own doing; but nevertheless, circumstances requiring decisive, determined, and

6

often violent measures. Some of the thrilling scenarios involving Tucker have been written about extensively, although oftentimes his particular participation has been innocently overlooked. In other instances, his taking part in eruptions of violence became local folklore, but never captured the attention of dime-novelists who were tilted toward melodrama, and acutely intent on capturing profit from a national audience.

If myths are to be made, and perpetuated, about such a disputable and inflated character as Wyatt Earp, it seems only fair to shine the historic spotlight on someone who by all accounts was considered the "real deal" when it came to bold enforcement tactics and resolute encounters. As this authentic lawman's story progresses, it is easy to discern that Dan Tucker was no paragon of idealistic virtue, but he never claimed to be! Evidence readily indicates he simply got the job done, resorting to six-shooter violence when necessary, and sometimes when it wasn't.

Historian Jack Burrows reveals it is not necessarily all to one's credit to have killed someone.[9] Nonetheless, counting notches carved in six-shooter handles seems to be how frontier lawmen are judged by twentieth-century journalists. Adding his two-cents, another writer summarizes, "In the case of the gunfighter, myth and legend have always had an incestuous relationship with fact and reality."[10] Understandably, recording the routine comings and goings of hard working frontier folk, regardless of their stabilizing societal contributions, are generally forced from historic pages by shattering gunshots and images of bleeding hardcases exiting the scene with a final spasmodic kick. When one frontier editor lamented, "Too bad the normal life of a community has no news value," even he underestimated a modern-era mania for the morosely titillating.[11]

In his prominent study and extensive research of frontier gunmen, *Encyclopedia of Western Gun-Fighters*, writer Bill O'Neal notes the inescapable arbitrariness in tagging a man with the sobriquet, "gun-fighter." Inclusion on the author's list was based on at least two *verifiable* shoot-outs, coupled with a vocation that necessitated the carrying of firearms. Accordingly, O'Neal chose not to classify the shootings, but included "encounters in which men fired at other men—spontaneously, from ambush or hiding, or face to face." And simply concludes, "They shot people and were shot themselves."[12] From his scholarly and statistical method a reasonably accurate ranking of frontier gunfighters can be extracted.

Illustrative of just how sadly dime-novelists, a few mendacious historians, and Hollywood scriptwriters have tricked the general public is artfully exposed by O'Neal's encyclopedic examination. Topping the list of genuine shootists are "Deacon" Jim Miller and John Wesley "Little Arkansas" Hardin, with twelve and eleven killings respectively;

two names which are familiar only to the more serious students of Western history. At the bottom of the list, with a zero marked on their scorecards, are the erroneously romanticized, but certainly better known, Wyatt Earp and Harry "Sundance Kid" Longbaugh.[13] Although usually ignored in modern writings, Dan Tucker's name can be inserted between those usually characterized as cold-blooded psychotic killers, and the manufactured heroes of movie and television fame.

Speaking of the frontier gunfighter O'Neal theorizes, "...idealists may feel that a gunfighter who killed few men during his career was an expert and generous shot, a more practical gauge of his skill is how many deaths he caused."[14] Unquestionably, counting corpses is the popular approach most used in appraising the effectiveness of the singular shootist; however, total reliance on this reckoning is intrinsically flawed. From a systematic perspective, once a shooter let the hammer drop his deed demanded consequence, but an antagonist's death in some situations may not have been the principal objective. During many bullet-spitting confrontations, especially from a defensive posture, the desired goal was simply to forcefully stop an adversary from doing something; if he died, so be it! So then, in taking true measure of the gun-carrying man, it appears more apropos to determine whether he would stand firmly anchored during a thundering storm, or seek safe passage through the nearest portal. Dan Tucker's bearings were fixed; he'd be damned before he'd cut and run from anybody!

If funerals are to be the benchmark for success, Dan Tucker's standing on the list of frontier gunfighters will prove rather high, and possibly somewhat surprising, but the final tally should be made toward the end of his story, not the beginning.

Dan Thrapp notes that little is known about the origins or endings of Tucker's life.[15] Compounding the problem and demanding cautious clarification is the fact that "Dan" was a nickname rather than a given name. Tucker's proper first name was David.[16] Susan Berry, Director of the Silver City Museum, first brought this information to the author's attention. Newspaper advertisements in the Grant County *Herald*, and other references to a Tucker business enterprise at the Point of Rocks on the Jornada del Muerto, prior to his alighting in Silver City, and the canvass of census records, newspapers, and courthouse documents after his Silver City debut, clearly reveal the man's real name was David Tucker.[17]

Where did the nickname originate? There is no conclusive evidence, but worthy of consideration would be the folk song "Old Dan Tucker" composed by Dan Emmett, which was written for, and introduced in a 1843 minstrel show, well before Tucker was born.[18] Lyrics such as, "*Old Dan Tucker was a mighty man, Washed his face in a frying pan, Combed his hair with a wagon wheel,*" etc. would have been just the ticket for playfully joshing the local lawman. In fact, on occasion regional newspapers did use the handle "Old Dan Tucker" when mentioning the Territorial gendarme.[19] For whatever reason, and regardless of where it originated, the nickname stuck. Apparently Tucker didn't mind. Few would have risked his wrath over a reference made in jest—if he had cared! Although generally well liked, nearly everyone knew, the prudent course was not to get too "fresh" with Dan.

In an effort not to offer further confusion, and to comply with generally accepted tradition, in this narrative the familiar first name "Dan" will be used exclusively. Although official documents usually refer to his true first name, most press accounts, local old-timer remembrances, and volumes of other primary and secondary source materials simply make reference to Dan Tucker.

The information is indeed sketchy, and in part based on census information, but it appears Tucker was born in Canada in 1849, raised in Indiana, and then migrated to Colorado when a young man in his mid-twenties.[20] From the purely historical perspective, it appears less than adequate to simply skip over Dan Tucker's childhood, but journalistic truthfulness now and again demands difficult choices. Also, to date no photograph of Dan Tucker has surfaced. Should the project of telling Tucker's story have been abandoned because of a paucity of early-life records or photographs? Assuredly not! Especially since there is a rich gold mine of historic details relating to Tucker's law enforcement life experiences in New Mexico Territory.

Suffice to say, the Indiana Historical Society put forth a sterling effort, and yes, some young Tuckers named David (and Daniel) can be identified through a review of admittedly incomplete census records, but none can be conclusively branded as the subject of this investigation.[21] Unquestionably it would be nice to know more of Tucker's beginnings, but not if the cost is wishful supposition.

Since data on Dan Tucker's geographical origins and just who his ancestors were is amazingly sparse, it is tempting to consider the possibility of his having used an assumed name in New Mexico, which was certainly not uncommon for the place and time. There are numerous accounts of both good and bad men making a western migration leaving one identity and the past behind, and for whatever reason embarking on a "fresh start" in a new land. There is no empirical evidence to indicate such was the case regarding Dan Tucker, but local gossip could be construed to have offered a possible motive.

Reportedly, at the age of twenty-five, he killed a black man in Colorado, and seeking refuge in a more healthful clime traveled to New Mexico Territory.[22] The probable source for this assertion is Dan Rose, early Silver City resident and chronicler of local history, but even he cautiously acknowledges the story was classified as hearsay. Rose who actually knew Dan Tucker, says "Rumor had it that he 'got his man' in Colorado."[23] As of yet, the rumor has not been confirmed, but by the same token, neither has it been refuted. Examination of the *Crime: Murder* file maintained by the Colorado Historical Society failed to produce a listing for Dan Tucker, nor does his name appear in the 1870 U. S. Census for Colorado, but this information in and of itself is not conclusive evidence that Tucker never was a Colorado resident, or involved in some serious altercation while there.[24] Dan Tucker's life prior to his arrival on the New Mexico stage for the most part remains a mystery.

Generally the impression is given that Tucker came straight to Silver City after leaving Colorado, and established residence in 1875. This is not correct. Although he may have visited Silver City as early as 1875, the stay was of short duration. The best information thus far developed indicates Dan Tucker saddled up and rode farther east, leasing Adolph Lea's old stage station on the Jornada del Muerto at a site known as the Point of Rocks, north of present day Las Cruces, New Mexico.[25]

Lea, born at sea to migrating German parents, and with later service in the United States Army's 1st Dragoons, Company H., had seemingly become a timeless fixture in New Mexico Territory's Mesilla Valley. Adolph Lea was Trinidad, New Mexico's founding father, but the site located on the southeastern corner of the Fort Selden military reservation would later become known to history as Leasburg, and a iniquitous town it proved to be.[26]

Named after Colonel Henry R. Selden, a West Pointer who had seen service in both the Mexican and Civil Wars, Fort Selden was established in 1865 for the express purpose of protecting north-south travel across the waterless Jornada del Muerto, and east-west traffic bound for or returning from Arizona and California.[27] From its inception, although strategically located for travelers, Fort Selden was too far removed from the operating bases of hostile Apaches, and consequently the usual complement of two companies spent more time policing the parade ground, languishing in the ten-bed hospital, loitering around the storehouse, inhaling pleasing aromas from the post bakery, or peering through guard house bars, than they did fighting Indians.[28] Inactive soldiers naturally drifted to Leasburg.

Curiously, as pointed out by Price, Adolph Lea retained a reasonably respectable reputation with military hierarchy, but the town itself was of wicked repute. As would be expected, there were saloons, gamblers, and prostitutes, but somewhat surprising is a signal fact—more soldiers lost their lives amidst drinking, betting, and whoring at Leasburg, than they did during Fort Selden's entire military combat history.[29] A military historian of the area reported, "Sometimes the soldiers fought with the settlers or with each other after which they often spent time in the guardhouse. As a result of such adventures, civilians killed at least seven Selden soldiers within the first year and a half of the fort's existence."[30]

One of the more notorious rows between citizens and soldiers occurred during the early morning hours of January 1, 1877, twenty-five miles to the south at Las Cruces, when John Kinney and some of his friends lost a battle of fisticuffs with 8th Cavalry enlisted men. Suffering bruises, abrasions, and bloody noses, Kinney's crowd, joined by border scoundrels Jessie Evans, Jim McDaniels, and Charles "Pony Diehl" Ray, slipped back to the New Years Eve dance, stationed themselves outside, and on signal, shot through the windows into the crowd of promenading celebrants, killing two soldiers and a civilian.[31] A rough crowd indeed!

As will soon be depicted, Dan Tucker seemed to fit right in with an element of frontier folk popularly known as the "sporting crowd."

Lea had earlier established a stage station on the Jornada, at a place known as the Point of Rocks, but after he removed from the location and obtained the position of Post Trader at Fort Selden he truly discovered financial success. Lea stocked a large general store.[32] "At his store the soldiers could purchase such luxury items as canned oysters and lobster, English dairy cheese, spices, canned fruit, and Cashmere Bouquet soap."[33] Additionally, Lea constructed a billiard hall and a seventeen room hotel.[34] At some point, Lea's old stage station was rented to a recently arrived New Mexican. Dan Tucker advertised:

Lea's Station

Having leased the above place on the Jornado del Muerto, on the road leading from El Paso, Texas, to Santa Fe, New Mexico, about twenty-five miles north of Fort Selden, I announce the fact that at all times I am prepared to furnish wayfarers with hay, grain, water and wood at reasonable rates.

DAVID TUCKER[35]

Probably not much to Lea's surprise, but perhaps a serious deflation to Tucker's dreams of an entrepreneurial empire, the young Canadian was again forced to decide on a change of address. Jack Martin, who would become known as "King of the Jornada" had successfully dug a deep water well, and over a period of time came to dominate business in the area.[36] "The water supply proved dependable. Jack Martin quickly developed his 'find' into an oasis in the desert for the many travelers going up and down the Camino Real…He built a hotel because travel by horse, buggy, and wagon was still slow and tiring, and ran his desert oasis with help from his wife and their three children. Soon a stage coach station opened at Martin's Well, as did an Army forage station and post office."[37] Tucker's business experiment was a financial flop.[38] Adolph Lea placed an advertisement in the Grant County *Herald* offering to sell or exchange his station for a "farm on the Gila," particularly noting that all territorial and county taxes had been paid.[39] Tucker needed work!

Supposition would indicate Tucker re-located to Silver City, New Mexico Territory at the invitation of Grant County Sheriff Harvey Howard Whitehill. Unsupported *supposition* in a historic context is of little value. Known facts reveal Whitehill, a Union Army veteran, had prospected in Colorado at Cherry Creek, Leadville, and Russell Gulch.[40] Politically active and a staunch Democrat, Whitehill had served as sergeant-at-arms in the first Colorado Territorial Legislature.[41] Later, after a five-year stay at Elizabethtown, New Mexico Territory, Whitehill and his wife Harriet moved southwest in 1870, settling in Silver City. Wayne Whitehill, one of Harvey's sons, was the first Anglo child born in the the town.[42] Papa Whitehill was appointed county coroner, and later was named Grant County Sheriff when the incumbent Charles McIntosh failed to return from a trip to Mexico, some say accompanied by a pot-full of county funds![43] Whitehill was later elected Sheriff.[44]

Sheriff Whitehill presided over an extensive chunk of New Mexico Territorial real estate. Created in 1868, located in the heart of Apache country taking up the southwestern corner of New Mexico Territory, and adjacent to the troublesome eastern Arizona line, Grant County was 7,000 square miles of rugged terrain, with budding mining camps and seemingly measureless open cattle ranges. Along a primary east/west travel route, and a shared international boundary with Mexico, it must have seemed to the newly appointed sheriff that he had landed slap-dab in the middle of some giant geographical conspiracy, designed to impede his conscientious imposition of the law.[45] Sheriff Harvey Whitehill had his hands full!

At the same time Dan Tucker was striving to capture a few dollars from some dehydrated travelers at his "rented" ranch on the Jornada, influential and independent Grant County citizens were aggressively instigating a secessionist movement to remove themselves from New Mexico Territorial rule, and transfer title to their county's rich mineral and agricultural assets to Arizona Territory. "The annexationist spelled out their dissatisfaction in clear terms. They considered the Territory of New Mexico badly governed, citing the fact that the legislature was controlled by the Santa Fe Ring, which was concerned with its own selfish interest. Considering the 'peculiar temper' and habits of the native New Mexicans, they saw no hope of relief in the near future. Furthermore, the laws of New Mexico were unsuited to their needs as a mining community, while those of Arizona, whose principal pursuit was also mining, were better adapted to the exigencies of this industry. As a county they had been denied equal representation and therefore had little or no voice in the enactment of laws so necessary to their welfare."[46] Ultimately the attempt proved abortive, but not completely without success, because Grant County gained new respect and prestige which prepared Silver City for its leadership role in furtherance of "local self-government, civic pride, and quality public education in the Southwest."[47] Grant County, more particularly Silver City, had brazenly shaped its future.

Although Harvey Whitehill led a truly exciting life, punctuated by spine-tingling adventures, complex criminal investigations, and civic contributions through various stints in elected offices, he is best remembered in twentieth-century writings as the first lawman to arrest the ill-famed "Billy the Kid." Young Billy, who had moved with his brother, mother, and stepfather to Silver City, had stolen several pounds of butter from Abel L. Webb, and was later arrested by Sheriff Whitehill, who released the youth on a pledge of future "good behavior."[48] Billy's good fortune in the first case was spoiled by his actions in the second. George "Sombrero Jack" Schaefer stole two six-shooters and some clothing from local Chinese laundryman, Charlie Sun. Afterward he solicited Billy's aid in secreting the stolen items which were valued between $150.00 and $200.00, a substantial sum at the time. Whitehill was furnished clues as to the suspects identity, and arrested Billy, while "Sombrero Jack" hightailed it just ahead of the law, leaving his after the fact accessory literally "holding the bag." The sheriff placed slender Billy in the local jail, but was soon astonished to learn the outlaw with "dancing eyes," had skinnied up the chimney, escaped, and ridden off into history.[49]

Did Dan Tucker know Sheriff Whitehill while both were in Colorado? Could a personal relationship have existed even before then? One newspaper account indicated Whitehill had operated a "old wood-burning locomotive" for the B & O railroad between Cincinnati and Indianapolis, while another report indicates Tucker was a native of Indiana.[50]

After Tucker's name dropped from Lea's Station advertisements in the Grant County *Herald*, there is a short stretch of time—the first half of 1877—before his trail is again detected. Interestingly, a recent search through an old storage shed produced a handwritten notation by late southwestern New Mexico researcher Pat Humble, which may offer a clue as to Dan Tucker's whereabouts. With emphasis added, the note simply says, "Dan Tucker *evidently* came to Silver City in 1877 from Point of Rocks and worked first at the Elephant Corral, about behind where Silver City Savings & Loan is now, but facing Main Street. Had a big Elephant painted on the wall. Life Size. Harry Carvil wrote much later that he should have stayed there, that a lot of men would have still been alive."[51] Certainly, if true, this type of employment paralleled Tucker's failed venture on the Jornada. But with an adventurous spirit, young Dan Tucker hungered for work more thrilling than saddling horses, mending harness, and shoveling manure.

Did Sheriff Whitehill recruit young Dan Tucker because he needed to fill a deputy position, or did Dan simply ask for a job? The answer remains elusive, but of little real importance. Whether they were friends prior to Tucker's arrival in Silver City for the time will remain a puzzle, but the record corroborates unmistakable facts—Sheriff Harvey Howard Whitehill deputized young Dan Tucker, and the two maintained mutual loyalty throughout their lifetimes.

Tucker left Silver City on May 28, 1877 in pursuit of two Mexicans who had stolen five horses from the herd of local resident, Richard Howlett. Tucker trailed the rustlers to Ascension, Mexico, but there the tracks disappeared, blotted out by the hoof-prints of everyday traffic. Dan Tucker made inquiries, and questioned villagers to no avail, but this did not seem "strange to those who are aware of the visual and moral blindness of Mexicans of the Republic where property stolen from the U. S. has been run across the line and is enquired (sic) for by *Gringos*."[52] After a fruitless search, Dan Tucker located the town's *Presidente*, offered a reward of $125 for recovery of the property, and arrests of the violators. Dan Tucker returned home—empty-handed.

Although Tucker's official status was not mentioned in the particular article, the same edition of the Grant County *Herald* carries an unrelated story which references Dan Tucker as being a Grant County Deputy Sheriff and the Road Superintendent for Precinct 3.[53] Technically, Dan Tucker held the position of Chief Deputy, and on occasion he is so mentioned, but in the overall crime fighting picture it was more a honorary title than indication of administrative finesse, although he did act as sheriff in Whitehill's absence from time to time.[54] While he may have indeed been the sheriff's number two man, Dan Tucker in point of fact was a legitimate working deputy.

Territorial period law enforcement historian Larry Ball advises, "The sheriff looked for certain qualifications in a deputy. The candidate for a deputyship had to be a person of known bravery, possess proficiency with guns, be able to ride horseback for long periods, and be familiar with the countryside."[55] Dan Tucker met these criteria. Sheriff Harvey Whitehill had made a good choice. Whitehill, like many other sheriffs of the time, because of tax collecting and administrative duties, most of the time went about his usual day to day business unarmed. And like many other sheriffs, he preferred to hire others to "go heeled," keep the peace, and arrest miscreant lawbreakers.[56] With specificity DeArment declares, "Whitehill was not a gunman himself, but he employed one of the best in Dan Tucker."[57]

From the best evidence thus far developed, Dan Tucker's physical appearance did not fit the generally accepted imaginary profile of the statuesque and stalwart "long arm of the law." "He was about 5 feet, 7 inches tall, slim built, blue eyes and light hair, and of a shy and retiring disposition."[58] Referring to his demeanor, another remarked Tucker was,

"...a very courteous, compliant man, a pleasant talker, and the last man I verily believe, that I would have singled out of a crowd, as a gun player."[59] Continuing characterizations seem consistent, "quiet in speech and never boasting," and a man with "cool unflinching eyes" was the phraseology adopted by one writer who had actually known him.[60] DeArment matter-of-factually characterized Tucker as a "soft-spoken young man," and "rumors were already afloat that the new county officer was a dangerous man, indeed."[61] And, an old-timer who knew him simply remarked, "he was a nice man...He wasn't quarrelsome, just a nice even tempered man."[62] Clearly, his appearance could prove dangerously deceptive! One area resident said of the appointment, "Dan Tucker was appointed Deputy sheriff and at once began to show what kind of stuff he was made of. Hitherto the bad element had 'painted the town red,' and 'shot it up,' at their own sweet will, but when Tucker took charge it was not quite such an easy job, especially after he had given the coroner two or three siftings."[63]

NOTES AND SOURCES

1. El Paso *Daily Times*, 05-04-1895. As a part of this letter written to the El Paso newspaper, Hardin went on to explain those characteristics he didn't admire, "Yet I contempt and despise a coward and assassin of character, whether he be a reporter, a journalist or a gambler."

2. Metz, Leon. *John Wesley Hardin—Dark Angel of Death*. P. 185-208.

3. Wichita *Daily Eagle*, 10-11-1884. This contemporary newspaper report places Dan Tucker in the class of gunslingers as Billy the Kid, Pat Garrett, and Curly Bill Brocious. The significance of this contemporary account is that it serves as indication of Dan Tucker's actual reputation during the time he was serving as a New Mexico Territory lawman, and was not made well after the turn of the century when so many of the tall-tales were concocted for the commercial marketplace.

4. Remarks of Wayne Whitehill, son of Grant County New Mexico Sheriff Harvey Whitehill. Courtesy, Zimmerman Library—Center for Southwest Research. University of New Mexico. Albuquerque. Pioneers Foundation interview. Transcript No. 503. Edited by Lou Blachly. Hereafter cited as Pioneers Foundation Interviews.

5. Silver City *Enterprise*, 09-05-1902.

6. Letter from O. W. Williams to J. C. Williams, 12-15-1924. Courtesy, The Center for American History. University of Texas. Austin.

7. Nelson, Susan and Ed., *Silver City Book I, Wild and Woolly Days*, P. 19. Hereafter cited as Nelson. Also see Silver City *Independent*, 06-12-1917 for the complete article from which the cited quotation was taken.

8. DeArment, R. K., "Deadly Deputy," *True West*. November 1991. P. 14. Hereafter cited as DeArment. This account is one of the few twentieth-century attempts to tell the Tucker story. The author recognized the importance of Tucker's contribution to the history of Grant County, New Mexico in particular and to a circumspect understanding of frontier law enforcement in general. Bob

L'Aloge's *Riders Along the Rio Grande* does indeed contain a chapter entitled
"Old Dan Tucker," but it is merely a rehash of information in DeArment's
article. Curiously, L'Aloge accuses Tucker of being an "outlaw turned sheriff,"
but not surprisingly, he offers no documentation to sustain the allegation.

9. Burrows, Jack., *John Ringo: The Gunfighter Who Never* Was. P. 17.
Hereafter cited as Burrows. Although specifically speaking of Wyatt Earp,
"There is no demonstrable evidence that he had ever killed anyone (which is all
to his credit) before coming to Tombstone." The author rightfully shunts the
larger questions to readers. Why is there such fascination with killing? Can a
frontier lawman's career be judged only by the number of cemetery plots he
filled? Should failure to take a life erase a name from the historic page?

10. Horan, James D., *The Gunfighters*. P. 6.

11. Clum, Woodworth., *Apache Agent—The Story of John P. Clum*. P. 269.
Also see, *Apache Days & Tombstone Nights—John Clum's Autobiography*, John
Clum, edited by Neil B. Carmony. Hereafter cited as Clum for text and Carmony
for annotations. Clum admits to his own tendency toward journalistic theatrics,
"There is no worldwide news in a church social or an amateur theatrical. The
headlines of the world's newspapers, then as now, yearned for a murder story."
P. 30.

12. O,Neal, Bill., *Encyclopedia of Western Gunfighters*. P. 4. Hereafter
cited as O'Neal. This volume contains recaps of 587 gunfights which occurred
after the Civil War, but before the century clock turned, as well as a wealth of
biographical and statistical data relating to a plethora of western frontier
personalities. Interestingly, many of the mythical misnomers about frontier
gunmen are dispelled. Such as, "Gunfighters whose reputation greatly exceeded
their accomplishments include Wyatt Earp, Bat Masterson, Doc Holliday, and
John Ringo." P. 5.

13. Ibid., P. 5-6. Contrary to popular opinion, Wyatt Earp was never
involved in a shooting incident by himself, but was always assisted by other
shooters, which in pure fact renders the absolute accuracy of his bullets striking
any mark as inconclusive.

14. Ibid.

15. Thrapp, Dan L., *Encyclopedia of Frontier Biography*, Three Volumes.
Volume III, P. 1442. Hereafter cited as Thrapp.

16. Tenth U. S. Census, Silver City, Grant County, New Mexico Territory.
P. 18, Line 28., June 6, 1880. This is the only Tucker listed in Grant Co. at a
time when it is known Tucker was employed as a Grant Co. Deputy Sheriff.
Additionally, Conrad Keeler Naegle, *The History of Silver City, New Mexico
1870-1886*, Master of Arts Thesis, University of New Mexico. 1943. Hereafter
cited as Naegle. The author cites Silver City Council Minutes, Book I, P. 2.
Tucker was the first City Marshal of Silver City and is frequently mentioned as
David Tucker. Also, in Grant County Mining Record of Deeds, Tucker uses his
true first name, David.

17. Interviews with Susan Berry, Director, Silver City Museum, Silver City,
New Mexico. March and May 1999. Additionally, Grant County *Herald*, 01-23-
1876 and the Silver City *Enterprise*, 09-05-1902. "He (Tucker) formerly kept a
ranch at Point of Rocks..."

18. Gustafson, C. A., "Dan Tucker—Deming's Lethal Lawman,"
Destination Deming, 1999 Luna County Visitors Guide. Hereafter cited as
Gustafson.

19. *Southwest Sentinel*, 05-31-1884.

20. Nearly all source material mentions Tucker was born in Canada. Curiously, Williams comments, "...Dan Tucker, who claimed to be a Canadian by birth." O. W. Williams to J. C. Williams, 12-15-1924. What Williams meant by use of the word "claimed is" undetermined. The 1880 Grant County New Mexico census does list Tucker's place of birth as Canada, as does the special 1885 census.

21. Correspondence to the author from, Carolyn Autry, Assistant Reference Librarian, Indiana Historical Society, William Henry Smith Memorial Library, Indianapolis, Indiana. August 17, 1999. And U. S. Census Records State of Indiana. Of his early life DeArment simply reported, "Born in Canada and a machinist by trade, he had been raised in Indiana and had come to Silver City from Colorado." P. 14.

22. Thrapp, Volume III, P. 1442., DeArment, P. 14., Nelson, P. 19. Most probably this information was developed from an undocumented article by Dan Rose which appeared in the Silver City *Independent*, 09-22-1931. The information is probably correct, and possibly came from the mouth of Tucker himself, although it is unconfirmed. Rose's assertion that he personally knew Tucker is not, nor has it been, historically disputed.

23. Silver City *Independent*, 09-22-1931, Rose.

24. Correspondence received from Barbara Dey, Reference Librarian, Colorado Historical Society, Denver, Colorado. September 11, 1999.

25. Price, Paxton P., *Pioneers of the Mesilla Valley*, P. 158. Hereafter cited as Price. Mention of the Point of Rocks refers to "low, rocky hills in the Jornada desert, used by the Apaches as a look-out point and observation screen for their attacks on travelers..." Also see Julyan, Robert, *The Place Name of New Mexico*. P. 199. "This conspicuous cluster of rock outcrops was an important landmark and campground on the Jornada del Muerto." Hereafter cited as Julyan. This Point of Rocks is referenced, and clearly identified on P. 104 in *The Roads of New Mexico*, and should not be confused with a similarly named rock outcropping mentioned by William French, *Recollections of a Western Ranchman*. French's reference, page 81, is to a locally known site off the road between Silver City and Alma, on the Western side of the Mogollon Mountains. Nor should the location be confused with the Point of Rocks in Colorado, prominently mentioned by Sallie Reynolds Matthews in *Interwoven—A Pioneer Chronicle*, or the site mentioned by Clum, which was located in Arizona Territory, "eighteen miles northwest of Tucson." P. 14.

26. Ibid. Also see Julyan, P. 201. "It (Leasburg) burned in 1883, and most of the inhabitants moved to nearby Fort Selden, where Adolph Lea had become post trader."

27. Frazer, Robert., *Forts of the West—Military Forts and Presidios and Posts Commonly Called Forts West of the Mississippi River to 1898*. P. 102-103. Hereafter cited as Frazer.

28. Giese, Dale F., *Forts of New Mexico*. P. 48. Hereafter cited as Giese.

29. Price, P. 158. "Indeed six soldiers died in Leasburg due to lawlessness, twice the number lost in the fort's combat history." Giese reports, "...in its 25 years of existence, only three men were killed in the line of duty." P. 48. Although Lea's reputation was generally good the Grant County *Herald* of 07-11-1876, during the time Tucker was leasing Lea's station, carried the following, "We are pleased to state that our esteemed and well known friend, Adolphe Lea,

has been acquitted of the charge of branding cattle not his own. The charge was too thin to bear the scrutiny of unprejudiced and intelligent jury."

30. Billington, Monroe Lee, *New Mexico's Buffalo Soldiers, 1866-1900.* P. 35. Hereafter cited as Billington.

31. Mullin, Robert N., "Here Lies John Kinney," *The Journal of Arizona History*, Autumn 1973. P. 226. Hereafter cited as Mullin. Also see, "Boss Rustler—The Life and Crimes of John Kinney," Part 1, by Fredrick Nolan, *True West*, September 1996. Hereafter cited as Nolan.

32. Price. P. 158.

33. Giese, P. 48.

34. Price, P. 158

35. Grant County *Herald*, 01-23-1876. The Jornada Del Muerto was a 90 mile stretch of waterless and barren desert which was frequently used by travelers on the north/south route between Mexico and Santa Fe. Sometimes chosen because it could shorten the trip by a day or two, travel on the Jornada Del Muerto (Journey of Death) could not be made absent risks of privation or Indian attack. See Julyan, P. 180. Sometimes the Jornada Del Muerto was referred to as "scalp alley." See Owen, Gordon, *The Two Alberts—Fountain and Fall.* P. 25. Hereafter cited as Owen.

36. Price, P. 157-159 for Lea and P. 137-139 for Martin.

37. Ibid. P. 139.

38. Grant County *Herald*, 1-20-1877. Tucker's name was dropped from the advertisements he had been running in the newspaper from December 1875 to October 1876. The add was, however, continued but over the name of Adolph Lea, clearly an indication Tucker had moved on—presumably to Silver City— but the first documented mention of his arrival there is a newspaper edition of June 9, 1877.

39. Ibid., 10-07-1876 & 10-21-1876. Additionally Lea noted the location was a "Government Agency and Stage Station," and that inquiries should be forwarded to him at Fort Selden.

40. Kildare, Maurice (Gladwell Richardson), "Saga of the Gallant Sheriff," *The West*, August 1968. P. 28. Hereafter cited as Kildare.

41. Ibid. Also see, Ailman, H. B., *Pioneering in Territorial Silver City—H. B. Ailman's Recollections of Silver City and the Southwest, 1871-1892.* Edited by Helen J. Lundwall. Hereafter cited as Ailman for text and Lundwall for annotations. DeArment says "Some said that he had fled Colorado after stabbing a black man to death; others were sure Whitehill had known Tucker in Colorado, had seen him in mortal action, and had sent for him." The author's comments are not necessarily incorrect, and Whitehill could have known Tucker in Colorado, but evidence indicates Tucker first leased the stage station before he settled in Silver City.

42. Silver City *Enterprise*, 11-03-1949. "I'll Never Forget" by Lou Blachly.

43. During an address to the Westerners' International, Silver City Corral No. 36, on 04-19-1983, Pat Humble, late southwestern New Mexico researcher and historian, takes issue with the generally reported accusation that McIntosh absconded with county funds. According to Humble, the sheriff had traveled to Mexico following outlaws, and south of Janos, Chihuahua was involved in a shoot-out, killed two brigands, but was wounded himself. Later he was placed in a Mexican jail, and languished for six-months before being released, eventually returning to Grant County and a much surprised populace. In his absence Harvey

Whitehill had been appointed sheriff. After learning the truth, the electorate, at a later date, elected McIntosh to the position of county commissioner. Hereafter cited as Humble, P. Audio tape courtesy of Terry Humble. Also see Silver City *Tribune*, 11-15-1873, "We are pleased to see Sheriff McIntosh so prompt in the discharge of his official duties. There has been nothing, so far, entrusted to his care, but what has been at once executed."

44. Kildare, P.28,

45. 1880 U. S. Census, Grant County, New Mexico Territory. And, Naegle, Conrad K., "The Rebellion of Grant County, New Mexico in 1876," *Arizona and the West*, 10 (Fall 1968) P. 226. Hereafter cited as Naegle (II). Without detailing specific geographical alignments, suffice to say that for the time frame covered in the Tucker narrative, Grant County included territory which would later be subdivided into Luna County (Deming) and Hidalgo County (Lordsburg), as well as a portion given up in the creation of Sierra County. From many perspectives at the time, especially for a law enforcement officer, Grant County was enormous, being about the size of the present state of New Jersey.

46. Naegle (II), P. 231.

47. Ibid., P. 240.

48. Weddle, Jerry, *Antrim is My Stepfather's Name—The Boyhood of Billy the Kid*. P. 24. Hereafter cited as Weddle.

49. Ibid. P. 26-30. Also see, Remembrances of Chauncey O. Truesdell, Silver City Museum Archives—Biographical Files. Silver City, New Mexico. Truesdell reports, "...so they locked him up in a little jail made of 2"x 6" and located in the north part of town. It had a fireplace in it and as Henry was only a small boy, he crawled out of the chimney and came to us." Reference to "dancing eyes" comes from the January, 2, 1902 Silver City *Enterprise* interview with Harvey Whitehill, "There was one peculiar facial characteristic that to an experienced man hunter, would have marked him immediately as a bad man and that was his dancing eyes. They never were at rest, but continually shifted and roved, much like his own rebellious nature." Whitehill describes the jail as "an adobe affair" having a corridor with a fireplace, behind "heavy oaken doors."

50. Blachly for remarks about Whitehill. And see, Silver City *Independent*, 09-11-1906, "As he (Whitehill) grew to manhood he learned the occupation of a locomotive engineer and followed railroading in the states of Ohio, Indiana, and Illinois until 1858 when he became imbued with the spirit of the west and came to Denver, Colo., when that city was a small town." Also see Silver City *Independent*, 09-22-1931 article by Dan Rose, which notes Tucker was a native of Indiana. In both the 1880 census and a special 1885 census, Tucker lists his place of birth as Canada. At face value it appears Tucker was born in Canada, but spent time in both Indiana and Colorado before migrating to New Mexico Territory.

51. Humble, Pat. Handwritten note from personal historical files. Copy courtesy Terry Humble, Pat's son, a enthusiastically competent researcher in his own right.

52. Grant County *Herald*, 06-09-1877.

53. Grant County Book No. 3, Register of Probate Court, P. 48., and on P. 68 the notation, "Court was opened by Deputy Sheriff Tucker by order of Hon. George W. Holt, Probate Judge." Also see, Grant County *Herald*, 06-09-1877. To date, this is the first mention found in newspaper files indicating Tucker was a deputy sheriff. The article simply states "Deputy Tucker" had been appointed

road superintendent for Precinct No. 3. A check for earlier newspaper comments, as well as investigation into locating Oath and Bond Books at the Grant County Courthouse has thus far proved futile.

54. Nelson, P. 19. Also see, Silver City *Independent*, 06-12-17. "Early Days of the Great Southwest"…"Chief Deputy, Dan Tucker."

55. Ball, Larry D., *Desert Lawmen—The High Sheriffs of New Mexico and Arizona, 1846-1912*. P. 27. Hereafter cited as Ball (S). Also see Ball (II), "Militia Posses: The Territorial Militia in Civil Law Enforcement in New Mexico Territory, 1877-1883," *New Mexico Historical Review*, 55:1 1980.

56. DeArment, P. 14.

57. Ibid.

58. Nelson, P. 19.

59. Silver City *Enterprise*, 09-05-1902.

60. Silver City *Independent*, 09-22-1931.

61. DeArment, P. 14.

62. Pioneer Foundation Interview {Wayne Whitehill}

63. Silver City *Enterprise*, 10-17-1902.

2

"STOPPED BY A BALL FROM TUCKER'S PISTOL"

Almost straddling the southern spine of America's Continental Divide at 5,900 feet, nestled between picturesque mountains gradually giving way to unforgiving Chihuahuan desert to the south, Silver City in the 1870s was fast eclipsing other mining communities in southwestern New Mexico and southeastern Arizona.[1] Formerly known as La Cienega de San Vicente (the marshes of St. Vincent), Silver City, and the surrounding area, already had a history rich with diverse cultural tradition dating to ancient times.[2] As far back as 10,000 years ago primitive hunters and gatherers were wandering the craggy canyons and slipping beneath shaded canopies of the spruce and pines in the monstrous Mogollon Mountains, just a few short miles to the north. Later, "around the beginning of the Christian era," the Mogollon culture temporarily flourished, but had disappeared by the twelfth century,[3] only to be replaced in the modern-era by a humankind unsurpassed at adapting to the beautiful, but brusque environment—the redoubtable Apache. A short distance to the east was the renowned Santa Rita del Cobre mine, which during the Spanish regime had provided 20,000 mule loads of precious copper for the slow-moving and vulnerable caravans destined for Chihuahua.[4] In fact, the mine proved so successful, partly due to the use of convict labor, that for the first four decades of the nineteenth-century most of the metal used in minting Mexico's copper coins came from Santa Rita.[5] Shortly after Mexican independence (1821), buckskin-clad mountain men such as Kit Carson, Ewing Young, Michel Robidoux, and the Patties, James and Sylvester, cautiously traipsed through the area in search of beaver.[6] About the same time, borderland rogue James Kirker hunted in the vicinity, first for felt, but later for flowing raven hair attached to Apache scalps, for which the Mexican government paid bounty.[7] And still later, Ninth Cavalry "buffalo soldiers" exhaustively scoured beneath sharply defined precipices, through mountain hogbacks, over lofty ridges, and across expansive desert floors, in search of the ever-elusive Apache—before they finally sauntered into town for a breather. Silver City, and her suburbs, do indeed lay on a bed of multicultural ashes.

But by the time Dan Tucker arrived and accepted the appointment as deputy sheriff, Silver City, the county seat, had a distinctly "American" disposition, and was clearly "American" in outward appearance.[8] Berry & Russell are right on target when commenting that "history is a prejudiced affair," pointing out the predominately Anglo influences of early Silver City.[9] Frances Boyd, a cavalry officer's wife speaking of New Mexico Territory, reflected that development of silver and gold mines, "caused the building of the only American town there, Silver City, which, with its one hundred beautiful red brick houses, is a wonderful place..."[10] Even period newspapers were thumping out a popular chorus—Silver City was "essentially eastern" and an "American town."[11] The Las Cruces *Borderer* proclaimed:

> No where in New Mexico—no where in the Southwest, can so striking an example of energy and enterprise be found as Silver City. The enterprising citizens of that go ahead town are determined to create a city that shall prove that American genius, enterprise and intelligence has reached this isolated frontier.[12]

The regional salesmanship compared to an earlier time when another southwestern mountain community, Prescott, Arizona Territory, was promoted as being thoroughly American. "Its (Prescott) inhabitants were Americans; American men had brought American wives out with them....The houses were built in American style; the doors were American doors and fastened with American bolts and locks, opened by American knobs,...there were American books, American newspapers, American magazines...The language was American, and nothing else..."[13]

In reality, the comparison between Silver City and Prescott did not end with an architectural analysis, or an assessment of the cultural and political power base. Both communities were founded because of rich mineral deposits in the area; because of the mountain setting both offered scenic vistas; both were completely encircled by vast reaches terroristically dominated by erratically hostile Apaches; both were heir to positive and negative influences from nearby military reservations; and both attracted a vast variety of frontier inhabitants—some cut from rougher edges of the cloth. And just as Prescott had its Whiskey Row, Silver City could well boast of fifteen saloons and three dance halls.[14] Deputy Dan Tucker soon became a seemingly permanent and prominent fixture in the darker side of Silver City's night life.

From the beginning there had been no guarantee, but the promise of wealth through exploitation of southwestern New Mexico Territory's mineral resources had beckoned, and the call was answered by a throng of promoters, speculators, and investors. For the optimistic capitalist, one sufficiently funded, the opportunities seemed unlimited, and financiers from the east invariably sought financial return from a jumble of monetary schemes; a few built on foundations of mysterious ethics, but the vast majority firmly supported by pillars of scrupulous honesty. In general, these architects of Silver City capitalism were men of stature, integrity, and an entrepreneurial spirit usually not associated with typical western mining camps. Most mineral municipalities born in the American West were knowingly conceived with short life-spans in mind; Silver City was "built to last."[15]

In fact, enduring stability was so much on the mind of city fathers' that a local ordinance was passed which prohibited wood frame construction of any kind within town limits. Quite naturally, limiting building materials to brick or adobe was touted as a fire-prevention measure—which it was—but additionally this prescribed cure for interdicting the construction of less substantially built structures served to inhibit the not so prosperous. A local editor wailed, "The effect of the ordinance is to prohibit the man of moderate means from building himself a home."[16] The Silver City *Enterprise* urged financiers to answer the demand for "dwelling houses," predicating the expenditures would "pay better interest than any thing we know of."[17] Several area businessmen predictably jumped at the chance to profitably close the housing shortage gap. Unlike sister mining communities of clapboard construction, Silver City could point with pride to *rental* property solidly built of brick, accentuated by exquisite architectural trim.[18]

Posted to the south nearby, however, was a neighborhood which stood in sharp contrast to the distinctly "American" appearance of Silver City. Chihuahua Hill, a predominately Spanish speaking locale of flat-roofed adobe construction, afforded hearth and home to many of the area Hispanics who worked in the mines or freighted fundamental supplies for the whole region. As deputy sheriff, and peace keeper for all citizens, Dan Tucker familiarized himself with the people, the customs, and assuredly danced during the fandangos, smoked corn-shuck cigarettes, and either sipped, or maybe even guzzled tequila while inspecting Chihuahua Hill's cantinas.[19]

Disregarding whether or not ancestral roots were deeply buried in Mexico's historically rich interior, or more recently sprouted from eastern seaboard shores, both Hispano and Anglo had planted seeds of permanency at Silver City.

So Silver City's population was comprised of a diverse gathering. Notwithstanding some journalist's efforts to elevate certain gun-toting law enforcing champions to positions of high prominence, reality reveals, at least in most cases, the peace keepers were recruited from a pool of candidates several layers removed from the community's social and economic power structure. Unless engaged in a posse out after callous criminals, or membership in Apache chasing platoons, both of which required only temporary duty, the leading spirits of governmental, economic and cultural affairs relied on others to maintain order and enforce the law. Certainly the dregs of society were at the bottom of the list, unworthy of consideration, and everyone was keenly aware preachers weren't particularly potent crime fighters, so from somewhere in between, the task fell to those who walked the fine line winding between barrooms, bordellos, boisterous *bailes*, and belligerency. Available evidence reveals Dan Tucker was never liberated from "middle class" status, nor did he ever appear inclined to disassociate himself from the sporting crowd; but it is equally indisputable that he was always successful in maintaining a healthy respect in the eyes of the community's elite, and a fearsome reputation with those disreputable characters who misspent their lives in the southwestern border country. In the words of an old-timer, Dan Tucker could be a "bitter enemy" or a "solid friend," but no matter the social strata, from the very bottom to the top, none questioned that Dan Tucker would stand his ground![20]

Oftentimes a deputy sheriff's presence was required outside town limits. In mid-June 1877, R. N. Calhoun was murdered at John Perry's ranch near the mouth of Mangas Creek. Based on some elementary detective work relating to spent cartridge cases, and just who possessed the corresponding type of rifle, suspicion was cast on four frontier vagabonds, "Wild Bill" Martin, Portuguese Jo (Jose M. Carrolla), Bob Nelson, and John Orr (aka Donaldson). The suspected brigands boldly vowed not to be taken alive—and so it was! In an ensuing shoot-out with posse members, three dead desperados fell on the spot, while Bob Nelson, although wounded, made good with his escape, eventually changing horses and disappearing. Shortly after the fireworks the rest of the posse returned to Silver City to celebrate "good deed and good riddance." Sometime later Deputy Dan Tucker rode into town leading the blood-splattered white horse last used by Nelson. Tucker reported he found the horse on Sycamore Creek, and no sign of a wounded outlaw.[21] Later it would it would be reported Nelson was found dead, supposedly only three hundred yards from where the bloody horse was discovered.[22] Had Deputy Tucker delivered a *coup de grace*?

On another occasion, or quite possibly just a different version of the same desperate encounter between the good guys and the badmen, a posse out after horse thieves picked up the rustlers' trail and followed it to the area around Cow Springs south of Silver City. "What happened there, the people as a whole never knew, except perhaps the sheriff and his deputies, but the posse returned, with every stolen horse and three extra ones with saddles on."[23] When questioned about the additional mounts, the lawmen, of which Dan Tucker was probably one, simply replied that the owners 'couldn't ride any longer,' and were left behind.[24] Follow up questions were ill advised!

Deputy Dan Tucker soon determined the business of law enforcement was to his liking, but the seemingly overwhelming civil and criminal tasks were monopolizing his time. At the Grant County Commissioner's meeting on July 2, 1877, Dan resigned his position as Road Superintendent.[25] Although Tucker would occasionally dabble in private speculative ventures designed to supplement his taxpayer funded income, for the next decade Dan would deliberately devote himself to peace keeping missions throughout Grant County environs. At the time, still suffering growing pains, southwestern New Mexico Territory could well profit from the services of implacable officers.

Deputy Dan Tucker was capable of letting the hammer drop and popping a cap whenever he thought it needful. On a particular summer night, performing his constabulary duties, but nevertheless taking pleasure in meandering through the crowd, Dan Tucker rationed his time between the gambling room at the front of the saloon, and the dance hall in back, although he no doubt periodically hesitated inbetween, where the "wet goods" were dispensed.[26] The Monday, Wednesday, Saturday and Sunday night dance schedule had been methodically maintained, and inhabitants "of almost every color and creed, gathered to dance and carouse and enjoy the one great joy of their life."[27] Oftentimes though, liquor fostered a collision of grating personalities. Typically a disturbance erupted, violent threats were allegedly made, and one of the parties sought the law for protection. What could Dan Tucker do but respond? Outside the dance hall, Tucker attempted to make an arrest, but one of the suspects, Atanacio Bencomo, opted for fight and flight over pacific surrender—a mistake of lasting consequence.[28]

The local newspaper announced, "On the 14th August, 1877, an inquest was held on the body of Atanacio Bencomo, who died from being struck by a pistol ball from a pistol held in the hands of Deputy Sheriff Daniel Tucker. His actions were justifiable as they were in the discharge of his duties as the Deputy Sheriff of Grant County, as the deceased was escaping from his custody."[29]

August would prove rather eventful for Dan Tucker. The Grant County *Herald* in a one-liner simply reported, "D. Tucker has been appointed county jailer in place of S. G. Bean."[30] Samuel G. Bean, ex-sheriff of Doña Ana County, and older brother of the waggish Judge Roy Bean, had been named turnkey earlier in the year, with the proud April proclamation that the newly framed and plastered jail was equipped and ready to accept boarders.[31] Why Tucker replaced Bean is not known. With the new assignment, Tucker would receive a fixed amount for the care and feeding of county prisoners.[32] In New Mexico Territory at the time, the rate was fifty cents per prisoner, per day.[33] Presumably, any left over funds would be pocketed, after a reasonable split with the boss, Sheriff Harvey Whitehill. In most studies, it is the frontier sheriff who receives reimbursement for jail operating expenses, but an examination of existing Grant County Commissioner's records indicates payment to "Deputy D. Tucker," stating he was paid for "feeding prisoners" and for "jail expenses."[34] Several years later, after a degree of monetary inflation, a local editor moaned, "The sheriff is compelled to feed these men (prisoners) at fifty cents per day, which amount will not buy the raw material alone. The greater number of prisoners the sheriff has to take care of the more money he loses."[35] Tucker maintained his status as a deputy sheriff, and continued to receive fees for specific tasks performed for Grant County, as needed—which was constantly![36]

Just a short time later, marital bliss was severely fractured in Silver City when Placido Cortez went berserk, and forced his wife from their residence, "using an ax as a gentle persuader." Summoned to the location by frightened citizens, Deputy Dan Tucker arrested the ax-wielding abuser, and placed him in jail pending a hearing.[37] Cortez was ultimately fined $10.00 and released, probably thankful he had been gifted with enough foresight not to resist a dead-shot deputy.[38]

Dan Tucker's scorecard as a gunman is sometimes innocently ratcheted upward in the retelling of scalding engagements about a white-hatted deputy and a whole cast of detestable rascals bent on evil. Often credited with as many as twenty-one killings *by others*, Tucker himself would later acknowledge eight in Grant County.[39] Since there is no indication, or more importantly no evidence, that Tucker was a braggart or self-promoter, there is a ring of truth to his assertion. As will be later explored, Tucker made these remarks to a Silver City *Enterprise* newsman while out on bail for a shooting—his only known press interview. On bond for one killing, it is unlikely he would falsely claim responsibility for others, unless they were justified, and already well known to an inquiring press. Logic would suggest one might "get away with" a erroneous and braggadocios statement in a faraway land, or at a time well removed, but not contemporarily to a newspaper editor already familiar with local news and area personalities. The creditability of the statement may be found in the motive for making it in the first place—frustration with the legal process!

Quite aptly DeArment declares, "Like most of the notch-sticks credited to notorious gunmen of the Old West, Tucker's has no doubt been over-carved."[40] On the same subject, Thrapp dropped the bomb directly on reality when he theorized about seemingly high figures which "may have been saloon gossip, but they suggest the mettle of the man."[41] Some of the killings attributed to Dan Tucker lack substantive documentation, and therefore readers are forced to make their own assessments as to validity.

However, in many other instances, historical investigation reveals Tucker was indeed a frontier figure to be reckoned with, oftentimes at the risk of great personal peril, and even a cursory review of primary and secondary source material suggests Tucker was no counterfeit man-killer. The legitimate question is not whether or not Dan Tucker killed anyone, but rather, just how many criminal careers did he terminate? There is a substantial body of evidence to support the claim that Dan Tucker would hold high rank among some of the much more publicized and better known gun-fighters of the nineteenth-century American West.

One writer who lived in Silver City at the time, and personally knew Dan Tucker, offers a thrilling but unsubstantiated story. Three horse thieves were ripping and roaring in a local saloon, while outside Deputy Dan Tucker was apprised by a hapless victim that his horse had been stolen, and now the equine was standing hitched to a post in front of swinging saloon doors. Dutifully, Tucker enters the barroom, challenges the scoundrels, and immediately the shooting begins. Skillfully, Tucker's shots from a .45 Colt mortally wound two of the brigands, while the third was "made helpless by a bullet that grazed his skull..."[42] From an investigative perspective, as the Tucker narrative continues, it becomes crystal clear that this episode should not necessarily be dismissed out of hand. But it wasn't just obstreperous outlaws who were misbehaving, and drawing Tucker's ire.

Ten miles to the east of Silver City, at the base of the Santa Rita Mountains, Fort Bayard housed blue-coated government sentinels charged with protecting the Pinos Altos mining district from depredations by Warm Spring Apaches.[43] Established in 1866 by General Carleton's command of California Volunteers, Fort Bayard played a meaningful role in the efforts to subjugate wayward Apache fighting men.[44] At the time (1877) Dan Tucker pinned the Grant County star to his vest, Fort Bayard had thirteen sets of spacious officer's quarters and comfortable adobe barracks which could accommodate four companies of enlisted men.[45] Two years later the post was staffed with "one brevet lieutenant colonel, a major, four captains, 11 lieutenants, 325 enlisted men (Companies A, B, and G, 9th Cavalry, and Company E, 15th Infantry), 14 laundresses, 14 civilian employees, 25 Navajo scouts, 280 cavalry horses (40 of which belonged to the Navajos), and 89 mules. By the standards of those days, it was a large post."[46] And by any standards, when military installations were near, intermittent law enforcement headaches afflicted area lawmen. From time to time, Deputy Dan Tucker was required to prescribe a dose of his own brand of medicine.

Tom Robinson, a black soldier stationed at Fort Bayard, was enjoying the day creating his own brand of havoc in front of Mrs. Miller's saloon at nearby Central City, which had become "notorious as an entertainment center for troops." Robinson was not in the least mindful of any deputy's presence. Stewed to his gills, Robinson chose not to comply with Tucker's order to submit to lawful arrest. Tucker pulled his six-shooter and shot Robinson. With his right arm wounded and out of commission, with his left hand the errant "buffalo soldier" was later forced to fork over a fine for resisting arrest.[47]

The following news item may very will be another version of a Dan Tucker arrest, although he is not mentioned. Nevertheless it clearly lays bare the sometimes rowdy behavior of partying soldiers which sometimes pushed lawmen into taking drastic action.

> Wm. Scouce, a soldier from Fort Bayard visited Central City a few days ago, and becoming somewhat intoxicated concluded he could run the town, and commenced by beating Mr. Miller, a saloon keeper, over the head with a pistol. He then went on the street and as a lady came riding by seized her horse by the bridle and then made indecent proposals. He was arrested by the civil authorities yesterday and brought to Silver City for trial.[48]

Possibly with a eye toward public relations, Dan Tucker cooperated with a newsman's request. "Through the kindness of D. Tucker, Deputy Sheriff, we have been furnished with the following list of Grand and Petit Jurors, summoned for the approaching (December) term of court."[49] The list of names provided by Dan Tucker was lengthy, indicating he had been quite busy in serving papers, and chalking up fees. Additionally, a dab of favorable political insurance (cooperating with the press) was just plain good sense, especially for those who from time to time were compelled to shoot to kill.

Sadly, and all too often at Silver City, the lights were prematurely snuffed out for men respected by all, those of a "pleasant disposition" and who were indeed "liberal to a fault." Such was the case of Richard Howlett, who in 1877 would lose more than a mere herd of horses to rustling Mexican thieves. At George Spears' saloon, Howlett engaged in a poker game with thirty-year-old Thomas Bowe. Bowe, who a year or two earlier killed a man at Ward's Ballroom, peered out from beneath the hat, which he typically wore "low down on his forehead." Howlett had not a premonition, nor forewarning of impending doom. The game seemed "good humored," but suddenly Bowe sprang upon the table and blasted Howlett with a six-shooter. Howlett lingered just a little while, and then "crossed over the divide." Bowe split for parts unknown.[50] Led by Sheriff Whitehill, all night "patrols" sought the whereabouts of the murderer, and even the next day private houses were searched, but to no avail. It was said that Bowe "had friends here who helped him to a horse, blankets, food, arms and ammunition, wherewith to make his escape."[51] Not even Dan Tucker always got his man.

But he got the next one. The story seemingly becomes routine. The music was reverberating through Don Juan Ward's dance hall on a pleasant 1877 August night, while young, blue-eyed Deputy Dan Tucker gazed longingly as brown-eyed beauties sashayed through a smoke filled room tinged with the sour scent of straight whiskey and stale perfume. Whatever thoughts he had, lustful or pure, were soon replaced with an urgency demanding resumption of a law enforcement frame of mind. One Juan Garcia had an altercation with one Belmudes. The deputy started to intervene, Garcia slashed Belmudes with a knife, ran from the saloon, and because he failed to heed Dan Tucker's warning, or *maybe* there was no warning; regardless, an eyewitness reported, "...'Tuck' was a dead shot and the bullet struck the Mexican 'dead-center' in the lower back."[52] The Grant County *Herald* confirmed, "Garcia was stopped by a ball from Tucker's pistol which struck him in the hip, close to the backbone."[53]

Dan Tucker is usually credited for waiting until the fleeing suspect illuminated himself by passing a lighted window, then making a two-handed shot at a distance of eighty-four steps, and when the bullet connected it "spun him like a top."[54] Regarding Tucker's marksmanship, Wayne Whitehill reportedly witnessed Dan Tucker, "put five bullets into a little ole tree with a .45 six-shooter and never stopped his horse," an anecdote which rings strikingly similar to dozens of first-hand reminiscences touting nearly every frontier gunmen's firearms proficiency.[55]

Likely the same incident, the killing of Garcia was elsewhere reported in this fashion: "The same year Sheriff Tucker had a narrow escape from an assassin, who sprang out at him from a doorway, attempting to drive a knife through him. He missed his lick however and ran across the street, and although it was pitch dark and drizzling, Tucker waited until the man passed in front of the Assembly rooms, across the patch of light that shone out from the glass front, then fired, bringing his man down. The distances was eighty-four steps. They buried him next day."[56]

Traditional folklore reveals Belmudes, whose intestines were hanging out, was attended by a local physician who repacked the extruding gut, took a gluttonous drink of cheap whiskey, used the remaining "snake-juice" as make-do antiseptic, and sewed the wound closed with common string.[57] Facts reveal Belmudes indeed survived, but Garcia his assailant did not, although not surprisingly he suffered from the wound, and possibly the cure, for months. The newspaper substantiates, "Juan Garcia the man who was shot by the deputy sheriff, while running away to avoid arrest, some seven months ago, died last Sunday."[58]

During the days of Tucker's reign in Silver City, indeed throughout Grant County, fleeing from an officer was tantamount to an admission of guilt, and if a suspected lawbreaker wouldn't stand arrest and subsequent legal examination, he could ill afford to anticipate any public sympathy. Likewise, a officer who cast a shadow of utter fearlessness, and showed a sheer willingness to shoot, could very well expect a degree of restrained compliance. Early frontier lawmen could little afford the niceties usually mentioned when alluding to "the code of the West." Writing of the early gunfights and gunfighters, historian Joseph Rosa rightly reminds that in a shooting confrontation "hesitancy could mean death or crippling wounds."[59] And despite examples of romantically penned litter, the author points out "the old-time gunmen had few rules; they were guided by instinct and experience, without which they could not have survived for long."[60] Speaking specifically of Dan Tucker, one old-timer expressed community sentiment "He never shot a man unless that man had broken a law."[61] It was just that simple!

Preposterous as it may appear in today's climate of political correctness and abhorrence to violence, early day Silver City citizens, "the men worth while,... the home builders, the law abiding" were pleased to have a dedicated deputy that they could depend on. Another of those early citizens commented on the generally accepted attitude toward Sheriff Whitehill's right-hand man, "They were convinced that Tucker was the right kind of a man for the job and never questioned the manner of his killings. He went single handed into these affairs, and it was up to him to use his own judgment; and he did so with an accuracy and precision probably unsurpassed in the West."[62]

Edgar Beecher Bronson, with tongue in cheek, offers his diagnosis regarding frontier characters of Tucker's ilk, finding they were afflicted with *Triggerfingeritis*, "an acute irritation of the sensory nerves of the index finger of habitual gun-packers; usually fatal—to someone."[63]

Amusing commentary to the side, historical investigation unequivocally demonstrates Dan Tucker was in fact a prime example of the stereotypical frontier lawman—outwardly devoid of fear, and not only proficient with firearms, but psychologically inclined to put them to use.

NOTES AND SOURCES

1. Berry, Susan, and Russell, Sharman Apt., *Built to Last—An Architectural History of Silver City, New Mexico*. P. 3. Hereafter cited as Berry & Russell.

2. Nelson, P. 5.

3. Ungnade, Herbert E., *New Mexico Mountains*, P. 19-20. Hereafter cited as Ungnade.

4. Ibid. P. 28.

5. Humble, Terrence M., "The Pinder-Slip Mining Claim Dispute of Santa Rita, New Mexico, 1881-1912," *Mining History Journal*, 1996. P. 93.

6. Berry & Russell, P. 6. Also see, John M. Moore, *Moore's Who Is Who in New Mexico*. P. 3.

7. McGaw, William Cochran, *Savage Scene, The Life and Times of James Kirker—Frontier King*. P. 112-113.

8. Naegle (II), P. 226. "Silver City became the county seat in 1871, and soon gained a reputation for its dynamic Anglo-American industry, ingenuity and perseverance."

9. Berry & Russell, P. 15.

10. Boyd, Frances Anne., *Cavalry Life in Tent and Field*. P. 214.

11. Berry & Russell, P. 17. Also see Las Cruces *Borderer*, 08-24-1872.

12. Las Cruces *Borderer*, 08-24-1872. As quoted by Naegle, P. 189.

13. Bourke, John G., *On The Border With Crook*. P. 158-159. Bourke contrasted the differences, "In one word, the transition from Tucson to Prescott

was as sudden and as radical as that between Madrid and Manchester." Hereafter cited as Bourke. Correspondingly, a similar contrast could certainly be made between Silver City and Mesilla or Santa Fe. O. W. Williams comments, "It (Silver City) was certainly the most substantially built of all the territorial towns other than Santa Fe; and while some of the towns in the Rio Grande Valley might have had a greater population, yet certainly it was only here that you could find two-story houses of brick or lumber in addition to the best class of adobe houses." P. 114-115. Williams, O. W., *The Personal Narratives of O. W. Williams, 1877-1902—Pioneer Surveyor, Frontier Lawyer*. Edited by S. D. Myres. Hereafter cited as Williams for text, Myres for annotations.

14. Berry & Russell, P. 13.

15. Ibid. The authors did a "bang-up" job in their comprehensive site specific historical examination of territorial Silver City. The architectural research, coupled with biographical comments concerning the community's "movers and shakers" conclusively validates their assessment, Silver City was indeed, "built to last."

16. *Southwest Sentinel*, 08-25-1883. Quoted by Berry & Russell. Also see Naegle, "In order to make even more certain that Silver City would not be laid waste by the ravages of fire as had practically every city of contemporary origin in the Southwest, the city council, on May 20, 1880, passed an ordinance prohibiting the construction of buildings of frame or other inflammable material anywhere within the city limits." P. 55.

17. Unger, Patti, {editor} *True Tales, 1882 & 1883—Volume I.* P. 14. Hereafter cited as Unger. Quoting the 11-23-1882 edition of the Silver City *Enterprise*. P. 14.

18. Berry & Russell. P. 20. Certainly in retrospect, foresight on the part of city fathers, and the passage of the fire prevention ordinance, were enabling factors which, in part, has accounted for the permanence of Silver City.

19. Ibid. P. 16-17. The authors accurately report the 1880 census clearly indicates the Hispanic population was evenly distributed throughout Silver City. Many of the Anglo elite in Silver City had Hispanic wives.

20. Silver City *Enterprise*, 09-05-1902.

21. Grant County *Herald*, 06-23-1877. Sycamore Creek empties into the Gila River three miles south of Cliff, New Mexico. Julyan, P. 344. Clearly the newspaper accounts describes the suspects; "Bill Martin, alias Jones, alias Wild Bill;" Portuguese Jo; Bob Nelson; and Donaldson." In his book *Outlaws of New Mexico*, Peter Hertzog lists "Wild Bill" Martin and his associate Bob Nelson as being Lincoln County outlaws, noting that Donaldson's true name was John Orr, and identifies Portugues Jo as Jose M. Carrolla. Hereafter cited as Hertzog. Jay Robert Nash in Encyclopedia of Western Lawmen & Outlaws, apparently merely repeats Hertzog's characterizations of the quartet. Hereafter cited as Nash. "Wild Bill" Martin should not be confused with "Hurricane" Bill Martin a desperado of some note who was active in Kansas, Texas, and finally New Mexico Territory, but there is documentation that his activities continued well after the date "Wild Bill" Martin was killed by the Grant County posse. See Thrapp, Vol. II, P 949.

22. Information concerning the subsequent discovery of Nelson's body is based on investigation and information furnished by Terry Humble, Grant County area researcher and historian.

23. Nelson, P. 31. Cow Springs located south of Silver City on the old Santa Rita-Janos Road was well known as a source for water in an otherwise desolated and dry section of Grant County.

24. Silver City *Independent*, 09-22-1931. In response to the burglary of a prospector's cabin, Tucker "mounted his horse and rode with the prospector to his camp. Here he took up the trail of the robbers and returned in two days with, not only the horse and other valuables belonging to the prospector; but the horses, saddles and guns of the two thieves." According to this report, Tucker advised Sheriff Whitehill, that he left the two criminal's bodies for a rancher to bury. Certainly, it is not unreasonable to question this report since it is undocumented, but on the reverse, the author did know Tucker, had personally observed him kill a fleeing suspect, and substantiated reports do indicate Tucker was quick to shoot, apparently without remorse.

25. Grant County Commissioner's Meeting Book. Page 51. July 2, 1877. Grant County Clerks Office. Silver City, New Mexico. The vacancy created by Tucker's resignation was filled by the appointment of D. Truesdale.

26. Silver City *Independent*, 06-12-1917.

27. Ibid.

28. Grant County *Herald*, 08-18-1877.

29. Ibid.

30. Ibid., 08-04-1877.

31. Price, P. 97-100. Reportedly Sam Bean had moved to Silver City to "escape further recriminations from having sided with the loser in the Civil War." He later moved to Las Cruces. And correspondence from Grant County researcher Terry Humble. Also see Sonnichsen, C. L., *The Story of Roy Bean— Law West of the Pecos*. P. 40-46. "After a while they (Sam and wife) moved to Silver City and then to Las Cruces, where Sam died nearly forty years later."

32. Grant County Commissioner's Meeting Book. P. 56. November 5, 1877. Grant County Clerk's Office. Silver City, New Mexico. At this meeting "Deputy D. Tucker" presented his account, it was approved, and warrants issued for the payment "for feeding prisoners and jail expenses."

33. Ball (S), P. 112. The fee was later raised to seventy-five cents per day after 1880.

34. Grant County Commissioner's Meeting Book, November 5, 1877 meeting, Page 56 as cited.

35. Silver City *Enterprise*, 03-01-1883. Quoted by Unger, P. 112.

36. Ball (S), P. 108-127. "The jailer also held a commission as a deputy and performed other tasks. He usually received a fixed income, since jailers did not have as much opportunity as other deputies to earn fees." P. 111. Although a small salary may have been paid to jailers in most instances, a review of Grant County records does not reveal that Tucker was paid in any systematic manner or compensated with a fixed income. It appears Tucker relied on sheriff fees for service and a fixed per diem per prisoner.

37. Grant County *Herald*, 08-18-1877.

38. Ibid.

39. Silver City *Enterprise*, 12-14-1882. At this time, this is the one and only known press interview with Dan Tucker, and was conducted because he was out on bond for a barroom killing. Tucker informed the editor, "in the course of his duty as deputy sheriff he has been obliged to kill eight men in this (Grant) county..." Tucker was complaining about having to be placed under bond to

await legal proceedings, as this "was the first time he was ever put under bonds to await examination."

40. DeArment, P. 14.

41. Thrapp, Vol. III, P. 1443.

42. Silver City *Independent*, 09-22-1931, "Dan Tucker, The Killer" by Dan Rose. That Dan Tucker carried a .45 caliber Colt is extracted from Blachly interview with Sylvester Stenson and Wayne Whitehill. Courtesy Western New Mexico University, Southwest Oral Histories. Silver City, New Mexico. Hereafter cited as Southwest Oral Histories.

43. Frazer, P. 95.

44. Ferris, Robert G., Series Editor, *Soldier and Brave, Historic Places Associated with Indian Affairs and the Indian Wars in the Trans-Mississippi West*. P. 223. Hereafter cited as Ferris.

45. Myres, Lee., "Military Establishments In Southwestern New Mexico: Stepping Stones To Settlement," *New Mexico Historical Review XLIII*: 1, 1968. P. 37. Hereafter cited as Myres.

46. Giese, P. 17. Also see, Miller, Darlis A., *Soldiers and Settlers, Military Supply in the Southwest, 1861-1885*. P. 59-60 for information on Fort Bayard's civilian supply contractors. Hereafter cited as Miller.

47. Silver City *Enterprise*, 12-12-1902. There is a possibility that the soldier "Tom" Robinson is in fact "James" Robinson, Sgt, Company G, Ninth Cavalry, at the time stationed at Fort Bayard. Robinson would be favorably singled out for his gallant action in a skirmish with hostile Apaches. Also lending credit to the account is the report of District Court Cases reported in *The Daily Southwest* for 07-28-1880, "*Territory vs. Thos. Robeson*, Assault. Plea of guilty. Fine $25 and cost." Also see Register of Prisoners Confined in the County Jail of Grant County. Courtesy New Mexico State Archives. Hereafter cited as Jail Register. For the remark characterizing Central City, see Myers, P. 38.

48. Unger, Quoting the Silver City *Enterprise*, 11-16-1882. P. v.

49. Grant County *Herald*, 11-24-1877.

50. Ibid., 10-06-1877. Also see Territory vs. Thomas Bowe. Grant County District Court Civil and Criminal Docket Cost Book. Courtesy New Mexico State Archives. Santa Fe.

51. Ibid., 10-13-1877. Also see, Nelson. P. 24. Eventually (1884) Bowe was arrested in Montana. See Silver City *Enterprise*, 05-23-1884 as quoted by Unger.

52. Silver City *Enterprise*, 06-12-1917.

53. Grant County *Herald*, 09-01-1877.

54. Silver City *Independent*, 09-22-1931. And Silver City *Enterprise*, 11-21-1902. Also see, Pioneer Foundation Interview {Wayne Whitehill}.

55. Southwest Oral Histories {Whitehill & Stenson}.

56. Silver City *Enterprise*, 11-21-1902. And Grant County *Herald*, 09-01-1877. The deceased, Juan Garcia, did not die instantly, but suffered from the wound for several lingering months before he died on 03-25-1878.

57. Interview with Susan Berry, Director, Silver City Museum, Silver City, New Mexico. March 1999. Certainly, Berry does not speak for the factuality of specific details which have become a part of Silver City folklore, but does concur with numerous accounts which report that Dan Tucker did in fact kill Garcia. Dan Rose, who was there at the time, said, "The Mexican had been slashed across the abdomen and his intestines were hanging out of his body,

touching the ground. The doctor gathered them in his hands, washed and replaced them; then sewed up the wound. The Mexican, Belmudas, lived forty years longer." Silver City *Independent*, 09-22-1931.

58. Grant County *Herald*, 03-28-1878.
59. Rosa,. Joseph G., *The Gunfighter, Man or Myth?* P. 111.
60. Ibid. "The so called 'Western Code' never really existed. Men bent on killing did so in the most efficient and expeditious way they knew." P. 162.
61. Silver City *Independent*, 09-22-1931.
62. Ibid.
63. Bronson, Edgar Beecher., *The Red Blooded Heroes of the Frontier*. P. 70. Hereafter cited as Bronson.

3

"HARD FACED AND BATTLE SCARRED"

Normally history is best revealed in chronological order. On occasion, however, parallel events must be examined separately, choosing one first, and then the other. While Dan Tucker was spitting lead at fleeing suspects, recovering blood-splattered horses, detaining "skunk-drunk" soldiers, and arresting abusive ax-wielding husbands in Silver City, ominous events were being played out to the southeast in El Paso County, Texas. These events propelled Tucker into the cyclone of a very public controversy.

Generically, the discord is labeled the El Paso Salt War because private ownership of salt deposits were entangled with conflicting cultural interests; but in reality the resulting melee was eloquently and best characterized by one respected historian as, "wasteful and unnecessary, unless to prove to a pessimist that men can die bravely in a bad cause."[1]

The commonly held perception, although not necessarily accurate, is that Anglos located and illegally appropriated rich salt deposits which heretofore had been held "in perpetuity" for the collective and common good of Mexican citizens and their descendants. These descendants included those living along both sides of the meandering international boundary known as the Rio Bravo (in Mexico), and the Rio Grande (in the USA). In actuality, the causes and origins of the resulting fracas were much more complex. The brewing cauldron of discontent contained a recipe of religious misunderstanding, cultural differences, criminal conspiracy, greed, inflated egos, partisan politics, patronage appointments, economic prelacies, finger-pointing, murder, bigotry, and in the end governmental scapegoating.

Theoretically and legally, 1877 El Paso County was a part of Texas. However, from a practical viewpoint El Paso County, because of geography and demographics was still an appendage of Mexico. There were but eighty Anglo faces in a crowd of about twelve thousand, seven thousand on the Mexican side of the river, the remainder in Texas.[2] And to the non-Anglo, the river as a boundary was of little consequence. Extended family members lived on both banks, crossing at their leisure—unrestricted. Inescapable appearances at fiestas, fandangos, and funerals on both sides of the river, seemingly erased any international border-line, real or imagined. Government? "El Paso County was beyond the reach of state protection…and the policy of the Federal government was expressed in definite language, but weak in execution."[3]

El Paso County's isolation from the seat of state government at Austin can be depicted by the choices offered a traveler intent on making the trip. Previously a stagecoach had made what was deemed a record run from El Paso County to civilization and comparative safety in central Texas—in *just* sixteen days.[4] The singular traveler, if he dared make the trip horseback, through a deceptively dangerous and almost waterless landscape studded with cacti, crawling with rattlers, and infested with hostile warriors, could expect to make the trip in thirty days. But the fastest route to Texas' westernmost county was curiously deceptive.

If in a hurry, one would ride the rails from Austin, Texas north to Topeka, Kansas, then catch a Santa Fe Railroad train, and click along the tracks into New Mexico Territory until the end of the line was accomplished, thence jump into a jostling stagecoach for a gallop into Old Mesilla, and finally a horse, stage, or buggy ride to Texas's westernmost tip. A quick ten day trip from departure to arrival.[5]

Although the river divided nations, culture disconnected the people. Compulsory education, the right to bear arms, private property rights, and a separation of Church and State were central to one group, completely foreign to the other. Right or wrong didn't seem to matter. The only factor of perceived importance was on which bank of the river one chose to stand. Little could the Hispano living on the Texas side comprehend the need to comply with fundamental constitutional concepts drafted by Anglos, especially those promulgated at faraway Austin. On the U. S. bank, Anglos demanded compliance with Texas statutes, and deference for a "superior" style of life. On the river's east bank civic meetings and verbal assaults on governmental policy was fundamentally perceived as a secured constitutional freedom; cross to the other side and public assembly was interpreted as a threat to a bureaucracy continually teetering on the brink of anarchy. On one side of the trickling current, separation between church and state was supreme, on the other, a priest dabbling in school and government affairs was customary, even expected. Exacerbating the already complex problem was not an insignificant amount of pure racism—on both sides. Anglos looked on a Mexican population as inferior and ignorant. From the other side, non-Anglos saw their superiority in numbers—it was not necessary to submit to unpopular regulation—overthrowing governments was routine! Famed southwestern historian Leon Metz fires a quick, but precisely aimed shot, "The Mexicans were the dynamite; and the Anglos were the fuse."[6]

It will not be necessary to comprehensively narrate the "Salt War" story in order to explain Dan Tuckers' participation. Suffice to say, Judge Charles Howard legally filed a claim on the disputed salt-beds 90 miles east of El Paso, which in turn further alienated the non-Anglo population, who were wickedly spurred toward unrestrained opposition and criminal misbehavior by a corrupt Catholic Priest. Judge Howard murdered Louis Cardis, a political voice for the non-Anglos, and all hell broke loose because of a perception that Howard would escape punishment and reap poisonous profit at Hispano expense. Reportedly to ensure that Howard would pay retribution, "four men were hired to come from the other side of the river (Mexico) and kill him," the alleged conspiracy incited by the Priest of Guadalupe, Mexico, Antonio Borajo.[7] Special Texas Rangers were recruited from local citizenry to keep the peace and protect property, but they along with Howard were placed under siege, and ultimately captured in an action which can best be simply described as a riot. While murder, mayhem, and looting was in progress, the remaining Anglo population cried out for help.[8]

El Paso County Sheriff Charles Kerber was indeed hamstrung from a manpower standpoint, unable to raise a sufficient fighting force. He urgently telegraphed Texas Governor R. B. Hubbard with the following request, "Allow me to raise 100 in New Mexico."[9]

The Governor replied, "Dispatch received. Raise 100 men at once, to resist invasion, put down insurrection, and re-enforce State troops..."[10]

Sheriff Kerber immediately sought aid in New Mexico, "I telegraphed in every direction. Was promised 40 men at Las Cruces (sic) and 50 at Silver City..."[11] His confidence rising with anticipation of reinforcements arriving Kerber penned, 'I expect 50 citizens from Silver City and then I will drive the scoundrels ahead of me like sheep....You will find I will not allow the greasers to pass unpunished."[12]

In New Mexico, Deputy Sheriff Dan Tucker helped raise a contingent of men which would become known as the Silver City Volunteers or the Silver City Rangers. Unfortunately for some, the Silver City Volunteers were made up of some of the roughest and toughest of the border country, including the notorious John Kinney, outlaw and livestock rustler extraordinare.[13] One historian generalizes, "The new recruits were hard faced and battle scarred...they nearly all had reputations."[14] Certainly not all of the Silver City Volunteers were outlaws and rustlers, but it would be reasonable to wager, all were itching for action, especially since they were to be cloaked in the officialdom of a rescuing posse, and the enemy was non-white. Although the rank and file were to be paid $40.00 per month and forage, most would have volunteered their service *gratis*, just to satisfy an appetite for adventure.[15] Primed with adrenaline, alcohol, and attitude, the crew from Silver City arrived in El Paso County on December 22, 1877, ready to "whip ass and take names."[16]

It should come as no surprise that Dan Tucker was chosen to lead this set of New Mexican mercenaries, and his selection is confirmed by several accounts. The Grant County *Herald* reported, "D. Tucker has been chosen captain of the Silver City Company now in El Paso county."[17] In a recent article on outlaw John Kinney, Frederick Nolan displays an actual copy of Kinney's discharge from Sheriff Kerber's posse, which refers to Kinney being a private in "Lt. Tuckers Company of Volunteers of State forces."[18] Numerous mentions of Tucker's leadership role are authenticated in *House of Representatives, Executive Document Number 93*, the U. S. Government report on the investigation into the ill-advised affair. On one hand, Tucker's lieutenancy possibly illustrates just how much of a reputation he already had garnered. By any standard this was a "hard crowd," and one not easy to falsely impress. On the other hand, ensuing events were not fundamentally aligned with well principled law enforcement, and since Tucker was the leader, he cannot be excused from an appropriate degree of responsibility.

Upon arrival in El Paso County the Silver City Volunteers were brought up to speed on the status of the dismal and tragic mess. Judge Charles Howard, John McBride, and John Atkinson had been executed by a hastily formed rag-tag firing squad; merchant Charles Ellis had been captured, dragged behind a galloping horse, and finally stabbed to death; and Texas Ranger C. E. Mortimer had been mortally wounded by sniper fire. Widespread looting was in progress, and Father Borajo was reportedly encouraging violence by declaring, "Shoot all the gringos and I will absolve you."[19]

Civil authorities in El Paso County had sought but not received aid from the U. S. Army, and their disappointment is simply illustrated in the caustic barb from Ranger Lt. Tays, "When I arrived here the greatest excitement prevailed and found Captain Blair (USA) making preparation to start to my assistance with his command of 18 men *some time next spring*."(emphasis added)[20] One chronicler of early military history theorizes, "Most, if not all, the bloodshed and property destruction could have been avoided if a federal officer, Blair, had been less timid and state officials less tardy in requesting necessary assistance."[21] In his report to William Steel, the Texas Adjutant General, Texas Ranger Major John B. Jones declared, "…Captain Blair could have gone into where the state troops were without meeting with serious opposition; and if he had done so not a shot would have been fired, and the trouble would have been ended."[22] Even back at Silver City the rift between military and civilian forces was recognized by the editor of the Grant County *Herald*, "We hear it stated upon good authority that quite an unfriendly feeling exists between the Rangers and United States troops stationed in El Paso county."[23]

Below what is now El Paso, but then Franklin, Mexican Nationals and their brothers from the Texas side of the river, were in complete possession of the towns of San Elizario and Ysleta, exhaustively caught up in a frenzy of ransacking and looting.[24] Insurrection and upheaval were seemingly boundless, as if the river had crested, washing helplessly terrified Anglos downstream in a surreal ethnological cleansing. But it was a miscalculation, and the backwash was to sweep over the "insurrectos" with ferocious retribution. Speaking of his deceased

Caucasian comrades, one rescuer spiritedly scribbled, "(they) met their fate like brave gentlemen fully believing we would avenge them, *and we will*."[25]

Ward hit the bullseye when he reported, "Sheriff Kerber had been promised the aid of fifty men from Silver City...thirty men from Silver City arrived; judging by their performance it is well that fifty did not come."[26] Ensuing events will definitely disclose the Silver City Volunteers came psychologically prepared for battle, and the dementia could not be cured by anything less.

Retaliatory bloodletting was the inescapable ethnocentric solution. "It is reported that the San Elizario mob have their pickets posted within two miles of El Paso, Texas, and that every movement of the United States troops and citizen forces is carefully noted. They are evidently preparing for a stubborn resistance, and as they are well armed, the conflict may be a serious one."[27] During the siege, mayhem and murderous rebellion telegraphic communications simplified transmitting news, and the Galveston *Daily News* enlightened their salty readership with a squalling forecast of the looming human hurricane, "The blood shed by the Mexican butchers at San Elizario will hardly be suffered to go unavenged for the flimsy technical reason that it was a purely local squabble over a salt pond."[28]

Three separate units took to the field with the purpose of quelling the disturbance, restoring order, arresting violators, recovering bodies, and depending on individual perspective, exacting revenge. Colonel Edward Hatch, Ninth Cavalry led the military detachment, inexperienced Lt. J. B. Tays led a contingent of local citizens designated as Texas Rangers, and the incensed El Paso County Sheriff Charles Kerber headed a small posse, which also included the Silver City Volunteers. The Campbell brothers, J. W. and I. F., cajoled the mules pulling a wagon containing the coffins reserved for the known deceased.[29] The blame game was about to begin.

Crescencio Yrigayen, a suspected mob leader was soon captured in possession of some of the arms stolen from the Rangers during the earlier siege.[30] Another suspected insurrectionist, Santiago Durand, likewise was arrested.[31] With the military unit operating ahead of the civilian forces, the El Paso posse and the Silver City crowd spent the night (12-22-1877) at the residence of local Ranger Price Cooper. Bright and early the next morning, the outfit struck out, the two prisoners with their hands bound riding atop the coffins as the wagon bucked and clattered toward the scene of expected action. Shortly thereafter, about a mile from Ysleta, the *escaping prisoners* were shot, at least that was the story according to the Rangers and Sheriff Kerber.[32] Colonel Hatch believed otherwise![33]

Nearing Socorro (Texas) one of the Rangers was reportedly wounded by a shot fired through a door from the inside of a house.[34] The response was immediate, Gregorio Holguin was killed, his wife left lying on the dusty floor, shot through the lungs. Toribio G. Rubio, a lad of thirteen years, was in the house at the time, and was "scared out of his wits."[35] Later, on site investigation failed to locate any bullet holes fired through, and from behind the door.[36] Mariana Nunez gave a similar account of what appears to be the same story, stating her husband was killed by the Rangers, she being shot in the side, but her account does not reveal her departed spouse's name, therefore there is at least the possibility of confusion on the part of Rubio, or maybe oversight on the part of Edmund Stine, Mariana's interpreter, or even slight plausibility that another murder went unrecorded.[37] In any event, there the matter ended.

Major Jones, although generally sympathetic to the realities of frontier law enforcement was forced to admit, "Other excesses and disorders by the state troops and the sheriff's posse are said to have been committed about the same time."[38] He wasn't wrong!

Jesús Telles, known insurgent and frenzied mutilator of Judge Howard's body, was then spotted by the Rangers. According to at least one report, Telles *charged* the posse and was fatally cut down, still holding one of the dead Texans' six-shooters in his hand.[39] Another unidentified rebel fired at the Rangers and he too was shot down.[40] Case closed!

With the lack of any resistance, organized or otherwise, the Rangers and the Silver City Volunteers encamped at Ysleta.[41] Idleness is often the father of misdeed, and the New Mexico contingent were soon to be labeled—border bastards.

Pedro Cauelario, a local Justice of the Peace, testified that he and his son were disarmed by pistol-pointing Rangers, but Lt. Tays finally recovered the weapons and returned them to him. He also named Rangers F. Johnson and J. Williams as committing an "outrage" on his sister-in-law, Salome Telles.[42] Salome confirmed Pedro's account, adding the Rangers shot her dog, pot shot at her chickens, stole money, and then one, "pointed the pistol at my breast and forced me to give up my person to him."[43] Antonio Cadena swore Rangers ransacked his house, pointed a revolver at him, stole his six-shooter, cartridge belt, saddle, bridle, spurs, and two horses.[44] Noverto Pais reported the Rangers "hit me with their pistols twice, and I have the marks yet."[45]

Even an Anglo, J. P. Miller, testified he was temporarily kidnapped, guns shoved in his face, and threatened with his life if he failed to point out the location of two women. Miller reported, "These men belonged to the Tucker crowd, who came from Silver City."[46] Moritz Lowenstein, Ysleta Postmaster, professed under oath that Sheriff Kerber, through him, "paid several citizens for corn, and corn-stalks and poles which were taken by Lieutenant Tucker's men, and for damages done by them."[47] Sheriff Kerber was forced to acknowledge, "Martin's horse was also taken by the Tucker men, and I ordered the horse given up, and he was returned to him. Some arms were also taken from Pedro Candelario and his son by Tucker's men, which I ordered to be returned to him, and they were. I also paid for corn and fodder taken from different parties by these men, and for damage done to the parties by the same men."[48]

Sonnichsen properly notes the feeding frenzy was getting out of control, Rangers fighting among themselves, noting that Sgt. Ford killed Sgt. Frazer, and then quite accurately postulates, "and other desirable homicides might have followed if the Silver City 'Rangers' had not been mustered out on January 10."[49] Possibly in a calculated effort at a finger-pointing and face-saving gesture, Texas Ranger Lt. J. B. Tays, remarked, "I wish they would clear out of here. Lieutenant Tucker's men, from Silver City, behaved very badly; not all of them, for some of them were very good men. It is well known here that those offenses, such as ravishing women, taking people's property, and breaking doors and windows were, committed by Lieutenant Tucker's men..."[50] Tays was forced to acknowledge the Silver City Volunteers "didn't appear to be under any restraint," and many of them were "bad" men," and in a transparent effort to separate himself from the New Mexicans, guilefully added, "I didn't consider they were in the service of the State, as they had not been mustered into the service of the State."[51] Tays was indeed needful of a degree of public support, and semblance of political deniability, for some contemporaries were already accusing him of initially surrendering, and therefore causing the execution of Judge Howard, McBride, and Atkinson. Although he could hardly be cognizant then, Tays would go down in history as the only Texas Ranger who ever surrendered, inviting Walter Prescott Webb to register, "The man lacked resourcefulness, initiative, and that combination of dash and judgment so essential in a crisis."[52]

Twentieth Judicial District Judge A. Blacker, in an attempt to absolve Texans of outrages, craftily scribbled, "These (New Mexico Volunteers) were not the State's soldiers; they were not enrolled, not mustered, not sworn, and have not been paid. These men, it is said committed some fearful excesses and felonies, and some have fled the country."[53] El Paso County deputy sheriff H. H. Harvey testified, "I know of American citizens—one instance—going to El Paso, Mexico, and having a shooting scrape there...There were ten or twelve in the party, but by my advice they left their arms here, with the exception of two pistols, which they took with them. Kinney was one of them. They belonged to the Silver City crowd, Tucker's or Kinney's 'gang,' but they had been discharged by the sheriff..."[54]

Not surprisingly, but assuredly out of character for a clergyman, the insolent and instigating Padre Borrajo was offering a $1000 reward for the heads of certain posse members.[55] Nobody was foolish enough to try!

Of the Silver City Volunteers, the military board later commissioned to investigate the affair reported, "...on December 22 another small force of about thirty men arrived from Silver City, who had been called into temporary service by Sheriff Charles Kerber, under telegraphic instructions from the governor. But, unhappily, as was natural and according to experience in raising volunteers along the border, when the exigencies of the occasion do not permit that delay which a wise discrimination in the choice of material would cause, the force of rangers thus suddenly called together contained within its ranks an adventurous and lawless element, which, though not predominant, was yet strong enough to make its evil influence felt in deeds of violence and outraged matched only by the mob itself."[56]

Texas Ranger Major John B. Jones disagreed, and filed a minority report, which in part read, "The majority, referring to the conduct of the sheriff and his party at Socorro on the 25th of December last, speak of what was done as 'wanton outrage' and say that 'in brutality they were not excelled by the atrocities of the mob itself.' In time of profound peace and quiet it might be proper to characterize these occurrences as has been done by the majority...the sheriff considered it his duty to make the arrest of several parties, leaders of and active participants in the mob, who were known to be in Socorro, and to search certain houses for arms. In doing this several men were killed and one woman wounded; and on the same day two prisoners were killed; but these occurrences, transpiring in the wake of a wild, fanatical, and brutal mob, in a period of excitement, closing up a reign of terror by the mob which is said by the majority to have been 'brutal and atrocious,' though not justifiable, were probably unavoidably incident to the duties which the officer in charged conceived that he was called on to perform."[57]

In his comprehensive study, *BORDER, The U. S.—Mexico Line*, Metz rightly emphasizes that "everyone on both sides of the border had disgraced themselves..."[58]

Actual hostilities were in fact over, but dawn was just breaking over a battlefield of faultfinding and rancorous rhetoric. One New York newspaper referred to Texas Governor Hubbard as a "imbecile" for even seeking assistance from the U. S. Military, characterizing the eruption of violence as a "mere local disturbance."[59] Others fired back, that if the strife was 'a purely local matter' it was so for entirely technical reasons because the troubles began on the American side of the Rio Grande.[60] Governments from each side of the river blamed the other for failing to bring lawbreakers to summary judgment. Military officials criticized local authorities for exuberant over-reaction, state authorities censured the military for action best described as "too little, too late," Mexicans bemoaned aggressive capitalism from across the muddy current, and Texans ridiculed non-Anglos as ignorant men, with little intelligence.[61] And *all* rebuked "Tucker's crowd" whose men "seem especially to be responsible for the rapes, homicides, and other crimes of which the people justly complained."[62]

Tucker's bunch were indeed chips off rough bark, but that fact had not been kept secret during their recruitment, when they were needed, and is simply clarified by just one contemporary press account, "The tradition of the country is that New Mexico was made up of the loose rocks and ends and ragged remnants of creation, after the world was completed, and that Mesilla is a fit capital for it. Now it is a land of refuge for numerous outlaws, driven from Texas and other States."[63] In response to a earlier request for help from New Mexico, Texas Ranger Major Jones received the reply, "I can raise the ten fighting men, but they are hard cases."[64]

At least one of the hardcases, John Kinney, must have thought El Paso County would produce a bountiful crop, ripe for "easy pickings," as he opted to remain in the area after his January 10, 1878 discharge from Sheriff Kerber's posse. Opening the Exchange Saloon, Kinney tried publicly to foster the belief that he was a legitimate businessman, but not with much success, due in part to association with nefarious comrades, and even wide-open El Paso frowned when he got into a shooting scrape with a man locally known as "Buckskin Joe."[65] Kinney gathered his cohorts and rode north into history, causing the perplexed Texas Ranger Lieutenant J. A. Tays to remark, "The mob of desperadoes that was around El Paso Texas have all left for Lincoln county."[66] Dan Tucker didn't make the trip, he had already returned to Grant County.

Unquestionably, at least at the time, Tucker's New Mexico squad was just what the Texans were looking for, but in the end, results seem to reveal they got much more than they bargained for. Careful review of all the investigative data does not specifically implicate Dan Tucker in atrocious acts, criminal behavior, or daring misdeeds, but since he was theoretically "in charge" he should not escape historic admonishment. He could have done better and he should have!

NOTES AND SOURCES

1. Sonnichsen, C. L., *The El Paso Salt War*. P. 61. Hereafter cited as Sonnichsen.

2. Ward, Charles Francis, "The Salt War of San Elizaro (1877)", Master of Arts Thesis, 1932., University of Texas, Austin. P. 10-12. Hereafter cited as Ward.

3. Ibid., P. 8.

4. Austerman, Wayne, R., *Sharps Rifles and Spanish Mules, The San Antonio—El Paso Mail, 1851—1881*. P. 33. Naturally as time went by, new routes were chosen, and roadbeds improved, thereby reducing the arduous stagecoach trip by several days, yet, prior to the advent of railroads, the trip from interior Texas to El Paso remained a major undertaking.

5. Sonnichsen, P. 36. Also see, Wilkins, Frederick. *The Law Comes To Texas—The Texas Rangers, 1870-1901*. "Governor Hubbard had decided to send help, but he was not sure about how to do so since it would take a Ranger company almost a month to reach the area, and none could be spared from their assigned locations. He decided to send Major Jones to observe conditions and make a recommendation for a solution. Jones traveled by train from Austin to Topeka, Kansas, and from there took another train west as far as it ran into New Mexico. Then he rode by stage down to Franklin, Texas, arriving days ahead of the usual mail stage across West Texas." P. 137. Hereafter cited as Wilkins.

6. Metz, Leon Claire, *The Shooters* . P. 217. Hereafter cited as Metz.

7. Report of Adjutant General, State of Texas, 1878. P. 23. {John B. Jones}. Hereafter cited as AG-1878. Courtesy Texas State Library and Archives Commission. Austin. Texas.

8. For an overall account of the "Salt War" see Sonnichsen and Ward as cited. For a synopsis see Metz as cited. Curiously, C. L. Douglas, *Famous Texas Feuds*, covers the subject but fails to include any mention of volunteers coming from New Mexico Territory. For more detailed review and analysis, including statements of actual participants, see *United States House of Representatives, Executive Document No. 93, 45th Congress, 2d Session, 1878*. Hereafter cited as HR-ED No. 93. {specific statement}.

9. HR-ED No. 93 {Keber to Hubbard, 12-14-1878}

10. AG-1878. P. 23. {Hubbard to Keber, 12-15-1878}.

11. HR-ED No. 93 {Report of Sheriff Charles Keber, 12-25-1877} Also see Grant County *Herald*, 12-14-1877, "Sheriff Kerber just received a dispatch from Governor Hubbard authorizing him to raise one hundred men in New Mexico and try to relieve the State troops."

12. Letter of Charles Keber to George B. Zimpelman, dated 12-19-1877 and published in the Galveston *Daily News* on 01-06-1878.

13. Tucker's participation and leadership role in the Silver City Volunteers is repeatedly, as will be observed, mentioned in HR-ED No. 93. John Kinney is occasionally mentioned. Also see, Mullin, and Nolan as cited. Curiously, Bob L'Aloge, fails to even mention Dan Tucker's leadership role during the "El Paso Salt War" in *Knights of the Sixgun, A Diary of Gunfighters, Outlaws and Villains of New Mexico*, although he devotes an entire chapter to John Kinney who was officially ranked as a private in the Silver City Volunteers.

14. Sonnichsen, P. 58.

15. Nolan, P. 18., reports the $40.00 per month and forage figure for the Silver City posse. Unfortunately a roster of the Silver City Volunteers has not be located as of yet. Nolan is most probably "right on the money" because an examination of the *Muster and Payroll* of Lt. J. A. Tays, Company C, Frontier Battalion, Texas Rangers, reveals privates were paid at the rate of $40.00 per month and that Lt. Tays was paid $75.00 per month. Undisputedly, Dan Tucker was the leader of the Silver City Volunteers, often referred to as Lt. Tucker in the official reports, and most probably paid at the rate of $75.00 per month, if paid at all. *Muster and Payroll*, courtesy of Donaly Brice, Texas State Library and Archives Commission. Austin, Texas.

16. Webb, Walter Prescott., *The Texas Rangers—A Century of Frontier Defense*. P. 363. Hereafter cited as Webb. Other documents confirm the 12-22-1877 date. Webb identifies Tucker and Kinney as leaders of the Silver City Volunteers.

17. Grant County *Herald*, 01-05-1878. Confirming Tucker's leadership role, the same newspaper edition carried a separate story which in part read, "...Last night at 9 p. m. as a man of Lt. Tay's company was returning from the quarters of Lt. Tucker's company, he met two men who halted him and immediately opened fire upon him, which he returned."

18. Nolan, P. 15.

19. HR-ED No. 93. P. 98 {Letter of J. N. Garcia} Also see, Sonnichsen, P. 49-58.

20. Tays to Major Jones, Frontier Battalion 12-20-1877, quoted in Ward P. 118., and Sonnichsen, P. 57.

21. Leckie, William H., *The Buffalo Soldiers—A Narrative of the Negro Cavalry in the West.* P. 190. Hereafter cited as Leckie.

22. AG-1878. P. 16. {John B. Jones}

23. Grant County *Herald*, 01-05-1878.

24. Ward, P. 121.

25. Sonnichsen, P. 58.

26. Ward, P. 122.

27. Grant County *Herald*, 12-22-1877.

28. Galveston *Daily News*, 12-26-1877.

29. HR-ED No. 93. P. 84-85. {Statements of J. W. and I. F. Campbell}

30. Sonnichsen, P 58.

31. Ibid.

32. HR-ED No. 93. P. 79. {Report of Charles Kerber}

33. Sonnichsen, P. 59. Also see HR-ED No. 93. P. 87. {Report of Colonel Edward Hatch} Hatch reported that the deceased prisoners bodies were examined and he found one had "five or six bullet-holes in his head, shot through the hat-band; the other was shot in the forehead and in the side. So near was the shot in the side it was evident the gun had been near his clothing....I was then assured in my own mind that these prisoners were killed without necessity..."

34. Ward, P. 126

35. El Paso Times, 01-31-1937.

36. Sonnichsen, P. 59.

37. HR-ED No. 93. P. 84. {Statement of Mariana Nunez}

38. AG-1878. P. 17. {John B. Jones}

39. HR-ED No. 93. P. 79. {Statement of Sheriff Charles Kerber}

40. Ibid. Sonnichsen identifies this subject as Cruz Chaves. P. 59.

41. Sonnichsen, P. 59.

42. HR-ED No. 93. P. 90. {Statement of Pedro Cauelario}

43. Ibid., P. 90. {Statement of Salome Telles}

44. Ibid., P. 93. {Statement of Antonio Cadena}

45. Ibid., P. 94. {Statement of Noverto Pais}

46. Ibid., P. 95. {Statement of J. P. Miller}

47. Ibid., P. 114 {Statement of Moritz Lowenstein}

48. Ibid., P. 117 {Statement of Charles Kerber}

49. Sonnichsen, P. 59. Also see, AG-1878. P. 23. {Telegram to Keber from AG Steele, January 9, 1878} "The emergency calling for the posse having passed you will discharge them. With the forces now in El Paso peace should be assured."

50. HR-ED No. 93. P. 114 {Statement of Moritz Lowenstein}

51. Ibid., P. 116. {Statement of J. B. Tays}

52. Webb, P. 367. Metz reports, "For the first and only time in history, a Texas Ranger Company had been taken captive." P. 227.

53. HR-ED No. 93. P. 126. {Report of A. Blacker}

54. Ibid., P. 64. {Statement of H. H. Harvey}

55. Grant County *Herald*, 01-12-1878.

56. HR-ED No. 93. P. 17. {Majority Report}

57. HR-ED No. 93. P. 22. {Minority Report}

58. Metz, Leon C., BORDER, The U. S.—Mexico Line. P. 172.

59. Galveston *Daily News* 12-26-1877.

60. Ibid.

61. HR-ED No. 93. P. 117. {Statement of Charles Kerber}

62. Ibid., P. 4. {Report of W. M. Dunn, Judge-Advocate General}

63. Galveston *Daily News*, 01-11-1878

64. Ibid.

65. Nolan, P. 14-21. Price reports the Exchange Saloon was the "hang-out for New Mexican *mal hombres* (bad men)," and "Shootings were frequent, and even Kinney was once wounded." P. 209. Thrapp says the Exchange Saloon was a "hangout for the most parasitical." Vol. II, P. 786.

66. Rasch, Philip J., *Warriors of Lincoln County*. P. 152. Quoting a letter from J. A. Tays to Major John B. Jones, 05-31-1879.

4

"I GUESS HE DONE A GOOD JOB KILLIN' HIM"

Deputy Sheriff Dan Tucker returned to duty at Silver City, but while in Texas, J. H. Mills had been named Grant County Jailer, an understandable occurrence—someone had to watch over pilferous prisoners.[1] Apparently in Tucker's absence, a dearth of tranquillity on Silver City streets, a lack of peace and harmony in emporiums of liquid refreshment, and general fractious misbehavior, had at last obliged city fathers to ante up. On April 11, 1878, Dan Tucker was appointed Silver City's first town marshal.[2] Dan held on to his Deputy Sheriff position, which under the fee system paid for work actually performed, but most of his time was now spent in town.

Ball clarifies how early lawmen were paid: "The income of the frontier lawman was based on the fee system, rather than on the present-day salary procedure. The sheriff was paid only when he and his deputies served process of court or performed some other duty, usually around the spring and fall court sessions. Even then he did not receive a monthly, or even daily, income as an officer of the court. Instead, the sheriff and his deputies earned a percentage of the fee for each item of work performed. A suspicious public believed that this 'piece-work' payment insured that the officer had indeed performed a particular service. Court business was often meager in the thinly settled southwestern counties and depended upon the number of crimes committed within the sheriff's jurisdiction. Many sheriffs maintained a private business and part-time shrievalty."[3]

Then as now, the question of law enforcement remuneration occasionally captured public attention, evidenced by these editorial urgings in the Silver City *Tribune*: "The fees of officers should be regulated and raised, and in all cases where the Territory or safety of the citizens requires any service of any officer, he should be reasonably compensated by the Territory or county."[4]

Likewise, it was expected, and in fact necessary, for deputies to supplement their income from other sources, and many were actively involved in mining or real-estate speculation, cattle ranching, transportation, both wholesale and retail mercantile enterprises, and not just a few added gambling to the list. Evidence reveals Deputy Dan Tucker financially dabbled in divers projects calculated to subsidize the fees paid by the city and county entities for his law enforcement services.

And Silver City recurrently required a touch of law enforcement service, but not all encounters were with the "badman from bitter creek," aptly illustrated by this local news blurb:

> A certain prominent executive officer of this county, who shall be nameless, was fined the small sum of five dollars and costs last Monday Morning for violation of city ordinance No. 6. The accused had been practicing at a mark within the limits, and came up and paid the bill like a little man. He pleaded guilty.[5]

Idle speculation could easily lead to an assumption that Dan Tucker was the "little man" and guilty culprit, and he *may* have been, but there the story must end. With a proven no-nonsense attitude, and a dead-shot reputation, it wasn't too long before Dan had the city back under reasonable control. The Grant County *Herald* proudly proclaimed, "Marshal Tucker under the city government has put a stop to the discharge of firearms upon our streets."[6]

That Dan Tucker played the dual role of both city and county lawman is clearly evidenced by examination of Probate Court records for the time period. As was often the case, Dan Tucker was forced to set aside city police business, don his Sheriff's hat and preside at sessions of Grant County court.[7] And with regularity he was forced to switch back to his police hat and lock up rambunctious spirits who had overindulged and were causing disorder in barrooms or on Silver City streets. Unquestionably Deputy Sheriff/City Policeman Dan Tucker had his hands full.

Tucker's sterling efforts at maintaining peace on municipal streets may have been lauded by frontier editors and local politicians who were promoting the boundless business opportunities offered by a permanent Silver City residency, but just like other booming Western communities, part of the population was drawn from a floating crowd which profiteered on a regular gambling circuit. And just like other sporting "hot spots" such as Las Vegas (N. M.), Tucson, Tombstone, San Antonio, Fort Griffin, and the Monte Carlo of the West, El Paso—Silver City with open arms and southwestern hospitality welcomed the gambling fraternity, who could be counted on to infuse the local economy with fresh capital and firsthand reports on the latest underground gossip, especially in winter months when northern snows forced a gentle heat-seeking migration southward.[8] DeArment reports the professionals "were known by sight wherever they went and were welcomed enthusiastically by the townsmen, for it was an article of faith on the frontier that the degree of prosperity of a town was in direct proportion to the number of high-rolling gamblers on hand at a given time."[9]

Two kindred spirits arrived in Silver City during 1879, one of which would later play a significant role in the saga of Dan Tucker. One wore pants, the other a skirt, but both were arrayed in the cloth of mystery, murder, and a murky past. Frank Thurmond, a "San Antonio gambler of renown," was accompanied by his wife Charlotte, an accomplished bettor in her own right, but more commonly known to history as Lottie Deno, the queen of Fort Griffin's gaming tables.[10] One prolific contributor to southwestern historical pages described Lottie this way: "She was a strange one. Cold as ice, warm as silk, silent as a passing ship…"[11] Besides Lottie, Frank Thurmond's constant companion was a Bowie knife. Reportedly he was an expert in its use, (subsequent events will confirm the assessment) and it was common knowledge that Frank "would give ground to no one."[12] At Silver City, Frank dealt faro and Charlotte "served as lookout" at the Gem, a combination dance hall and barroom.[13] That Dan Tucker knew and favorably associated with Frank and Charlotte is of little doubt, and history records that when the time came for Frank to step forward and back his friends—he did! But for now, Dan Tucker had Silver City lawlessness pretty much under the control of his hammer-cocking thumb.

Outside of town, however, a murder most foul! In truth the dastardly deed had occurred in November of the preceding year, but during March, 1879, the grisly story developed into a full scale, and very public criminal investigation. Sheriff Whitehill received information from a not too confidential source, Kitt Conn, that H. F. Dwenger had not been seen of late, and was reportedly on a trip back to visit his Missouri home. Remarkably though, all of Dwenger's livestock was still grazing in the pasture at his place east of town—down to the last solitary mule.[14] A particularly peculiar circumstance for a man making a long trip? Besides, as the sheriff was informed, William "Parson" Young and Dwenger's wife were "getting kinda thick." Sheriff Whitehill did some skilled sleuthing, determined something was indeed amiss, and aided by good fortune was successful in extracting a murder confession from Dwenger's fifteen year-old son, Billy. Not much to the sheriff's surprise, Billy acknowledged he had not acted alone, and he had been assisted by William "Parson" Young, all the evil doing committed at the urging of his mother, Dora Dwenger. The conspirators had buried the deceased in a unmarked grave between the Hanover mine and Georgetown, a few miles east of Silver City.[15] Sheriff Whitehill upon locating the grave had the body exhumed.[16]

On April 5th the Grant County *Herald* reported the results of the Coroners Jury, which in part read: "After due deliberation and examination upon our oaths do find that the deceased Henry F. Dwenger, came to his death from a gunshot wound in the hands of his son William (Billy) Dwenger, assisted by William Young; the ball entering the back of the head and coming out at the right eye…" During the July term,

murder indictments were returned for William "Parson" Young, Dora
Dwenger, and her son William, by the Grant County Grand Jury.[17] All
three were later convicted for the murder, Young sentenced to be
hanged, Billy receiving a life term, and Dora caught ten years.[18] The
Whitehill family took in the remaining Dwenger child, a toddler, three
year-old Josie.[19]

Young offered the assertion he was insane, based in large part on a
claim his skull had been previously injured, and he now had a steel plate
in his head, thus explaining his nickname of "Silver Plate Dick."[20]
Concerned that he might be forced to hang someone lacking sufficient
mental faculties to comprehend what was happening, Sheriff Whitehill
instigated and pushed for an examination (sanity hearing) in which four
physicians were present. The sheriff's brother, Perrine P. Whitehill, who
often served as a jailer, testified that Young had the "capacity to judge."
In the end, medical men agreed, and the execution order stood, pending
Territorial Supreme Court appeal.[21]

Seemingly with no appreciation or recognition of the chances he was
taking in making arrests and maintaining order, Tucker was forced to
resign the position of Town Marshal, "largely a result of the fact that up
to that time he had received no remuneration whatever..."[22] Still, he was
eking out a living under the fee system—"Deputy Sheriff Tucker is busy
summoning jurors for our next term of court."[23] Finally in March of
1879, the city council approved payment to Tucker in the amount of
$91.66 as partial payment for previous work performed.[24] Likewise, the
County Commissioner's paid Tucker for jail expenses dating back to
December of 1877.[25]

The errors of the past council gave way in May 1879, and a newly
elected slate of Silver City Councilmen re-appointed Tucker town
marshal.[26]

While Sheriff Whitehill took off for Fort Wayne, Indiana on an
altruistic mission to deliver the orphaned Dwenger child to relatives,
City Marshal Dan Tucker was making sure city streets were being
repaired utilizing "chain gang" labor from the jail.[27]

Fortunately for Silver City residents, the next few months appear
rather quiet and mundane in an analysis of the city's crime problem.
Unfortunately for modern historians, Tucker's next six-shooter exploit is
not too well documented. A brief notice in the local paper recounts what
was now becoming a seemingly dull, and all too familiar story—"Deputy
Sheriff Tucker, charged with killing a man who resisted arrest, had a
hearing in front of Justice Givens, last Thursday. It was a case of
justifiable homicide."[28]

Certainly this shooting should not be confused with Tucker's earlier
killing of Juan Garcia, who as reported suffered for months before
expiring, but died seventeen months before this article appeared in the
local paper. The circumstances too, are quite different.

It is highly plausible this episode was the one referred to by Sheriff Whitehill's son, Wayne, who reported he witnessed Tucker in action: "...there was a Mexican went haywire there and he was in one little room in a little old 'dobe shack and had a door and just a couple of windows and every time anybody would go by he'd throw frying' pans and everything he had out at anybody. So somebody run up the street there and called Tucker and he come down there and Tucker walked over and he threw somethin' at him and Tucker popped him and killed him right there...That Mexican, I guess, would have harmed somebody if he hadn't of been killed. He was sure a wild man. I guess he done a good job killin' him. Everybody thought so anyhow."[29]

Well not quite everybody! One old-timer was to remark over fifty years later, "Had he (Tucker) been a more restrained and cooler officer, most of the killings he was responsible for need never have taken place."[30] The majority, however, were on the side of Tucker.

Dan Rose wrote for the Silver City *Independent*, "Tucker was called to a house where a Mexican was murdering his wife and son. He had beaten them with a club, and had begun to demolish the furniture when Tucker arrived. Through a window the Mexican saw Tucker coming, and stepped behind the door. As Tucker, with his gun in his hand, entered the door, the Mexican brought his club down on the deputy's arm, knocking the gun to the floor. Quick as a flash Tucker picked up the gun with his left hand and shot the Mexican dead."[31]

And just *maybe* the following account refers to the same shooting, "...attempting to arrest a Mexican at Silver City, in the month of September, Sheriff Tucker received a severe blow on the arm with a rock, that lamed him for several weeks. His six-shooter was brought into play, and the coroner had a job for the next day."[32]

Assuredly, as evidenced by his past performance, and on this occasion, when Deputy Dan Tucker advised "you're under arrest," it was no poker faced bluff! One local anecdote is illustrative of how having the reputation as a lethal lawman made Tucker's job less strenuous; and although conveniently amusing, it is honestly feasible and was reported as truth.

Sitting in front of the jail, Tucker had removed the cylinder from his pistol, and was in the process of cleaning the weapon, while at the same time talking with several gold-buttoned soldiers who had ambled by. Down the street, "a Mexican and his wife were quarreling," the husband pulled a knife, severely cut his wife, and thinking he had committed murder ran from the scene, still holding a knife dripping blood. The woman's screams attracted Tucker's attention. Springing into action, he quickly assessed the situation, saw the man running away holding the bloody knife, heading for the hills obviously intent on escape. Although Tucker's revolver, lacking the cylinder was utterly useless, he pointed it anyway at the fleeing suspect, and authoritatively hollered "stop or I'll shoot your ass," or something equally understandable. Looking over his shoulder, and seeing just who was pointing a six-shooter in his direction, the sprinter abruptly applied the foot brakes, turned "on a dime," and "trotted back to Tucker, his hat in his hand."[33]

Just a short time later, three suspects being held for murder assaulted a jailer, locked him in a cell, cut their shackles with an ax, stole a revolver, "scaled the prison walls" and fled to the hills east of town. With citizen informants pointing out the direction of travel, Deputy Dan Tucker quickly organized a squad of fellow armed citizens and gave pursuit. With characteristic decisiveness Dan Tucker maneuvered his posse into the advantageous position, and then made the escaping killers an offer they best not refuse. They didn't. A reporter simply said, "There was quite an excitement for a little while. They are now heavily ironed."[34]

While Tucker was trailing dangerous escapees through the piñons and junipers, cattle rustlers stole sixty-five head of rancher Dan Coomer's cattle. In the company of a black fellow rancher, and for whatever reason unable to get help from Sheriff Whitehill, Coomer followed the outlaw's trail for twenty-four days. The trail led through the Burro Mountains south of Silver City, down the Gila, through the Carlisle Range, and finally on into Arizona Territory, and then back into the Burro Mountains. Coomer overtook two of the rustlers, and killed them. One of the outlaws had "lit out" the day before, and Coomer who was busy gathering his stolen stock, sent word to Dan Tucker, who promptly arrested the beleaguered rustler at Lone Mountain. After completing his round-up, and returning cattle to his home range in the Santa Rita Mountains, Coomer "hunted up Acting Sheriff Tucker, and offered to give himself into custody, if any warrant had been issued or complaint been made against him, on the score of killing cattle thieves."[35] There hadn't been, nor would there ever be! In a later day interview about lawlessness and rustlers, Coomer who was at political odds with Sheriff Harvey Whitehill, remarked, "He (the sheriff) had but one good deputy that I know of, and that was Tucker."[36]

Certainly Tucker was leading a thrilling life, involved in numerous instances of gunplay, arresting cattle rustlers, capturing escaped murderers, and performing in a manner which fit the sort of profile that would later capture the attention of twentieth-century writers and movie-makers. But routine business also plays a part in any lawman's life. Tucker was seemingly constantly serving summons for Grand and Petit jurors for Grant County and presenting bills to the city government for services rendered.[37] And the work simply did not end upon service of a subpoena. As a servant of the court, the sheriff (and deputies) was responsible for storing evidence, providing security for both prisoners and witnesses—and the court. Additionally, the chief county lawman was expected to care for juries, providing "bed and board," all the while maintaining privacy and providing security. Naturally lawmen were under obligatory oath to offer testimony and appear as witnesses themselves when assisting in the prosecution of criminal cases. Civil lawsuits between battling litigants who were fighting for monetary damages, or seeking redress for actual or perceived wrongs created nearly as much heartburn for the local lawman as did trying to criminally penalize felons and misdemeanants. And just as one court session ended—it was time to began preparations for the next.[38]

Never far removed from danger during his New Mexico days, Tucker was nearly killed in late December 1879 while attempting to arrest a drunken Carpio Rodriquez. The arrestee, jerked a pistol, fired, and the "ball passed through the Marshal's clothing," but did not strike flesh or bone.[39] Although information is sketchy as to what happened next, it would not inordinately stretch the imagination to speculate, Rodriquez quite probably received a thump on the head—at a minimum—before being thrown in jail.

In early 1880, the deputy was temporarily relocated to the southwest portion of the county.[40] The Grant County *Herald* reported:

> D. Tucker, City Marshal started for Shakespeare on this morning's coach. We understand that for the present, Tuck will remain at Shakespeare, he having received the appointment of Deputy Sheriff for that section of the county.[41]

Located about two and a half miles southwest of present day Lordsburg, and a reasonably short horseback trip from the Arizona line, Shakespeare was a place of many names, many mines, many money-makers, and many misfits. Originally known as Mexican Springs or Pyramid Station, then Grant, still later as Ralston, and finally enduringly christened Shakespeare to escape being tarred forevermore as the birthplace of the Great Diamond Hoax, the collection of mud-formed buildings on the mining camp's single street gradually metamorphosed to a consequential community.[42] The town quickly became a welcome oasis for those traveling east or west, and a seemingly safe refuge for lonely prospectors who tried to maintain connection with some semblance of civilization. There was indeed psychological urgency in maintaining a resolute link with familiar humankind, for renegade Apaches threatened, "...most of the time."[43]

Shakespeare became a thriving center for activity, and could by 1880 brag of a post office and a telegraph operator, as well as an assortment of businesses designed to cater to public needs, real or recreational.[44] And yet, there was a transitory atmosphere. "There were no churches or Sunday schools, no lodges or fraternal organizations, and no social clubs in existence at Shakespeare; so it naturally resulted that those desiring amusement or recreation gathered together at the saloon."[45]

Early resident Emma Muir described the Roxy Jay Saloon as "cool as a cave" in the summer months and as "hot as an incubator" during the winter, and at all times "the center of Shakespeare's social life."[46] Adding, "It occupied the longest adobe building there, and its bar ran from one end to the other,. It was of polished mahogany, that bar, and was made to order in St. Louis, then shipped in one of the toiling freight wagons. On the wall behind it hung a great mirror, in which the prospector of the rugged Pyramids, the cattleman of the grama ranges, the pony mail-rider of the Indian trails, the rustler of the San Simon and the merchant of the town could watch themselves drink Roxy's bountiful offerings and find as much comfort in what they saw as what they drank. Occasionally six-guns disturbed the noisy calm of that fellowship, but no stress ever made anyone throw lead in the direction of that mirror....Wherever a light could be hung, there a light was, so that the place was a blaze of kerosene."[47]

One area resident reported a typical evening's diversity of conversation at the Roxy Jay, where interested observers could learn about the latest mining strike, be repulsed by ghastly details of the most recent Apache depredation, laugh at crude camp jokes, or listen to debates about the "respective mineral merits of different geological strata."[48] However, the chronicler did acknowledge, "here the miner lost his wages, and the prospector his mining claims...here was planned and often carried out all that was evil in the camp."[49]

Although there are indeed many thrilling stories erupting from Shakespeare's seemingly impenetrable and forbidding landscape, in telling the Dan Tucker story it will not be requisite to elaborate about Robert "Arkansas" Black's last minute harangue which timely untied the hangman's knot; of "Happy Bob" Fambro's death at the hands of an exasperated barkeep; or of "Bean Belly" Smith fatally filling Ross Woods full of lead during a dispute over the last egg to be found in camp.[50] Nor will it be necessary, or possible, to recite with pin-point precision just when each one of a number of colorful frontier characters made their appearance on the Shakespeare stage. Traveling between the isolated settlements in southeastern Arizona and southwestern New Mexico territories, and in and out of Shakespeare at the time, were such notables as "Curly Bill" Brocius; John Ringo; Joe Hill (Olney); Sandy King; Johnny Barnes; "Russian Bill" Tettenborn; the Clanton clan; the McLaury brothers, Frank and Tom; "Slim Jim" Crane; "Billy the Kid" Grounds; Harry Head; Charles "Pony Diehl" Ray; Billy Leonard; Zwing Hunt; the Haslett boys; and the "Sweetheart of the San Simon," Jim Hughes;—just to name a few.[51]

Suffice to say, the countryside was "plumb full" of players, many of which would later capture the idolizing attention of various twentieth-century historians and journalists. There should be no doubt, Deputy

Dan Tucker must have been personally familiar with part of this cast of rambling border badmen, and they with him.

Janaloo Hill disputes Tucker's reassignment to Shakespeare, "True, it had been said by a neighboring newspaper that Shakespeare was going to hire Dan Tucker as marshal, but there is absolutely no record of this becoming a reality. The total lack of any criminal cases from Shakespeare in the court records of Grant County during this period leads one to conclude that Shakespeare was, as it had always been, the town with no law."[52] Due to the paucity of records, just how much time Dan Tucker actually spent enforcing the law in and around Shakespeare as a deputy sheriff will have to remain undetermined. Indications, backed by reasonably solid evidence for this particular time period reveals Deputy Dan Tucker was seemingly in constant motion throughout the whole of old Grant County, not just in one locale. Clearly, Shakespeare was a community absent *much* law, but on occasion the blind mistress of justice did reach out and embrace the recalcitrant resident.

And sometimes her choice of deputies could in and of itself seem incongruous, simply illustrated by but one example. William A. "Billy the Kid" Grounds, a Texan by birth, a Shakespeare area resident by happenstance, and a disreputable character by choice, would sometimes walk the fine line between blameless and blameworthy.[53] With regularity, however, he would stumble, infrequently landing at the doorstep of law and order, but more generally falling across the threshold of illegality.

Whether or not Dan Tucker temporarily deputized Billy Grounds is not certain, but at least for a time, the youthful Billy played the part of a faithful frontier lawman, and transported a prisoner from Shakespeare to Silver City, receiving $6.50 from Grant County coffers for the trip.[54] While *official* law and order may have been in short supply at Shakespeare, careful examination of admittedly sparse evidence does seem to refute a claim of utter lawlessness. Tucker may have been busy elsewhere, and surely he appreciated "Billy the Kid" Grounds law enforcement efforts, but even he probably knew the youngster was playing both ends against the middle, and was not headed down the right road.

More than once, Billy chose the alternate route. One author reports Billy and his partner Zwing Hunt stole thirty head of cattle from the Persley and Woolf ranch in Arizona Territory's Sulphur Springs Valley.[55] An old timer alleges that Billy, along with others, robbed a church in "Old Mexico."[56] History does indeed record, that death would finally claim young Billy Grounds in a shoot-out with Arizona Territory lawmen at Chandler's Milk Ranch near Tombstone.[57]

Evidencing there was at least a smidgen of police work being done at Shakespeare is also illustrated by the arrest of Charley Williams.

Reportedly a cattle rustler from somewhere in Texas, Williams idled away his time drinking at Shakespeare, apparently with little or no constructive attention directed toward gainful employment.[58] Another account simply labels Williams an "old prospector."[59] Whether Charley was intermittently slipping out of town to trip a steer and burn his brand into the hide, or was picking and chipping away at promising rock outcroppings is of little real significance. Certainly consumption-suffering F. W. Mollitor didn't care one way or the other, all he desired was to lay in front of the Roxy Jay napping and soaking up the desert heat to ease his physical discomfort.[60] Outside the saloon Mollitor dozed in a habitual siesta, inside Charley William's eyes were open, but bloodshot and blurred. Staggering outside into the noonday sun, and brandishing his six-shooter, William's "eyes fell upon the prostrate man lying on the bench, he turned the pistol down on him and fired. Not a word passed at the time between them."[61] Mollitor died! And although data is indeed sparse, it can be confirmed that Charley Williams was arrested and taken to Silver City.[62] Sheriff Whitehill was advised by telegraph to be expecting the prisoner.

> Shakespeare, N. M. June 2nd.
> F. W. Mollitor was shot last night by Charley Williams. I have Williams prisoner, and in irons, under guard. Will send him in by coach to night.
> P. B. Graves[63]

By the middle of the month Charley Williams had posted bonds to the amount of one thousand dollars, pending his appearance at the July term of Territorial District Court.[64] That the citizens of Shakespeare were at least making an attempt at compliance with the rule of law is further reinforced by the fact that William Carroll who had earlier shot "Happy Bob" Fambro was also arrested, removed to Silver City, and after a preliminary hearing released on $2000 bond.[65] Evidence clearly reveals that on specific occasions or with particular suspects Shakespeareans demanded a degree of selective enforcement.

Probably because Deputy Dan Tucker was "hanging out" in the southern part of Grant County, per Sheriff Whitehill's instructions, on March 16, 1880, the office of Silver City town marshal was declared vacant.[66] Certainly indicators from previous council meetings indicate Tucker was not too enthralled with the way he was being remunerated for services performed on behalf of Silver City. Likewise, at the March 18th council meeting it was ordered that the City Clerk in conjunction with the City Attorney investigate ex-marshal Tucker's account, and if it was found deficient, to proceed against his bondsmen.[67] Naegle remarks, "Evidently Tucker was found short in his accounts for on May 20, 1880, the council ordered that demand for payment be made of his bondsmen. Some satisfactory settlement must have been made as there is no further reference to the matter in the minutes of the council."[68] Although, at least to date, no records have been located which indicate what Tucker thought about the entire affair, reasonable speculation would indicate he was finally glad to sever any financial marriage with the city; it had been a unsatisfactory arrangement from the beginning.

Public controversy over Silver City police salaries was to continue for several years, based in part on the fact city fathers were paying monthly settlements with warrants which were worth only sixty-cents on the dollar. At least one reporter took a positive law enforcement stance, "We would suggest to the council that they double the salary or pay cash, as they cannot retain good men on the force under the present condition of affairs."[69]

Even divorced from city marshal affairs Tucker stayed busily engaged with the law enforcement mission throughout the county, and history records he did not spend all of his time in and around Shakespeare. On a trip back from the mining community of Hillsboro, Tucker reported he had found the trail of six Indians in Gavilan Canyon, leading toward the Mimbres River.[70]

On July 17, 1880, Dan Tucker found time to join up with a prospecting party made up of men from Shakespeare, Central City, Silver City, and Fort Cummings. The hardy crew of adventurers bivouacked at Carrizalillo Springs in the extreme southern portion, in a dangerously isolated reach of old Grant County down by the Tres Hermanas (Three Sisters) Mountains.[71] O. W. Williams, who would later receive recognition as a noted author and ecologist, and who was a member of the hopeful fortune hunters, described Tucker as "the deadliest of all the deputy sheriffs who had ever served Grant County."[72] In another account he added, "Deputy Sheriff Tucker left off his official duties but not his guns and, regardless of all lawbreakers who might cross his path, came hurrying down the Old Copper Trail to hunt down the most elusive fugitive of all his experience."[73] At least on this excursion, Dan Tucker wasn't on the lookout for a desperado's trail, but he did have to keep one eye focused toward the horizon in search of plundering Apaches, and at the same time, scan the ground before him for rattlesnakes.[74] Whizzing arrows didn't pierce the prospecting party, but venomous fangs did. Coincidentally, one diamondback struck a Mr. Crittenden on the hand, and another "fanged" his steed on the nose. The "horse's head was swollen as big as that of a hippopotamus."[75] Both survived.

Like most everyone else of the time and place, Tucker was not immune to mineral fever, and careful examination of courthouse records corroborates several mining and real-estate transactions. One such example of geological enterprise is evidenced by Tucker locating and filing on the Bulzebuh Mine, in the Victoria District, near the area of present day Gage, New Mexico, and just two days later (Sept. 25, 1880) selling the property to J. E. Price for $2000.00.[76]

Dan may have preferred prospecting on the Old Copper Trail, but reality dictated he take up the trail of a thief. Sam Eckstine's house was burglarized, money and "a lot of jewelry" was taken by a former employee, identified as a Mexican boy. Tucker was hot on the trail when a local paper went to press, predicting the probability of capture.[77] While on the trail, Tucker reported that he had it on good authority that fresh Indian sign had been seen to the east in the Black Range.[78] However, there was apparently nothing Tucker wanted to impart to the ever inquiring press regarding his chase after the burglar. Eventually, the suspect's lifeless body was found along the banks of the Mimbres.[79] The circumstances are strikingly similar to those relating to the earlier death of desperado Bob Nelson. Coincidence?

One aspect of a sheriff's duty was obligatory, and to most thoroughly distasteful—execution! Hanging the condemned man was a task most sheriffs dreaded. Naturally, custodial care of an inmate scheduled to pay the supreme penalty maximized security concerns, but other considerations were interjected into the equation. Providing for extra guards, purchasing raw materials, hiring carpenters to construct gallows, and ordering "special" ropes, were just a few worrisome details of a financial nature that mandated attention and a drain on scanty funds.[80] It was a horrendous hassle for the local sheriff. Ball jerks the noose on reality: "The sheriff was as much under public scrutiny as the victim. A botched execution could blemish his standing and have political repercussions. Macabre scenes were possible on the gallows, and these legal executions could take on the atmosphere of a circus sideshow."[81] Subsequent events clearly reveal Sheriff Whitehill, when required, would step up and perform his sworn duty—Dan Tucker faithfully by his side.

Convicted of first degree murder in District Court, Charles Williams (Barney O'Tool), who had killed a man in Georgetown, and Louis Gaines, who had murdered a fellow black soldier from Fort Bayard on Christmas Eve, reportedly with a common table knife, were sentenced to be hung in Silver City.[82] To avoid any unintended confusion it must here be pointed out that there are two Charles Williams, and the one scheduled for execution was not the Charley Williams who had murdered Mollitor at Shakespeare and was out on bail bond.[83]

For the most part Williams received little or no public sympathy, save from a vocal group of rabble-rousing friends, but there was a movement underfoot to petition the Territorial Governor to commute Gaine's death sentence. *The Daily Southwest* cried foul and editorialized, "Too many murderers have already gone unpunished in Grant county. This community cannot longer afford to allow a groundless feeling of pity or a culpable indifference to stand in the way of justice. We owe it to ourselves to see that the sentence of the law is executed to the letter...Justice should always be tempered with mercy, but mercy like charity, begins at home. We must protect ourselves."[84] The imposition of the death penalty for Williams and Gaines faced an added obstacle.

Whether bound by a legally mandated schedule, or simply "trying to kill two *jail-birds* with one stone," Sheriff Whitehill had announced both Gaines and Williams would be hung the same day, at the same time, "on the flat near the northeastern limits of Silver City."[85] Still harboring grudges from the not too distant Civil War, and overflowing with unadulterated racism, a group of citizens declared they would see "hell" before they would let a black man share the scaffold with a white.[86] Stubbornly determined not to show weakness, and deadly serious in his resolve not to exchange calendar dates, Sheriff Whitehill deputized a posse of sixty well-armed citizens. As the chosen date drew near, "it looked like war for sure" and even some of "the women had guns."[87]

Even the local press was picking up rumors of a possible rescue and prison liberation for Williams. Whether it was merely drunken mouthing from the condemned man's friends or indeed a indication of a more serious threat made little difference. The air was thick with animosity, spiked by intrigue, and fraught with legitimate danger.[88]

During the afternoon of August 20,1880, seemingly oblivious to a chorus of cat-calls, jeers, and verbal threats, the two prisoners were marched toward the gallows. Resigned to their fate, the condemned Williams boasted that his true identity would forevermore remain secret. Gaines acknowledged his "entire life had been a very evil one."[89] The protective posse knew not what to expect from a crowd which numbered four hundred. Sheriff Whitehill was determined not to dishonor his oath, although he may have pondered the political implications, and Dan Tucker with equal resolve had chosen to back his boss.

On the scaffold, Tucker adjusted the nooses around the prisoners necks, placed black hoods over their heads, and "just twenty minutes before four, the drop fell with a dull thud, and Charles Williams and Louis A. Gaines were swung into Eternity. Every arrangement was perfect..."[90] The crowd, having thought better about defying Sheriff Whitehill's order and wary of testing Deputy Dan Tucker, chose to disperse quietly.

Just a couple of days later, Dan Tucker, characteristically working alone, initiated a search for four stolen horses which had been taken a day or two before.[91] A short time later, Tucker rode into town, driving the four missing horses before him. The owner was pleased to have the rustled livestock returned, and the local newspaper editor exhibited intelligence enough not to overindulge in fact-finding. As usual the unflappable Dan Tucker maintained stoic silence. The horse thief or thieves were not then mentioned, or missed, nor ever found! Or had they been?

The Grant County Commissioners weren't asking any impertinent questions, either. At the October 4th (1880) meeting the county dads settled up with Deputy Dan Tucker in the amount of $200, not a insignificant payment at the time.[92] Analysis of previous fee payments, although in lesser amounts, reveals Dan Tucker was continuously engaged in area law enforcement affairs.

Although the disturbance is not particularly described, it would seem that Dan Tucker, accompanied by "Cherokee" Jim Bowman, who was described as "a mixed blood, half colored, half Cherokee, and all man," along with George Parker, and the Wood brothers, were taken into voluntary custody, and hauled before Justice of the Peace Rilea, where it was determined they had "merely acted with a view to suppressing disorder."[93] Certainly this was not an unusual occurrence for the time period. Many frontier lawmen freely submitted to arrest, or voluntarily presented themselves before a magistrate, had a simple hearing, and were later released or paid some nominal fine for minor infractions of the law. The question that remains unanswered concerning this specific disorderliness is whether Tucker & Co. were "instigators" before they became the "suppressers."

In March 1881, Richard Remine, who had been convicted of murdering Patrick Rafferty near Georgetown, New Mexico Territory, four years earlier, was scheduled for execution at Silver City, and once again Dan Tucker would be called upon to do the job. Dick Remine had killed his mining partner in a drunken rage, some say beating him to death with a single-jack, others claiming he chopped the deceased into kindling with an ax.[94] When sober, Remine was a hell-of-a likable guy, but the crime had been gruesome, to horrible to just forget. Dick had danced, and now community standards demanded he pay the fiddler! He was generally considered harmless, and although incarcerated without bail, the prisoner was given free run of the town, enjoying a "trusty" status, oftentimes shopping in Silver City grocery markets for the jail kitchen, and sometimes charged with preparing the meals for jail inmates.[95] At least one report, if accurate, details the freedoms granted Remine: "It was stated that he was allowed to go out at nights to gamble in the town, and having stayed out until after 11 o'clock one night he was sternly notified by the sheriff that this could not be allowed as it made too much (noise) after bedtime, and that thereafter if he did not come back by 10 o'clock he would 'damned sure be locked out'."[96]

In any event, Remine had not much to lose by simply running off, but he didn't, some say because he had been mesmerized by the "personal attractions, considerable shrewdness, and devilish disposition" of murderess Dora Dewnger who was also confined in the Grant County Jail awaiting appeal of her conviction.[97]

Maybe he had second thoughts about scampering off after he finally read the newspapers: "The prisoners Richard Remine and Parson Young are to be hung, the Supreme Court having sustained the verdict given in the Court below. These men since the decision was rendered have been confined and shackled. The time for the Execution has not as yet been stated.[98] And later a newspaper simply reported, "Sheriff Whitehill received a dispatch from the Governor last Thursday to the effect that warrants for the Execution of Young and Remine, had been mailed..."[99]

One March 14, 1881, Deputy Dan Tucker "moved the man over" so that he finally stood on the slide between the two upright posts and under the noosed rope. Then the prisoner's ankles were bound together and his hands were tied behind his back.[100] Before he met death Remine spoke up saying he had been treated with "uniform kindness" by Sheriff Harvey Whitehill and his deputies.[101] Tucker then placed the black hood over his head, placed the noose around the neck of Remine, and as the "last move before the end, the knot of the noose was turned so that it rested just under the ear of the doomed man."[102] Dan Tucker stepped back, looked toward the Sheriff, who gave the requisite signal, and Remine was hanged by the neck—until dead.[103] Two weeks later the drama was reenacted, for the benefit of William "Parson" Young, and Deputy Dan Tucker hung his fourth man.[104] And unlike Remine, Young had no kind words—for anyone!

Grant County researcher Terry Humble reports the chapter on "Parson" Young did not quite close with his death at the end of the hangman's knot. Later, (1882) when the cemetery was being relocated from the middle of Silver City to its present location, and for whatever other reason, Young's casket was opened. To everyone's astonishment the deceased lay face down in the coffin, leading to immediate speculation that he had been buried alive, and had "turned over in his grave." Hastily an investigation was begun, and much to Sheriff Whitehill's relief, several witnesses were finally located that recalled seeing Young dumped into the coffin "face down," clearly establishing that he had been hanged by the neck until he was dead-dead-dead![105]

Silver City resident Usher C. Garrison may not have been as broad-minded as the condemned Remine in praising the sheriff. For the time period, an occasional firearms accident was not uncommon. Sheriff Harvey Whitehill's carelessness almost ended in disaster when his six-shooter slid out of his coat pocket, struck the floor, discharged, and the ball inflicted a "painful but not serious" wound to Garrison's face.[106] Or by some other accounts, the pistol was actually in the sheriff's pocket, and fired through his clothing when he bumped the revolver into a piece of furniture in the Probate Clerk's office at the courthouse.[107] Either way, a close call indeed! Whitehill had foolishly loaded all six-chambers of his six-shooter, ignoring the hazard of allowing the hammer to rest on a live round. Common sense dictated loading the weapon with only five loads—resting the hammer on a empty cylinder. Whitehill's counterpart in Arizona Territory, Sheriff John Harris Behan, also had the same type of stupid accident, his wayward bullet nearly striking one of his deputies.[108] And even the unerring Wyatt Earp caught the attention of newsmen when "his revolver slipped from its holster and in falling to the floor the hammer which was resting on the cap, is supposed to have struck the chair, causing a discharge of one of the barrels. The ball passed through his coat, struck the north wall then glanced off and passed out through the ceiling."[109]

The above citation to Whitehill's accident is clearly in conflict with numerous reports professing that he was a prime example of the *unarmed* Sheriff.[110] In truth many frontier lawman, especially the Sheriffs, opted for middle ground between being constantly loaded down with artillery and charging into serious encounters with just bare fists. Most frontier sheriffs saw themselves as politicians, administrators, tax-collectors, and members of the community's elite rather than as shootists. Out in the brush was one thing, but within in the confines of town limits, it was a simple matter for the chief lawman to step into the office and retrieve his pistol before responding to the difficulty down the street or making an arrest.

History abounds with instances of noted lawman having to hustle up a six-shooter, or in some cases resort to more primitive weaponry. At Santa Fe, well-respected Sheriff, and future United States Marshal, Romulo Martinez, was unarmed and obliged to "throw rocks" at a culprit.[111] Later, New Mexico lawman Dee Harkey pled with suspect Carl Gordon, "...I am an officer and want to arrest you, but I left my gun this morning at the wagon, and that is my hard luck." Exercising common sense, Gordon surrendered his weapon to the officer, replying, "Here take mine, I can't hit anything with it."[112] In Arizona Territory, while he was the elected sheriff of Yavapai County, an *unarmed* John Behan doggedly waded into the eye of a storm, and arrested several drunken soldiers at Wickenburg, one of which had fired three shots in his direction.[113] Wyatt Earp was forced to *borrow* a revolver from Fred Dodge, before he sneaked up behind "Curly Bill" Brocious on a Tombstone street and thumped him over the head.[114] In the case of Sheriff Harvey Whitehill, it is safe to say he "normally" did not carry a gun.[115] Dan Tucker went "heeled" all the time!

NOTES AND SOURCES

    1. Correspondence from T. Humble, Grant County researcher and historian. 11-03-1999.
    2. Naegle, P. 180. The author correctly reveals city council minutes refer to the appointment of "David" Tucker, but the more common use of "Dan" was used when the story was carried in the Grant County *Herald* on 04-11-1878,

"Dan Tucker was appointed first Town Marshal of Silver City at the city council meeting."

3. Ball, Larry D., "Frontier Sheriffs At Work," *The Journal of Arizona History*, No. 27, P. 291. "Each time the sheriff or a deputy served the process of court or performed any other official task he filled out a voucher. Every three months or so, the sheriff collected these vouchers and presented them to the board of supervisors for 'settlement.' When the board paid the sheriff, he, in turn, paid his deputies and settled the bills for his office."

4. Silver City *Tribune*, 11-08-1873.

5. Grant County *Herald*, 06-15-1878.

6. Ibid., 07-20-1878.

7. Probate Court Records, Grant County Clerk's Office, Silver City, New Mexico. Examination of these records clearly reveal that Dan Tucker, in his role as Deputy Sheriff frequently opened court from 1877 through 1879. The last entry for this type of duty was September 19, 1879, just before he was reassigned to Shakespeare.

8. DeArment, Robert K., *Knights of the Green Cloth—The Saga of the Frontier Gamblers*. P. 113. Here after cited as DeArment (II).

9. Ibid.

10. Ibid., P. 264. Also see Charles Robinson III, *The Frontier World of Fort Griffin—The Life and Death of a Western Town*. P. 85-91. Although the author offers details regarding Deno's life at Fort Griffin, he ends his account by simply saying she "then vanished from the scene as suddenly as she had appeared, leaving nothing behind but her legend." P. 91. He does not report about her involvement with Frank Thurmond, her travels to Silver City, or finally alighting at Deming, New Mexico. Carl Coke Rister, *Fort Griffin On The Texas Frontier*, does not mention Thurmond by name but does refer to him as, "a notorious local gambler and saloon man." P. 138. For a unvarnished look at Lottie Deno see, Ty Cashion, A Texas Frontier, The Clear Fork Country and Fort Griffin, 1849-1887. P. 196-198. The author identifies Lottie as Charlotte Thompkins, and likewise does not mention her connection to Thurmond, or her later life in New Mexico. Thrapp characterizes Lottie Deno (Charlotte Thurmond) as a madame, and closes his summation with, "Lottie moved on to Silver City, New Mexico, where she operated a restaurant, and was married to a gambler and saloon man. When he died, she joined the Episcopal Church, became known for social welfare work, and died at Deming, New Mexico." Vol. I, P. 393-394. For more information about Lottie Deno and Frank Thurmond's lives in New Mexico see *Lottie Deno—Gambling Queen of Hearts* by Cynthia Rose. The author correctly gives Lottie's true name as Carlotta, although in New Mexico she was indeed sometimes known as Charlotte. The last few chapters of the book deal with the relocation of the Thurmonds to Deming, New Mexico—their final resting place. Hereafter cited as Rose, C.

11. Stanley, F., (Father Stanley Crocchiola), *The Deming, New Mexico Story*. P. 15. Hereafter cited as Stanley.

12. Rose, C., P. 34.

13. DeArment (II). P. 113.

14. Silver City *Enterprise*, 10-27-1949, "I'll Never Forget" by Lou Blachly. And Pioneer Foundation I {Wayne Whitehill} In the newspaper account the informant is identified as Kit Conn. In the interview transcript he is identified as Kitt Collins.

15. Grant County *Herald*, 03-01-1879. Some reports list the age of William "Billy" Dwenger as eighteen years of age at the time of the crime.

16. Ibid., 03-15-1879.

17. Ibid., 07-19-1879. Also see Grant County Civil and Criminal Court Cost Docket Book. Also see Jail Register.

18. *The Daily Southwest*, 04-17-1880.

19. Grant County *Herald*, 08-09-1879. Also see, Silver City *Enterprise*, 10-27-1949. "I'll Never Forget."

20. Silver City *Enterprise*, 09-22-1931. Reprint of a letter from O. W. Williams to J. C. Williams, January 25, 1926.

21. Ball (S), P. 154. Also see, Grant County *Herald*, 03-05-1881, "The commission appointed to inquire into the mental condition of Parson Young, consisted of several physicians and one or two non-professionals. They found that Young could scarcely be classed among rational beings; and we understand that their report with the proceedings in the case, will be submitted to the Governor for such actions as the circumstances may warrant." Young may have suffered a undetermined degree of mental incapacity, but in the final analysis, any diminishment he had did not overcome a decision to proceed with the execution. And see above cited newspaper edition of the Silver City *Enterprise*, "After his death it was found that he had no such plate..."

22. Naegle, P. 180.

23. Grant County *Herald*, 11-23-1878.

24. Naegle, P. 180. Also see Grant County *Herald*, 03-15-1879.

25. Grant County Commissioner's Book. P. 62. 04-03-1878. Grant County Clerk's Office. Silver City, New Mexico. Sadly for Tucker there was a dispute concerning an overpayment of his accounts, "The board and its late clerk, hearing that an error was made in overpaying Danl. Tucker $133.50 for feeding prisoners in October 1877, the Board took the note of the said D. Tucker for said amount payable on demand and the same was placed in the hands of the sheriff for collection and it was charged up against said sheriff in his account with the County of Grant." P. 77-78. January 1, 1879.

26. Grant County *Herald*, 05-03-1879. And Naegle, P. 180., Council Minutes, Book I, P. 2.

27. Ibid., 08-09-1879. With the youngster's father deceased, and the mother in custody unable to make bond, the child was referred to as an "orphan" in newspaper accounts. In all probability Tucker's prisoners on work detail were not actually chained together, but assuredly, each knew the probability and the weight of the penalty to be exacted for attempted flight before Dan Tucker's revolver.

28. Ibid., 08-30-1879.

29. Pioneer Foundation Interview {Wayne Whitehill}

30. Silver City *Enterprise*, 06-11-1953. "I Saw the Early Days of Silver City" by Harry M. Carvil.

31. Silver City *Independent*, 09-22-1931.

32. Ibid., 12-26-1902. The shooting in question was reported in the newspaper on August 30, 1879. The author of this account places the shooting in September 1879, certainly not too much of a historical discrepancy to discount the author's veracity or accuracy.

33. Ibid., 11-14-1902.

34. Grant County *Herald*, 09-06-1879.

35. Ibid., 10-11-1879, and Silver City *Enterprise*, "The Rustlers of '79 And '80." The same issue of the Grant County *Herald* in a unrelated story about city marshal fees, refers to "David" Tucker, Marshal. The Burro Mountains compose of the Big Burros and Little Burros lay parallel to each other southeast of Silver City, separated by the Mangas Valley. The Big Burros were home to numerous frontier mining camps and the mountain range had long been frequented by Apaches. Ungnade, P. 135-136.

36. Silver City *Enterprise*, 10-01-1886.

37. Ibid., 11-29-1879 & 12-13-1879. Also see Grant County Commissioner's Meeting Book for June 2nd and October 6th (1879) P. 88 and P. 92., respectively.

38. Ball (S), P. 89-105.

39. Thrapp, Vol. III, P. 1443.

40. Grant County *Herald*, 01-24-1880.

41. Ibid.

42. Hill, Rita & Janaloo, "Alias Shakespear—The Town Nobody Knew," *New Mexico Historical Review*, XLII: 3 1967. P. 211-227. Hereafter cited as Hill (R&J). For additional information on the Great Diamond Hoax see the book *Diamonds in the Salt* by Bruce Woodard. Also see Emma M. Muir, "The Great Diamond Swindle" *New Mexico Magazine*, August, 1948. And, Rita Hill, "Mysteries Set With Diamonds," *True West*, September/October 1980.

43. Muir, Emma M., "Bonanza Days at Shakespeare," New Mexico Magazine, September 1948. P. 27. Hereafter cited as Muir.

44. Hill (R&J), P.222,

45. Williams, P. 122.

46. Muir, P. 45.

47. Ibid. The Pyramids mentioned by Muir refer to the nearby Pyramid Mountains. Approximately 22 miles long, running north-south, and from three to seven miles in width. The mountains, at times, have been mined for copper, gold, silver, lead, and zinc. The highest peak is North Pyramid Peak with a summit at 6,002 feet. See Ungnade Herbert E., *New Mexico Mountains*. P. 166. Hereafter cited as Ungnade.

48. Williams, P. 122.

49. Ibid., P. 123.

50. Hill, Rita.,*Then and Now, Here and Around Shakespeare*. P. 30-34 & 44-46. Hereafter cited as Hill (R).

51. Muir, Emma M., "The Stage to Shakespeare," *New Mexico Magazine*, July, 1948. P. 25. The author does not list all of the characters frequenting Shakespeare, but she does furnish the nickname for Jim Hughes. Later the Silver City *Enterprise*, 04-11-1884 edition will characterize Pony Deihl as "one of the worst and most notorious outlaws that has ever cursed this frontier." Also see, Hilliard, George, *Adios Hachita—Stories of a New Mexico Town*. P. 2-3. "Warned that Leonard and Head were on their way, the Hasletts (Bill & Ike) lay in wait, rifles loaded and cocked, and shot the two outlaws dead." Unfortunately for the Haslett brothers, revenge was just around the corner, as reported in the *Arizona Weekly Star*, "They followed the Haslett boys for some twenty miles from Eureka before they overtook them, and as soon as they came up with them the fight to the death commenced. The Haslett boys were game and made a brave fight, killing two and wounding three of the Crane (Jim) party; but being overpowered were finally killed."

52. Hill, Janaloo, "The Sad Fate of Russian Bill. Why Was He Hanged?," Three part series appearing in the Silver City *Enterprise*, 10-20-1983. Hereafter cited as Hill.

53. Hill, Janaloo, "Yours Until Death, William Grounds," *True West*, April, 1973. P. 15. One of the few article devoted to Grounds, and interestingly contains a series of letters from young "Billy" to his mother at Dripping Springs, Texas. Hereafter cited as Hill (II). Also see Thrapp Vol. II, P. 593, who classifies Grounds as a "desperado," suspected of rustling and murder. William MacLeod Raine, *Famous Sheriffs & Western Outlaws*, P. 102, characterizes Billy Grounds as a "known rustler and suspected road agent." Hereafter cited as Raine.

54. Grant County *Herald*, 01-10-1880. The county commissioners also authorized a like payment to J. R. Cunningham for either the same or a similar prisoner transporting assignment.

55. Hill (II), P. 57.

56. Pioneer Foundation Interview {Anna Ownby}.

57. Hill (II), P. 60.

58. Williams, P. 146.

59. Hill, Rita and Janaloo., *Shakespeare Cemetery—Resting Place of Our Pioneers*. P. 10. Hereafter cited as Hill (R&J—C).

60. Williams, P. 146.

61. Ibid., According to Hill (R&J—C) Williams stabbed Molliter. P. 10.

62. Ibid.

63. Grant County *Herald*, 06-05-1880. A subsequent notation confirmed the prisoner arriving at Silver City, "Charley Williams, who shot F. W. Mollitor at Shakespeare night before last was brought in on the coach this morning, and is now in jail."

64. Ibid., 06-12-1880.

65. Ibid., 06-05-1880. William Carroll failed to make his scheduled court appearance, his bond was forfeited, and a warrant for his arrest was ordered. See Grant County *Herald*, 07-31-1880. Later the case was dismissed. See Grant County Civil and Criminal Cost Docket Book, *Territory vs. William Carroll*.

66. Naegle, P. 180.

67. Grant County *Herald*, 03-20-1880. Also see, *The Daily Southwest*, 03-17-1880, and Naegle, P. 180

68. Naegle, P. 180-181. The author reports that during the next four years, the Silver City Marshal position changed hands nine times. The controversy and displeasure concerning how the Marshal was selected, how the office was administered, and how the City Council acted with their oversight authority would continue for years.

69. Silver City *Enterprise*, 05-30-1884. At one time Harvey Whitehill served as Silver City Town Marshal, but he too had a public dispute with city fathers' causing him to publicly declare the position was one which he disdained, and he said, "I do not depend on a city marshalship for my bread and butter." Silver City *Enterprise*, 01-18-1884.

70. *The Daily Southwest*, 06-15-1880.

71. The Tres Hermanas Mountains near present Columbus, New Mexico have summits in the 5000 ft. range, and were in the past actively mined for gold, silver, and copper. Ungnade, P. 163.

72. O. W. Williams to J. C. Williams, 12-15-1924.

73. Williams, P. 152-153.

74. Phelps, Frederick, "Frederick E. Phelps: A Soldier's Memoirs," *New Mexico Historical Review*. April 1950. P. 122. Edited by Frank D. Reeve. Earlier Phelps had traveled the same area and commented, "I do not think I saw less than fifty (rattlesnakes) in the twenty miles we made that day, and what in the world they lived on has been a mystery to me to this day. Rattlesnakes live very largely on frogs, toads, rabbits, and other small animals, but not a sign of life did we see that day except snakes."

75. Williams, P. 155-156. The editor, S. D. Myers, eludes to more than one snakebite victim, "Some of the men were bitten by rattlesnakes." P. 176.

76. Grant County Book of Mining Locations, Book 3., P. 169-170. & Grant County Mining Records of Deeds, Book 7., P. 41. T. Humble proffers what very well may be an accurate theory concerning many of the early day mining transactions. Humble believes the actual sale price of real-estate and mining interests to be much less than normally listed. Especially in light of the fact that there were no real-estate property taxes prior to 1884 in Grant County, and "it was considered a favor to one's neighbor to give an inflated price on any land transaction." The intent of such overvaluation naturally being to increase the property value for all nearby parcels, and for future financial transactions on the same survey.

77. *The Daily Southwest*, 08-06-1880.

78. Ibid., 08-07-1880.

79. Interview with T. Humble, Grant County researcher and historian. May 1999.

80. Ball (S), P. 147.

81. Ibid.

82. Silver City *Enterprise*, 12-12-1902. Also see, *The Daily Southwest*, 07-27-1880. "Territory vs. Chas. Williams (No. 2)—Murder. Convicted in 1st degree, and sentenced to be hung August 20th." And, "Territory vs. Louis Gaines—Murder. Convicted and sentenced to be hung Aug. 20." During his interview with historian Lou Blachly, Wayne Whitehill confuses Gaines with another soldier who shot a comrade in the abdomen, the bullet entirely passing through the intended victim and killing a innocent bystander.

83. Correspondence from Terry Humble, 01-09-2000. "As it turned out, there were two Chas. Williams tried at this term of the Territorial Court. The one who was sentenced to hang was from Georgetown. The other Charles Williams had his case continued." Also see Jail Register.

84. *The Daily Southwest*, 07-27-1880.

85. Ibid., 08-20-1880.

86. Silver City *Enterprise*, 10-27-49. "I'll Never Forget."

87. Ibid.

88. Grant County *Herald*, 07-31-1880.

89. *The Daily Southwest*, 08-20-1880.

90. Ibid. On 02-12-1881 the Grant County *Herald* reported, "Barney O'Tool was the real name of the man who was executed here last August under the name of Chas. Williams. His father lives some twenty miles east of Wheeling, West Virginia." Also see Jail Register.

91. Ibid., 08-23-1880.

92. Grant County Commissioner's Court minutes, 10-04-1880. Grant County Clerk's Office. Silver City, New Mexico.

93. Grant County *Herald*, 02-19-1881. "Cherokee" Jim Bowman was a former civilian scout with the U. S. Army. Silver City *Enterprise*, 10-03-1902. Additionally, he is given credit for the discovery of the rich silver float at the north end of the Burro Mountains, which led to the development of the Blue Bell Mine, later known as the Alhambra. Also see, Sherman, James E. & Barbara H., Ghost Towns and Mining Camps of New Mexico. P. 12. Hereafter cited as Sherman. "Cherokee" Jim Bowman should not be confused with Sam Bowman, who was also of mixed ancestry and who also scouted for the U. S. Army in Arizona Territory. Whether the two were related is undetermined. "Cherokee" Jim Bowman "was a good-hearted, good natured, clever man, and had as many friends as anyone in that country....He had a wife and family living in Silver City..."

94. O. W. Williams claims Remine used an ax. Wayne Whitehill asserts that the murder weapon was a "single-jack." The instrument can best be defined as a 4 to 8 pound, short handled sledge-hammer, designed to be operated by one man, using one hand. Whether a "single-jack" or a ax was used probably made little difference to the victim, nor does it matter much in the presentation of Tucker's story.

95. Silver City *Enterprise*, 10-27-1949. "I'll Never Forget." Remine's name is sometimes spelled Rhemine. Located northeast of Silver City, Georgetown was at one time a thriving mining community of 1,200 but due to a smallpox epidemic and the eventual decline in silver prices the camp finally fizzled. Julyan, P. 146.

96. Silver City *Independent*, 09-22-1931. Reprint of a letter from O. W. Williams to J. C. Williams, January 25, 1926.

97. Ibid.

98. Grant County *Herald*, 03-23-1880.

99. Ibid, 02-05-1881.

100. Silver City *Independent*, 09-22-1931. Williams to Williams.

101. Grant County *Herald*, 03-19-1881.

102. Silver City *Independent*, 09-22-1931. Williams to Williams.

103. Grant County *Herald*, 03-19-1881. Also Jail Register.

104. Ball (S), P. 374. William "Billy" Dwenger received a life sentence for his part in the murder and his mother, Dora, received a ten year sentence. See *Daily Southwest*, 04-17-1880. Wayne Whitehill advised Lou Blachly that he personally witnessed Dan Tucker's participation in all four hangings, which certainly appears reasonable in that his father, the sheriff, was officially charged with seeing that the executions were carried out.

105. Correspondence from Grant County historian and researcher Terry Humble, 10-31-1999.

106. Ball (S), P. 199. Also see *Southwest* 03-12-1881. Ball reports Garrison's face wound as "serious" and the newspaper account says "painful but not serious." Ball's reading is correct. Any gunshot wound is serious.

107. Grant County *Herald*, 03-12-1881.

108. Breakenridge, William., *Helldorado—Bringing the Law to the Mesquite*. P. 206. Brown, Richard Maxwell {editor} Hereafter cited as Breakenridge for text, Brown for annotations.

109. Miller, Nyle H. & Snell, Joseph, W., *Great Gunfighters of the Kansas Cowtowns, 1867-1886*. P. 83. Quoting the 01-12-1876 edition of the Wichita *Beacon*.

110. Accounts that Sheriff Whitehill didn't carry a firearm, can for the most part be traced to the remarks of his son, Wayne. During an interview, Wayne advised Lou Blachly that his father spent fourteen years as a sheriff and that, "During all that time he never wore a gun. He would never take a posse after a murderer. He would walk up to the murderer with his hands out like this," holding his hands in front of himself. "But he always brought his man in." Silver City *Enterprise*, 10-27-1949. Sheriff Whitehill most probably went about his day to day business unarmed, but historic certainty does reveal the sheriff on occasion armed himself.

111. Ball (S), P. 181.

112. Harkey, Dee., *Mean as Hell—The Life of a New Mexico Lawman*. P. 162.

113. *Arizona Miner*, 05-14-1872.

114. Erwin, Richard E., *The Truth About Wyatt Earp*. P. 165-175. Hereafter cited as Erwin.

115. DeArment, P. 14.

5

"KEEPS THAT TOWN FREE OF ROUGH CHARACTERS"

South of Silver City, standing naked in shadows of the Florida Mountains, the new railroad town of Deming haughtily commenced revealing her charms—such as they were![1] Originally, a few settlers filled with expectation, but somewhat lacking in patience, had christened a tent city "New Chicago," in anticipation of the Southern Pacific and the Atchison, Topeka, and Santa Fe Railroads joining tracks at the Mimbres Junction, and creating a "major urban" center.[2] A tad premature with their municipal plans, the promoting pilgrims were "outraged" when the Southern Pacific chose a depot site—several miles to the west.[3] A new community was then born, and given the name Deming, in honor of "Mary Anne Deming, the wife of wealthy railroad magnate Charles Crocker."[4] Grant County citizens with confident expectation, in fact a nationwide audience, awaited news which would signal that civilization had finally arrived. On March 8, 1881, the Southern Pacific and the AT & SF Railroads joined the last rails, and America's second transcontinental connection opened the gates for southwestern commercial development.[5]

"Soon an army of mechanics was busy erecting round houses, station houses, railway tenements, putting down the big wells; switching yards three miles long were laid out: soon the handsome and commodious depot hotel was in course of construction—then the finest railroad building between Kansas City and San Francisco—Deming, the division point for both roads; lay over station for all Pullman employees, train crews and express messengers; everything indicated that here the railroads would make the great town of the Southwest, and 'it was good to be here.'"[6] So said one early resident.

Correspondingly, Deming was awash with railroad men, locomotive mechanics, busy construction workers, speculating capitalists, and a traveling public, all of which required bed, board, and diversion. With real promise of becoming the Southwest's dominant railroad hub, Deming was quick to lay claim to mercantile establishments, a post office, eateries, newspapers, hotels, and saloons. And in but a very short time, the well-known Fred Harvey had established another in his chain of restaurants and hotels at Deming, which quickly became known as the "finest of its type."[7] But in the beginning, there were growing pains, succinctly and rather politely explained by former Deming *Headlight* editor Edward Pennington, "At the advent of the town the population was of the usual well assorted kind—good, bad and not indifferent—for

70

the indifferent don't come until the town is established."[8] Speaking of
the influx of disreputable characters habitually following the laying of
rails, one author offers, "...when it became necessary for the early
parasites to find nourishment, they went to work on specimens of their
own kind...these in turn practiced their cannibalism on later-comers and
so *ad infinitum*."[9] Ball, absent a public relations agenda, once again pulls
the trigger on historic reality, "As the Santa Fe and other railroads
approached the Southwest, much flotsam and jetsam of the frontier
accompanied the construction gangs. Rustler bands pillaged herds of
livestock to feed these hungry workers and to supply several new mining
camps in the southern counties."[10] Grant County was one of these
southern counties.

By April 1881, developments south of Silver City were beginning to
pop out of control. Many of the undesirable riffraff had simply
transferred their parasitical vocation from the Mimbres Junction water-
tank to Deming. An early saloon operator was contemporarily
characterized as the "most desperate white savage in the entire valley."[11]
From reports Sheriff Whitehill was receiving, Deming was almost under
siege from a band of lawless brigands who were making it
uncomfortable for area residents and the traveling public at best, and
sometimes even downright dangerous. Con-men, and disreputes of
varying degrees were getting the best of "even one or two knowing ones
from Silver City."[12] Of Deming, one journalist penned, "Deming morals
are not to be discussed in a newspaper—till she has some."[13] He
continued the analysis, "The cow boys, or roughs and thieves, are so
numerous that no man ventures any distance from the village (Deming)
without his Winchester rifle, ready to repeat 12 or 16 times without
reloading. With this element constantly on the watch for plunder, a
man's life goes for naught."[14] Another observer just penned, "One must
admit that saloons and gambling houses were a power in Deming during
those early years."[15]

Although the lawlessness was fast becoming a very real public
image dilemma, the Deming *Headlight* resorted to humor with diffusing
witticism:

How to Tell a "Tenderfoot"

Here comes a young man with a red satchel and a "biled"
white shirt with a Piccadilly collar attachment. He talks
considerably about the way they do things back east. He is a
decidedly fresh looking youth and presents a biblical smile and
Sunday school appearance. He pities the people of this country
from the bottom of his heart and wants to know how people
live with so little farming being done. He has about $150 cash
money left with which he expects to buy New Mexico and a
part of Arizona. Remorseless Time speeds on, and one

month's board reduces his pile to fifty dollars. He never drinks, swears or chews, while the glorious uncertainties of draw poker, faro, keno and monte are unto his untutored ken as is Latin to an Apache. He frequently remarks that he did not come here for his health. About this time he begins to realize that prices are high in this country and finally, donning a fresh Piccadilly becomes a chronic kicker. He carries a pocketful of recommendations and love letters. He hears that a man wants to hire some miners for $4 per day in Poverty Gulch, and having been unable to secure a position as a book keeper, or bank cashier starts for the "Gulch." On arriving, the superintendent of the mine asks him if he is a "top" or "bottom" man. He replies that he never gambled in his life. The superintendent seeing that his feet are tender, is more explanatory, and explains: "I mean, sir, do you prefer to work at the windlass or down in the shaft?" "Oh, yes I see—well, I don't care which. Tenderfoot goes below where they put him to striking. He makes a miss, and big Mike's hand suffers in consequence; whereupon the mighty Mike beats him over the head with a pick handle, loads him into the bucket as "country rock," and, giving the signal to "hoist away," Tenderfoot is ingloriously retired from further active operations as a miner. He then returns to town, after forty-eight hours' walk, thoroughly disgusted and his money reduced to $38.40. He talks overmuch about the brick homes and evergreen trees in his father's yard, and as he is about finished his conversation in steps "Big" Ed Burns—the notorious "top and bottom" fiend—disguised as a miner, and who has just sold a mine for $50,000. Ed has got more money than he knows what to do with, and wants to shake somebody the dice for the treats. Tenderfoot don't drink liquor of any kind, but would not object to a soda water. At this stage of the proceedings in steps a stranger from Tenderfoot's home, fresh with news from the evergreen spot. The dice are introduced and the "sure thing" game of "top and bottom" catches Mr. Tenderfoot for $38.40. After this he sleeps many weary nights to the leeward of a convenient water-tank or within the shelter of a friendly box-car, and the measly, mangy, heartless emissaries of the devil known as railroad men call him a tramp and provokingly ask him how he likes the "overland" route. Finally, arriving at his native village, he seeks the cover of a neighboring grove, and, coaxing a small boy to do the deed, dispatches the annexed note—or something similar—to his loving sire:

DEAR FATHER—Meet me at dusk at the picnic grove on the outskirts of town. Bring a shirt and a pair of pants and a coat. Your destitute son.
Charles C.
P. S. I've got a hat.

> After this he becomes a valued mining correspondent of the
> New York *Herald* and writes up New Mexico or Colorado as
> he views it.[16]

In part, this early newspaper account was somewhat whimsical, but
"Big" Ed Burns was indeed the genuine article. He was known
throughout Colorado, Arizona, and New Mexico as a notorious killer,
con-man, and "floating" tinhorn gambler.[17] "Big" Ed was especially
adept at figuratively roping in tenderfeet, and dragging them into the lair
of "top and bottom men;" who, as prominent historian Paula Marks
explains, were "men who used loaded dice to trick the gullible into
betting against the possibility of the tops and bottoms of three rolled dice
adding up to twenty-one. Since the tops and bottoms would add up to
twenty-one every time with unloaded dice, this was known as a real
sucker trick."[18]

Another of the depraved characters haunting the area around the
Mimbres Junction railroad tank-stop, just a few miles east of Deming,
was James W., "Six Shooter" Smith, or so he was known throughout the
Southwest; his mother called him John Henry Hankins.[19] "Six Shooter"
Smith was well known for shooting at people to see how close he could
come without hitting them, and his nefarious crony John Jefferson
Harlan, better known as the "Off Wheeler" joined in the fun.[20] At
Deming, with typical rambunctious spirit, Smith *accidentally* shot a
fellow sport in the foot, at least so says one report.[21]

Regarding Smith, Wayne Whitehill recalled a childhood trip he
made to the area with his father, the sheriff, "...in there was a fellow
named Six-shooter Smith. He was supposed to have been a real expert
with a gun and they had on the ground there little tables, card tables all
around the saloon and the bar was up here at this end. So this Six-
shooter Smith and my father and a bunch of 'em was up here talkin' and
he was gonna show some tricks with this six-shooter. And I was settin'
at a table way back pretty near to the end and there was an old fella
settin' right across from me, just settin' there in his chair, and I was
settin' right over here. After while this fella was whirlin' this six-shooter
over his finger like that and it went off and, god, the bullet went right by
my ear and hit the front of the building. And this old fella settin' there
with me he just fell over and begin to holler 'I'm shot, I'm shot.' And I
thought sure he was killed, but they come and picked him up and he
didn't have a scratch on him. But I know that the bullet just didn't miss
me very far and it hit right in the front of the building...He was twirlin'
this gun on his finger somethin' like that and the thing went off."[22]

In a description of early Deming, Pennington makes mention of the
local cemetery, reporting the first customer worthy of ceremonial
interment was a man killed by Andy (Anthony) Price.[23] Interestingly, in
a separate note, another writer tells of the day when Price and his buddy

loaded up on tonsil tonic at Warder's Café. Filled to the gills, bordering on the comatose, Price flipped out his six-shooter and his comprade inquired, "Does she pop?" With drunken dexterity the gun owner thumbed back the hammer, pointed at his pal's head..."and she popped!"[24] Defended by Albert Jennings Fountain, Price was eventually successful in pleading he remembered very little, the six-shooter was defective, and that if he had indeed shot his partner it was done in a "playful mood."[25]

Interestingly from the perspective of the Dan Tucker story, and adding details regarding Tony "One-arm" Price, are Wayne Whitehill's remembrances, which in part are validated by a newspaper comment, "Anthony Price, the Grant county murderer, is to be tried at the present term of the court in Mesilla."[26] The sheriff's son remarked, "Well, I know he killed somebody up there and my father took him to Las Cruces to try him, for a trial, and I went....he took me along and over here at Rincon we stayed there, with the team we got that far in one day from Silver City and that night they put a handcuff on me and this Price and made a pallet down on the floor and we slept there and Tucker and my father slept in a bed that night there, but they had me handcuffed to his good arm. We went to Cruces and they tried him down there...they give him a small sentence somehow for killin' somebody up here. It was murder."[27]

Murder or accident, it made little difference, and Andy Price would soon kill again, before he eventually sobered up and jumped the dividing line between ruffianism and righteousness. Price became a peace officer. "Andy Price the man twice tried for murder in this county, is constable at Eureka. It is said that he is a very good officer and that the rustlers give that section of the county the go-bye."[28] But in the days before he made the switch from polecat to policeman, Deming was wild and wooly—a wide-open frontier town!

Grant County's elite were becoming quite alarmed, especially in light of some territorial newspaper reports indicating that at Deming, "Six-Shooter Smith was 'the big dog with the brass collar.'"[29] Reportedly, at least one responsible citizen prescribed a cure for the outlaw ailment, "We've got to kill maybe two and maybe six desperadoes and then the thing's settled."[30]

The Grant County Grand Jury gave Sheriff Whitehill the political nudge:

> There seems to be a very bad state of affairs existing in the southern part of this county, near the border of Old Mexico. It almost seems that a law abiding citizen can hardly live there with any safety to himself or property. There seems to be a band of men living in that section of the county, who live by robbing and stealing, and defy the authorities. We ask that our Sheriff and law abiding citizens use every effort possible to

suppress this lawlessness, and if it cannot be done otherwise, to call on higher and more powerful authority to assist in so doing, as such a state of affairs seriously effect the prosperity of our county.[31]

The sheriff had to act. Taking deputies Tucker and Farrell, the trio of Grant County lawmen embarked on a peace keeping mission at Deming.[32] After a stay of several days, the lawmen made several arrests, one of which was "Three-Shooter" Smith, a real-life hombre who was so nicknamed because he was only half as bad as his cohort "Six-Shooter" Smith.[33] Deputy Dan Tucker "vowed" to stay at Deming until the rowdiness and misbehavior was brought under reasonable control.[34] With at least a semblance of law and order in place, Sheriff Whitehill returned to Silver City, leaving Dan Tucker behind.[35]

One writer informs that within three days after his arrival at Deming, Dan Tucker had killed three men, and wounded two others.[36] It is fair to question such a bold declaration. Historic truth belies the assertion regarding the time frame, but it is not necessarily erroneous when finally tallying marks on Tucker's notch-stick. But before he had to kill anyone, Deputy Dan Tucker simply ran "Six-Shooter," "Three-Shooter," and some of their hell-raising side-kicks smooth out of Deming town.[37] Attaching moralistic or righteous motives to Dan Tucker's hard-core enforcement stratagem might prove erroneous. A clearheaded examination of extant evidence, however, can support a rational conclusion: Sheriff Harvey Whitehill demanded the law be enforced at Deming, and employee Dan Tucker complied in his usual manner.

At least part of Tucker's calming influence is usually attributed to his choice of weapons. DeArment advises, "Tucker strode the streets with a double-barreled shotgun under his arm..."[38] And clearly from time to time, as will be illustrated, Dan Tucker did make use of a shotgun; indeed, he was proficient at killing people with both six-shooter and scattergun. Much more critical than the choice of weapons, Dan Tucker had the "grit" to get the job done, causing one commentator to announce, "if he wanted to arrest a desperado he was sure to either arrest or kill him."[39] Writing the history of Deming, another writer simply offered, "Lawlessness took a foothold. But Marshal Dan Tucker narrowed the dimensions."[40] Regardless of armament, Dan Tucker played a lead role in subduing rowdy behavior, and by the end of the month, one southwestern news-sheet proudly proclaimed, "Thanks to Sheriff Whitehill and his deputies, the most perfect order now prevails at Deming."[41] Tucker temporarily returned to Silver City.

By the middle of June, the Grant County Commissioners had paid fees to Dan Tucker for night watchman's duty at the county jail.[42] Surely, Tucker found time to prop his feet on the desk, lean back against the wall, and read the Grant County *Herald*; a story was dominating the pages of New Mexico news-rags, attracting nationwide interest. The newspaper reported, "The vulgar murderer and desperado known as 'Billy the Kid' has met his just deserts at last. He was shot and killed at the house of Pete Maxwell, near Fort Sumner, at midnight Thursday, the 14th instant, by Sheriff Pat Garrett, of Lincoln County."[43] Although Tucker's and the Kid's paths may have at sometime crossed, there is no evidence of such, but surely Tucker would have been paying attention to the tale. And Sheriff Whitehill may well have mulled over his earlier management of the youth's brief confinement in jail at Silver City, and how he had dealt with the rebellious juvenile.

By the end of the next month (July, 1881) Deputy Dan Tucker was off to Maricopa, Arizona Territory on undisclosed business.[44] According to at least one knowledgeable researcher, Dan Tucker made the trip to Maricopa to partake of hot mineral baths as a treatment for previously inflicted "wounds."[45]

Tucker was back in Deming by the end of September, 1881. Historian David Johnson, who is quite familiar with this group of southwestern borderline personalities, confirms by quoting a local newspaper story, "At Deming on Wednesday evening last {September 28, 1881}, Deputy Sheriff Tucker shot and killed one Charley Hugo who had been deporting himself in a riotous manner, and who resisted arrest."[46] This author soundly theorizes that Hugo must not have been a "gang member or noted outlaw," or the newspapers would have expanded on the story more precisely and covered it in depth.[47] Correspondingly, applying the same logic, one can suspect area reporters were now editorially anesthetized by another legally justifiable shooting at the hands of their prominent deputy. Wayne Whitehill indifferently remarks, "He (Tucker) killed two or three here in Deming."[48]

Fully cognizant of the bubbling liveliness at Deming, Grant County Commissioners at their October 3, 1881 meeting created Precinct 11, naming a Justice of the Peace, J. P. Wilson, and appointing John Warden as precinct constable.[49] Subsequent events, coupled with investigative analysis, reveals that although others were sometimes granted deputy status in southern environs of the county, Dan Tucker had been, and was at the time considered the primary lawman for the area. Apparently Sheriff Whitehill liked having Tucker concentrate his enforcement activity around Deming, the voting public enthusiastically endorsed the decision, and Deputy Dan Tucker willingly obliged both.

About this time, although exactness remains elusive, Deputy Dan Tucker added to his income by becoming an express messenger on the stage operating between Silver City and Deming. James H. Cook, then manager of the "WS" ranch near Alma, New Mexico wrote, "...one of Wells, Fargo & Company's most noted shotgun messengers, Dan Tucker, helped guard the passengers and treasure by the stages. Tucker had some thrilling experiences with stage robbers in the Southwest. He had the reputation of being one of the bravest of the many gun-fighters of the southwest borderlands. Guarding treasure entrusted to the care of Wells, Fargo & Company was a pretty hazardous occupation in that bandit-infested country at that time."[50]

Cook fails to enumerate or explicate the "thrilling experiences with stage robbers," but the significance of his remarks lays not in diminutive details, but rather in the overall reputation projected by Dan Tucker. Similarly, in Ben W. Kemp's biography of his father, *Cow Dust and Saddle Leather*, Tucker is reputed to have killed seven of Curly Bill's gang in front of a Deming saloon during a scalding shoot-out in 1884, in which Dan "appeared at a street corner and blasted them down in a hail of buckshot."[51] The story is a figment of unbridled imagination, but once again clearly allegorizes the depth of Tucker's man-killing reputation. At the time of the alleged hair-raising incident, 1884, Tucker's dexterity in handling handguns was cited in the Wichita *Daily Eagle*, "There are few men that can do that trick. I have been ten years on the southwest frontier, among the worst classes, and don't know more than half a dozen."[52] The writer mentioned four who were proficient at "twirling the pistol around his forefinger and cocking and pressing the trigger the moment the butt came into the palm of his hand." Dan Tucker, deputy sheriff at Deming was one.[53]

Doubtless, a portion of Dan Tucker's action-packed adventures were inordinately sensationalized, but that in-and-of-itself should not distract from those exploits firmly established by fact. In Western history, many of the "lesser lights" became famous only after their escapades were fantasized, magnified, and glorified during life's twilight years—or after. Ironically, it appears Tucker was better known in his own time than in ours. As a lawman, he earned a "reputation" in his day. Later, Western history largely missed or forgot him.

Adding to the volatile mix of southern Grant County rowdies, at least on a few occasions, were soldiers stationed at nearby Fort Cummings. Established in 1863, near Cooke Springs, a crucial watering hole for travelers bound for or returning from California, the fort, like its cousin Fort Bayard, was strategically located, which when translated means—right in the middle of Apache country. After watering at the spring, many a traveler had been ambushed by lurking Apaches while traversing the four-mile stretch through nearby Cooke's Canyon.[54]

Unlike most southwestern military installations, Fort Cummings was completely enclosed behind ten foot adobe walls, "measuring 320 feet from east to west and 366 feet from north to south."[55] Typically, the fort maintained a bakery, guardhouse, hospital, officer and enlisted men's quarters, and corrals, but somewhat atypically, "a storehouse with a capacity of two years' supplies for 100 men."[56] The fort was evacuated in 1873, but because of recurring Apache depredations, reoccupied in 1880.[57] Often charged with escort duty, patrols, and at times actual

Apache chasing, the soldiers upon their return to post would seek rest and relaxation in town, and sometimes trouble.

It wasn't too long before the *New Southwest* reported that lightening-rod Dan Tucker had once again drawn a few sparks. With emphasis added, the news report stated:

> A few days since, as we were reliably informed, five military officers from Cummings went over to Deming on a little jaunt, and three of them got boisterously drunk. Deputy Tucker started to arrest and disarm one of them, but he resisted, and in the struggle, the drunken officer's pistol went off, slightly burning Tucker's hands. The latter effected the arrest however, *as he usually does*, and while he was taking off his prisoner, another drunken officer made a feint with two Indian scouts, who were of the party, as though to rescue the prisoner. Meanwhile two military prisoners whom these scouts were detailed to guard, made their escape, and general confusion ensued among the officers, Tuck keeping up the march of his prisoner to the calaboose. The whole affair was of the most disgraceful character and an investigation would be in order were not whitewash too plenty. Deming has enough trouble with professional ruffians, and it would seem as though officers of the army should not seek to earn distinction by being of this class.[58]

Whether Dan Tucker returned to Arizona Territory after the shooting for medical reasons concerning powder burned hands, or for official Grant County Sheriff's business, or because he just wanted to plunge into a hot mineral bath, is not known. Soon, however, rumors were running rampant. At Silver City a local paper reported a rumor that Dan Tucker had been killed.[59] Interest in the gossip was also reported further down the line, the El Paso *Lone Star* reported, "The shooting of Tucker, deputy sheriff of Grant County, at Benson, A. T., last week has not been confirmed."[60]

Indeed there was cause for concern! Under the headline "Deputy Sheriff Tucker Shot," the Tombstone *Epitaph* reported the story of a frantic shoot-out between Tucker and George Brown at Benson, Arizona Territory.

> A desperate shooting affair is reported as having occurred at Benson, Sunday night. The particulars thus are very meager. It appears that during a dispute between Deputy Sheriff Tucker and Geo. Brown, the latter drew a revolver and shot the other in the leg and abdomen. As Tucker fell he fired twice at Brown but neither bullet hit its mark. The Deputy Sheriff was in town last Friday. His wounds were pronounced fatal.[61]

Apparently, Tucker who had been in town several days, had a dispute with Brown over some undisclosed matter, Brown jerked his revolver, blasting away at Tucker, hitting him in the leg, the second missile punching somewhere through Tucker's mid-section. As Tucker fell to the ground, wincing in pain, he popped two caps at Brown, but both shots missed their mark. Initially, Tucker's wounds were declared mortal, but miraculously, as was often the case in an age of imprecise medical diagnosis, Dan pulled through, although he would be burdened with suffering and discomfort from the wounds for the rest of his life.[62]

Apparently, no additional information on this shoot-out has been developed. This may be due to the fact that just a few days later Wyatt Earp and crew would be involved in the Tombstone gunplay commonly dubbed the "Gunfight at the O. K. Corral," which immediately captured the attention of frontier journalists. Of course, it is understandable how public attention and newspaper correspondents' fascination with such a sensational story would quickly snuff out any local coverage of what had the appearance of just another barroom brawl.

Admittedly, the newspaper story does not identify "Deputy Sheriff Tucker" by first name, but the recital does indicate the wounded lawman was from out of town, due to the remark, "the Deputy Sheriff was in town last Friday." Certainly, Dan Tucker being repeatedly in and out of Arizona Territory for one reason or another, is easily established by review of old newspaper files, and clearly the El Paso *Lone Star* referenced "deputy sheriff of Grant County."

In an effort to clarify the story in Arizona, Christine Rhodes, Cochise County Recorder, made investigation, examined county oath and bond books, and reported there was no record of a Cochise County Deputy named Tucker at the time this melee took place.[63] A check with the Pima County Recorder's office also failed in the effort to identify this "Deputy Sheriff Tucker" as someone other than Dan Tucker of New Mexico Territory. Without additional information, this report cannot be absolutely confirmed, but on the scale of probabilities, it certainly dovetails with Dan Tucker's *modus operandi*—when in doubt, charge! Or as one old-timer said of Tucker, "he was just a nice man, quite, didn't bother anybody, but don't bother him!"[64] Evidently Brown bothered Tucker! Nursing his wounds, and undoubtedly thankful to be alive, Dan Tucker returned to Deming.

NOTES AND SOURCES

1. The Florida Mountains, named by the Spaniards for flora found in hidden recesses, lay just to the southeast of the railroad junction which would become known as Deming. Lying in a north-south configuration, the mountain range was directly on the well worn Apache trail which ran from Mexico to the Black Range in New Mexico Territory. The Floridas contain several summits over

7,000 feet, and at one time provided prospectors with low grade lead-zinc ores, and occasionally small veins of gold and silver. Ungnade, P. 162.

2. Unpublished typescript, with notation, "Dr. Jeffrey Brown's historical survey of downtown buildings-1986." Courtesy Art Roman, Deming Luna Mimbres Museum Archives. Deming, New Mexico.

3. Ibid. One of the reasons for the move away from "New Chicago" was so that the Southern Pacific Railroad could retain ownership of land "near the station." "New Chicago" citizens protested, but to no avail.

4. Ibid. Other reports indicate the town of Deming was named for Theodore Deming, Charles Crocker's father-in-law.

5. Greever, William S., "Railway Development in the Southwest," *New Mexico Historical Review*, Vol. 32. 1957. Also see, Myrick, David F., *New Mexico's Railroads—A Historical Survey*. P. 12. Hereafter cited as Myrick.

6. Pennington, Edward., 1902 unpublished typescript on the history of Deming. Pennington was a former editor of the Deming *Headlight*. A native of Fort Smith Arkansas, Edward Pennington became a prominent Deming citizen and later became postmaster. "In Deming he was known as the Colonel because of his erect figure and goatee." He died in March 1930. Stanley, P. 9. Typescript courtesy of Wayne B. Humphrey, husband of Pennington's great-granddaughter. Hereafter cited as Pennington.

7. Stanley, P. 5

8. Pennington.

9. Casey, Robert J., *The Texas Border And Some Borderliners*. P. 189. Hereafter cited as Casey.

10. Ball, Larry D., "Militia Posses:: The Territorial Militia in Civil Law Enforcement in New Mexico Territory, 1877-1883," *New Mexico Historical Review*. January 1980. P. 48.

11. Gustafson, P. 8.

12. Grant County *Herald*, 04-09-1881.

13. Chase, C. M., *The Editor's Run In New Mexico and Colorado*. P. 127. Hereafter cited as Chase.

14. Ibid.

15. Stanley, P. 6.

16. Deming *Headlight*, 03-25-1882

17. Thrapp, Vol. I, P. 196.

18. Marks, Paula Mitchell., *And Die in the West—The Story of the O.K. Corral Gunfight*. P. 195. Hereafter cited as Marks.

19. Bartholomew, Ed., *Western Hard-Cases or Gunfighters Named Smith*. P. 74-78. Hereafter cited as Bartholomew.

20. Ibid. Also see Thrapp, Vol. III, P. 1330, for Smith and Vol. II, P. 616, for Harlan. And, Rasch, Philip J., "'Six Shooter' and 'Three Shooter' Smith," *Quarterly of the National Association and Center for Outlaw and Lawman History*, (NOLA). Vol. IX, No. 4, Spring 1985. Hereafter cited as Rasch. Rasch explores the possibility that 'Six-Shooter' Smith's real name could have been James Jenkins.

21. Ibid. P. 78.

22. Pioneers Foundation Interview { Wayne Whitehill}.

23. Pennington. Also see Grant County Civil and Criminal Court Cost Docket Book, *Territory vs. Anthony Price*.

24. Gustafson, P. 8.

25. Ibid. For a more complete synopsis of the case see Owen, P. 86.

26. El Paso *Lone Star*, 04-01-1882.

27. Pioneer Foundation interview. {Wayne Whitehill}

28. Unger, P. 103. Quoting the Silver City *Enterprise*, 02-22-1883. Eureka was a settlement near the Little Hatchet Mountains, south of Deming. Interestingly it got it's name from the traditional exclamation used by miners upon discovering pay dirt, "Eureka!" Julyan, P. 128.

29. Rasch, P. 9. Quoting the March 22, 1881 edition of the Las Vegas *Optic*.

30. Ibid., Quoting the March 20, 1881 edition of the Las Vegas *Gazette*.

31. New Southwest & Grant County *Herald*, 07-30-1881. The report was signed by George W. Holt, Foreman of the Grand Jury.

32. Grant County *Herald*, 04-09-1881.

33. Rasch, P. 9.

34. Stanley, P. 7.

35. Grant County *Herald*, 04-16-1881.

36. Rose, Silver City *Independent*, 09-22-1931.

37. Rasch, P. 9, reports that "Three-Shooter" after his initial arrest, returned to Deming, created a disturbance by shooting up a saloon, was subsequently arrested, and then hauled to Silver City and placed in jail.

38. DeArment, P. 17.

39. Ibid.

40. Stanley, P. 3.

41. The New Southwest & Grant County *Herald*, 04-23-1881.

42. Ibid., 06-18-1881.

43. Grant County *Herald*, 07-23-1881. As quoted by Harold L. Edwards, *Goodbye Billy the Kid*. P. 86. The author furnishes numerous interesting versions of how the press treated "Billy the Kid's" death.

44. Southwest, 07-30-1881.

45. Humble, P. in address to Silver City Westerners' Corral, on 04-19-1983. The speaker's information indeed may be accurate, but it should also be mentioned that between Deming and Silver City were the Faywood Hot Springs, (also known as Hudson Hot Springs and earlier as Mimbres Hot Springs) which were widely known and believed to provide healthfully relief to a variety of maladies.

46. Johnson, David., *John Ringo*, P. 121. Hereafter cited as Johnson. Quoting The New Southwest and Grant County *Herald*, 10-01-1881. Hereafter cited as Johnson. There is indeed the distinct possibility Johnson is confusing this shooting with the shooting of Jim Bond by Tucker just a short time later. In fact, P. Humble in a taped address to the Westerners' International, Silver City Corral No. 36, distinctly separates this Tucker killing, from the later Tucker killing of Jim Bond at the Deming depot. P. Humble is not hesitant, and after giving a recount of the Bond killing at the depot, says "Dan Tucker got a cowboy in a saloon down there the same way." Copy of 1983 audio taped address courtesy of T. Humble. In his remarks to historian Lou Blachly, Wayne Whitehill says, "Sil Stenson up here, you know, said he (Tucker) killed two down here but he only killed one down here in this depot hotel." Clearly, Whitehill is convinced that Tucker only killed one man at the depot. In this instance, the author concurs with Humble's conclusion, Dan Tucker killed at least two lawbreakers at Deming.

47. Ibid.

48. Pioneers Foundation Interview {Wayne Whitehill}.

49. Grant County Commissioners Meeting Book. Meeting 10-03-1881. Grant County Clerk's Office. Silver City, New Mexico.

50. Cook, James H., *Fifty Years on the Old Frontier*. P. 139. Additionally, newspaper reports refer to Tucker as shotgun messenger on the Silver City to Deming run. Also see DeArment, P. 17., and Thrapp, Vol. III, P. 1443.

51. Kemp, Ben W., with J. C. Dykes., *Cow Dust and Saddle Leather*. P. 49.

52. Wichita *Daily Eagle*, 10-11-1884.

53. Ibid.

54. Myers, P. 29-35. Fort Cummings was designed to accommodate one hundred officers and men, plus sixty-five horses and mules.

55. Giese, P. 18.

56. Ibid. And Julyan who advises the fort was named in honor of Major Joseph Cummings, 1st NM Cavalry, killed by Navajos during the summer of 1863. P. 134. Also see Myers, P. 29-35. Actual stockade walls were a rarity at southwestern military installations. Outside stockade walls, soldiers so inclined could visit "hog ranches" offering "booze, women, and gambling—mostly bad, degenerate, and crooked—that set up just outside the post reservation..." After the birth of Deming military men drifted in and out of town. Likewise, a whole cadre of the "sporting businesses" sprouted up to serve their entertainment demands.

57. Frazer, P. 98. Also see Ferris, P. 225.

58. New Southwest, 10-15-1881.

59. Daily Southwest & Grant County *Herald*, 10-29-1881.

60. El Paso *Lone Star*, 11-02-1881.

61. Tombstone *Epitaph*, 10-20-1881.

62. Ibid.

63. Conversations with Christine Rhodes, Cochise County Recorder, Bisbee, Arizona. August 1999. After examination of records available at the Cochise County Courthouse, Ms. Rhodes determined, that at the time of this shooting there was not a local Arizona deputy named Tucker. The reasonable deduction, barring the development of new information, is New Mexico Territory Deputy Dan Tucker was the wounded party in this particular violent affray. Additionally, a check with the Arizona Historical Society failed to produce any results which would indicate otherwise. Correspondence to author from Rose Byrne and Scott B. Denlinger, AHS, 05-10-1999 & 06-15-1999.

64. Southwest Oral Histories {Sylvester Stenson}.

6

"PEACEFULLY SLEEPS BENEATH THE DAISIES"

Although the story of "Russian Bill" and Sandy King has been repeatedly scribbled in numerous accounts, for some unexplained reason Dan Tucker's role in the drama is often innocently omitted.[1]

Sandy King, aka Red Curly, aka Ferguson, was a desperado of local note along the lower stretches of the New Mexico/Arizona line. One author describes King as a "pure-quill badman."[2] Another simply says, "He was a rustler and thief."[3] O. W. Williams claimed King had committed a murder, and was out on bond.[4] Sharman Apt Russell adds that King was "...in trouble for killing a man in Silver City."[5] There would probably not be too much disagreement, King was "a hard, dangerous man of courage and a record..."[6] Sandy King, when not out misappropriating creatures of the bovine variety, could frequently be unearthed from the dust and grime while quenching his thirst at Shakespeare saloons.

William Rogers Tettenborn, a import from Russia, who fittingly answered to the moniker "Russian Bill," is more of an enigma.[7] Most accounts attempt to make a connection between Bill and Russian nobility, such as "he purportedly was the son of a 'Teuton' subject of the Czar and the daughter of William Rogers, a Scot sea captain."[8] Or, "Among these beleaguered traditionalists was the future Russian Bill, an officer in the Imperial White Hussars, which was then a glamorous regiment known for its high boots, sabers, and tailored coats."[9] Regardless of genetic lineage, "Russian Bill" hobbled onto the southwestern scene, after he was "lamed" in a Fort Worth shoot-out, and stabbed in the shoulder by a rascal at Denver—so they say.[10]

One account describes "Russian Bill" as having a "fierce blond mustache and blond hair which hung to his shoulders; he carried a six-gun at each hip and a long knife in his boot, and was always telling how tough he was."[11] Another early area resident accuses Tettenborn of "vaporing braggadocio."[12] Of the two, Sandy King was considered "much worse" and a "respected member" of the wicked outlaws who were allegedly plying their trade up and down the territorial line, and on occasion invading the Mexican states of Sonora and Chihuahua.[13]

Usually defined as a wanna-be badman, "Russian Bill" never did make the roster reserved for premier gunfighters, and most versions simply leave it at that. Upon closer inspection by Janaloo Hill, his actual reputation was somewhat elevated, when she revealed Tettenborn was quite actively involved in legitimate mineral speculation, owned interests in numerous mines, and served as official claims recorder for the Stonewall Mining District.[14] Despite the depths he may have fallen to, or the heights he might have attained, history had a inglorious spot reserved for "Russian Bill" Tettenborn.

The careers of Sandy and Bill abruptly came to a close, almost simultaneously, during their last pirouette on the Shakespeare stage. It seems Sandy had undergone a transfusion at a local saloon, and the red-blooded buckaroo was functioning at the ninety-proof level. Incensed that a store clerk would expect currency for a purchase—in place of slurred utterances—Sandy simply settled-up with the man by shooting off his finger.[15] Stumbling proudly, flourishing the fruit of his crime, a new scarlet neckerchief, Sandy King mounted a horse, *possibly* his own, and fled from the scene of the crime, only to be snagged by the Deputy Dan Tucker, who forthwith hauled him back to Shakespeare.[16]

Not to be outdone, "Russian Bill" left town on horseback, but *definitely* not his own. And while the act may have been a psychological attempt to "prove himself to the gang" in some "symbolic" medium as one author writes, the steed's owner didn't require psychoanalysis to declare the daring deed anything but horse theft—pure and simple.[17] Bill became a fugitive. At Deming, Dan Tucker was notified of the "all points bulletin" demanding arrest of the aristocratic desert pirate. Whether Tucker tracked down "Russian Bill," was tipped off by concerned citizens, or merely bumbled into him, is not historically clear, but in the end the deadly deputy found Tettenborn hiding in a sidetracked boxcar, and hastily decorated him with handcuffs and leg irons.[18]

Another rendition reports, "Russian Bill" and Sandy were involved in "some sort of fight," and that King was knocked down by gunfire, but only "creased," which resulted in his capture, while Tettenborn scratched-out to the east, "hoping to make it to the finished railroad and a one way trip *paya*."[19]

Deputy Dan Tucker, accompanied by a unidentified assistant, returned "Russian Bill" to Shakespeare, after stopping for a meal prepared by Anna Ownby, who reported the prisoner "ate with his handcuffs on."[20] At Shakespeare, Tettenborn was "thrown" into a room with Sandy King at the Grant Hotel, and there the pair languished, ineffectually guarded by Jack Rutland. What happened next is best explained by contemporary newspapers. Picking up the story from local reports, the Santa Fe *New Mexican* declared:

> They (King and Tettenborn) were brought here a few days ago and lodged in jail. Yesterday (Monday) they were loud and demonstrative in their threats against the citizens, declaring that the people of the town would have an opportunity to dance to their music inside of twenty-four (hours) days. During the small hours of the night the jail was visited by an armed force,

the guard was over-powered, and in an hour or so afterwards two pulse-less bodies, stiff and cold, could be seen suspended by a cord to a girder in what was formerly the barroom of the old Shakespeare hotel. We have a funeral here today at the expense of the citizens. These are extreme measures but it seems a necessity, and I fear the end is not yet...[21]

Jack Rutland advised Ownby he had been lying on a mattress while guarding the prisoners, and the vigilante crowd "threw him back in the corner and threw the mattress over him. And they hung those two men right in there."[22]

Of the hanging, Hill reports, "Since there was no newspaper in Shakespeare and since the town's hangings were something to be hidden, nothing appeared in any neighboring town's paper until a small item in the Dec.11, 1881 Tombstone Arizona *Epitaph* announced five men had been hanged at Shakespeare."[23] This assertion is not quite correct as revealed by a circumspect audit of newspaper archives. From the account cited above, the reader is advised as to what happened, and from the next report, Deputy Dan Tucker's personal involvement is mentioned. The November 16, 1881 edition of the El Paso *Lone Star* reported:

Two "rustlers," "Russian Bill" and "Sandy King" from the southern part of Grant county, were arrested last week by Deputy Sheriff Tucker and lodged in jail at Shakespeare last Monday. They were taken from jail that night by the citizens, who overpowered the guards, and hanged. "Russian Bill" has often declared that no man living could arrest him, but when he found Tucker was on his track he gave himself up without any resistance. Their fate has no doubt engendered the enmity of the element to which they belonged against Shakespeare and the people there will organize a safety committee as a means of protection. The two men hanged were noted horse and cattle thieves.

On November 12, 1881 a Silver City newspaper reported:

On the night of Tuesday, the 8th inst., Russian Bill and Sandy King were taken from the jail at Shakespeare and lynched by the vigilance committee of that place. King had been for some months past confined in the county jail in this city, and was released but a few days ago. He seems to have gone direct to Shakespeare, when he stole a horse and was again imprisoned to await trial. On last Saturday Dep. Sheriff Tucker, at Deming, received a warrant for the arrest of Russian Bill on the same charge for which King was held. He was arrested at Separ on Monday last and taken to Shakespeare by Deputy Tucker. On Tuesday they were given a hearing before a justice of the peace at that place, and Deputy Woods ordered to bring them to the county jail on Wednesday, but the citizens of Shakespeare, who had evidently tired of such character, concluded to mete out justice themselves, so King and Bill were quickly taken from jail by a party of seventy men, and hanged. The friends of the deceased have been warned that if they attempt revenge, they will be treated in like manner.[24]

Emma Muir repeated local gossip, revealing Sandy King was "so game that the committee almost commuted his sentence" but, pathetically, Tettenborn "begged for his life, as might have been expected of a horse thief."[25] The Law and Order Committee, disbursed, leaving the strangled bad boys to dangle all night suspended from rafters in the Grant Hotel dining room. The next day, a traveler passing through Shakespeare curiously inquired about the obvious. Pointing to "Russian Bill," the hotel proprietor replied, "he was a horse thief, the other one— a damned nuisance."[26]

Notwithstanding traditional local humor, it is clear Dan Tucker played a pivotal role in the capture of "Russian Bill," and Sandy King. Unfortunately, a little historic haze hangs over a particular, but unanswered question. Did Deputy Dan Tucker have any inkling about the intentions of the Shakespeare crowd? One cannot say, but historic evidence clearly reveals, Dan Tucker had not the slightest degree of sympathy for livestock rustlers, murders, thieves, or damn nuisances!

The calamitous chapter on "Russian Bill" Tettenborn's brief life cannot be closed, short a recitation of folkloric trivia. Allegedly, from Bill's mother in Russia, inquiries were made as to why she no longer received correspondence from her nobly bred, but admittedly wayward son. The "lady of means" probed, and if all are to be believed, evidently everyone answered, but of course, none dared report the truth, and break her distraught motherly heart. Generally the sad replies go something like, "he died from a shortage of breath due to a sudden change in altitude," or, "I am sorry to inform you that your son died of throat trouble."[27]

In repeating tales of Sandy King and "Russian Bill," it is impossible to avoid reporting the endeavors at coarse frontier humor, but a return to reality reveals that while Dan Tucker may have smiled at amusing anecdotes, he was decidedly sincere with regard to maintaining peace and tranquillity. His efforts were not unnoticed! "Deputy Sheriff Tucker of Deming, keeps that town free of rough characters."[28] Evidently, Tucker felt the need to flex some law enforcement muscle, for in one twenty day period, he arrested thirteen of the "cowboy gang" that had plagued southern Grant County and gave them their "walking papers," at least so reported the El Paso *Lone Star*.[29]

Tucker didn't issue walking papers to Jim Bond! "Three weeks ago a cow boy rode his horse defiantly over the depot hotel platform, and was about to ride into the dining room, when he dropped off his horse with a charge of buckshot in his back. The first charge struck the dining-room door, and remains there as a reminder of Deming customs. The cow boy was buried without ceremony. He is indebted to Deputy Sheriff Tucker for his change of abode..."[30] From the way this particular account is worded, it would appear Tucker sought compliance, punctuated his demand with a warning shot, then shot Bond who failed to heed the decree. Stanley disputes the warning shot theory simply stating, "Some took exception to Tucker's action, claiming that he shot the man in the back. Tucker was not the type to shoot men in the back. What happened was that the deputy missed the first charge, hitting the dining room door instead of the cowboy."[31] DeArment writes that Bond, "threw his Winchester rifle across the saddle and leveled it at the officer."[32] In recounting his version of a story which quickly became local folklore, Wayne Whitehill declared the errant cowboy rode his horse into the depot dining room, pulled a six-shooter on the deputy, but Dan Tucker "had this old shotgun so he just let him have it, shot his head off and the brains went up all over the ceiling."[33]

The story was retold in the Wichita *Daily Eagle*, "A darn fool went and rode through the dining-room in the railroad hotel at Deming flourishing his pistol, and frightened the lady passengers bound west nearly into fits. Dan Tucker found the fellow on the street, covered him with her (shotgun) and called 'hands up.' The blasted idiot makes a motion for his six-shooter and Dan filled him chuck full of buckshot. He failed to get there, Eli, and now peacefully sleeps beneath the daisies."[34]

Just after the century clock turned, the notorious train-station shooting was still in the news, as evidenced by these comments from the Silver City *Enterprise*, "...Sheriff Tucker was employed to keep order. The border terrors flocked there (Deming) in great numbers, and in an altercation with one named Jim Bond, Tucker armed with a shot gun came off victor. This occurred in the Depot Restaurant."[35]

In his efforts to add corroboration to the story, historian Lou Blachly ultimately located a letter written in 1906 by E. F. Keough. Keough explained, "Several killings took place in the town, and the railroad companies hired Dan Tucker, who was deputy sheriff under Mr. Whitehill to come there and keep the peace. The first thing he did was to demolish Jim Bond, a discharged Texas ranger, with a double barreled shotgun in the depot door. After that things went along somewhat smoother."[36] Some say that within just a short time, Tucker's impact had converted Deming into a "Sunday School."[37] An overstatement to be sure!

The shotgun used by Dan Tucker to end Bond's rambunctious rowdiness was a W. Richards, imported from Belgium with the double-barrels chopped off to a length of 19½ inches.[38] Tucker used this weapon for years during his law enforcement career and while guarding stagecoaches making the run between Silver City and Deming. Eventually he gave the weapon to a Grant County old-timer.[39]

Regardless of any added local color and flavor, or how the story is occasionally spiced up, Dan Tucker killed Jim Bond at the Deming depot. In a rough and tough bailiwick, the incident further cemented Dan Tucker's reputation as a "stone cold killer"—if necessary!

Even good cowboys could occasionally misbehave. In fact, errant and inebriated cowboys riding their trusty steeds into frontier barrooms was not necessarily uncommon, as depicted in just one bulletin: "Buck Tyson, a well known lower Gila cowboy, painted El Paso a rich carmine tint on Friday last. He was full to overflowing of tarantula juice and ran his horse through a plate glass door..."[40]

Keough's remark—"and the railroad companies hired Dan Tucker"— is not inconsistent with common practice for the time and place. Certainly, at least in the Territories, private enterprises frequently contributed financially for part, or occasionally, all of a deputy's salary. In these instances the positions were known as *subscription deputies*, and best explained by Ball: "That businesses, such as mining or cattle companies, desired resident deputy sheriffs was not uncommon. These organizations often lay in remote locales and kept large sums of money or valuable ores that enticed would-be bandits. Such companies offered to pay the wages of a deputy sheriff outright or requested that employees be commissioned, presumably at no extra pay."[41] Whether or not Dan Tucker fit into this classification is immaterial; from a legal perspective, Dan Tucker was officially commissioned a Grant County Deputy Sheriff.

Possibly because of the wounds he received in the shoot-out with George Brown in the Benson fight, Deputy Dan Tucker traveled to Tucson for medical treatment, but by January 7, 1882 he had made the return trip to New Mexico Territory.[42] At Deming, his professional assessment was, "everything quiet."[43]

Although Dan resided in Deming he continued with his shotgun messenger duties on the run to Silver City, frequently over-nighting in that city. And like cowboys from the Gila, soldiers from the forts, and a healthy smattering of "city folk," Dan Tucker invested much of his free time in the enjoyment of Silver City's night spots.

At Silver City, things were not quite so quiet. On the night of March 4, 1882, Tucker was attending a *baile* at the Coliseum, when a barber from the Centennial (saloon) named Fred, and a "Mexican" cook for the Tremont (hotel) had a fight. Fred and the cook vied for a dance with the same partner—at the same time! Evidently, Fred was not to be denied, and kept persisting until a point was reached where several of the cook's agitated friends decided to thrash him. Tucker jerked his peacemaker, ordering the combatants to separate. One pulled a knife and sprang forward. Tucker "sent him rolling into a corner with a blow from the butt end of his revolver." Then with characteristic frontier style, apparently Tucker let the two original disputants scrap it out, unaided by friends. Fred got whopped severely on the side of the head, and his challenger received a cut hand and had part of his nose bitten off. Tucker was lauded by the local press for preventing a race riot.[44] Who finally got the dance went unreported.

NOTES AND SOURCES

1. The New Southwest & Grant County *Herald*, 11-12-1881. The story was also carried in the The El Paso *Lone Star*, 11-16-1881.

2. Thrapp, Dan, "Shakespeare's Lively Ghosts," *Westways*. March. 1961.

3. Nash, P. 203. And see, Hill (R&J—C), P. 10. The authors report "Jefferson" may have been King's true first name, and that he was possibly related to King Fisher, the notorious Texas gunman.

4. Williams, P. 95. Also see *Grant County Register of Prisoners Confined in Jail*, P. 11. This entry indicates "Sandy King" was Jailed on Jan. 17, 1881 for Affray, and was released on February 26, 1881. Interestingly, this once again illustrates that there was at least a minimal degree of official law enforcement at Shakespeare.

5. Russell, Sharman Apt., "Russian Bill: the True Story of an Outlaw," *Journal of the West 23*. (April 1984) P. 92. Hereafter cited as Russell.

6. Thrapp, Vol. II, P. 783. Anna Ownby (sometimes spelled Owenby) characterized Sandy King as a "petty thief." Pioneers Foundation Interview {Anna Ownby}

7. Hill, 10-20-1983, The author correctly asserts, all accounts agree Tettenborn was from Russia, but after that acknowledgment there is a wide divergence of journalistic opinion.

8. Thrapp, Vol. III, P. 1411.

9. Russell, P. 91

10. Thrapp, Vol. III, P. 1411. The author's remarks no doubt come from Williams, who said, "He ("Russian Bill") had a bullet in his leg, received in Fort Worth, and he bore a scar from a knife slash in the shoulder as a receipt for a difficulty in Denver. Many had been his marvelous escapes." P. 94.

11. Muir, Emma M. "Shakespeare Becomes a Ghost Town," *New Mexico Magazine*. October. 1948. P. 26. Hereafter cited as Muir (II).

12. Williams, P. 94.

13. Ibid., for "much worse," Muir, P. 26, for "respected member."

14. Hill, 10-20-1983. The author's in-depth three part series relies heavily on actual primary source material, with special detail to courthouse recorded mining claims.

15. Russell, P. 93.

16. Thrapp, Vol. II, P. 783.

17. Russell, P. 92.

18. Nearly all accounts report that "Russian Bill" Tettenborn was arrested in a boxcar near Deming. Many, many accounts of the arrest have been penned, and depending on the source, the person or persons responsible for the arrest vary. In all likelihood, Dan Tucker at least participated in the arrest, he was the Grant

County deputy sheriff, at the time, posted at Deming, and even private parties making a "citizens arrest" would have probably sought Tucker's assistance. Furthermore, as reported, contemporary newspaper accounts credit Tucker with the arrest.

19. Hill (R), P. 36.

20. Pioneer Foundation Interviews {Anna Ownby}.

21. Santa Fe *New Mexican*, 11-12-1881, as quoted in *The Shakespeare New Mexico Story*, by F. Stanley, P. 14.

22. Pioneers Foundation Interviews {Anna Ownby}.

23. Hill, 10-27-1983. Also see, Russell, P. 93. The author cites the 11-12-1881 edition of the Santa Fe *New Mexican*, which in part reads, "The civic law seems to be impotent to protect us against those desperadoes that are preying on our rights and property, but it is my opinion that this community is determined to show the world that it is able to protect its property and lives and the lives of its families. Shakespeare is on the mettle and woe betide the unfortunate who raises the next row at that place." Russell places the capture of "Russian" Bill near Deming, New Mexico by an "impromptu posse." White, Majorie, "STAGE STOP," *Frontier Times*, April-May 1964. P. 63 reports that "Russian" Bill and Sandy King were hanged on November 8, 1881. Thrapp, Dan, "Shakespeare's Lively Ghosts," *Westways*, March 1961, P. 17., credits the hanging to a "newly formed Law and Order Committee, a group obviously dissatisfied with the more formal workings of Territorial justice."

24. The New Southwest & Grant County *Herald*, 11-12-1881. F. Stanley, The Shakespeare New Mexico Story, reports "Russian Bill" arrested at Deming by Deputy Sheriff Jack Rutland. P. 16. Raymond F. Adams, *Six-Guns and Saddle Leather*, disputes Stanley's assertion, although he himself somewhat adds to the confusion, "The author says that Russian Bill was arrested by Deputy Sheriff Jack Rutland in Deming, but contemporary newspaper accounts reported that he was arrested by Tom Tucker." P. 612. Tom Tucker, who also led an exciting and colorful life is sometimes confused with Dan Tucker. Tom Tucker is best remembered for his role in Arizona's Pleasant Valley War, and Oliver Lee's troubles in southeastern New Mexico, both of which occurred after Dan Tucker's tenure as a Grant County lawman and Deputy United States Marshal. See O'Neal, P. 328 and Nash, P. 305. Clearly the contemporary newspapers mention Dan Tucker. In reality, based on contemporary accounts, it would appear that Dan Tucker arrested "Russian Bill," and may have received assistance from other area lawmen or local citizens.

25. Muir (II), P. 26.

26. Ibid., P. 25. Interestingly Thrapp, Vol. III, P. 1411, purports the attributions to have been reversed, Tettenborn being the "nuisance." Consequential? Gatto, Steve, *Wyatt Earp—A Biography of a Western Lawman*, does make an intriguing, but undocumented assertion, "Nothing had been heard about Curly Bill since December 1881, when it was reported he was leaving the country. He may have had a good reason to leave the area since there is some indication that he was almost lynched with Russian Bill and Sandy King in November 1881." P. 191. The "some indication" is replaced by "some reports" in the endnotes, somewhat devaluing the citation. Hereafter cited as Gatto.

27. Most accounts of the hanging of "Russian Bill" contain a different version of the letter of inquiry and the reply. Thrapp says Sheriff Whitehill received the inquiry and local citizens replied with the "high altitude" remark.

Vol., III, P. 1411. Ball (S) concurs that Whitehill received a request from "Russian Bill's" mother, indicating that Whitehill replied that her son had committed suicide. P. 274. Williams reports he wrote back that her son "had met with a serious accident." P. 95. Hill advises that John Evensen of Shakespeare replied with the "throat trouble" response.

28. El Paso *Lone Star*, 12-03-1881
29. Thrapp. Vol. III, P. 1443. This information is confirmed by remarks made in the November 11, 1881 edition of the El Paso *Lone Star*.
30. Chase, P. 127.
31. Stanley, P. 7. The author does confirm that the deceased cowboy's name was Bond.
32. DeArment, P. 17. Also see Chase, P. 127-128. The identification of the cowboy as Bond, is mentioned by James B. Gillett, *Six Years With The Texas Rangers*. P. 198, although the author uses the first name "Jack," and most other reports indicate it was "Jim." Gillett reports that Bond was a "San Simon Valley rustler," ex-Texas Ranger, and spy for area crooks. Gillett mentions Dan Tucker by name, as the officer who attempted to arrest, and then had to kill Bond. Gustafson simply says Bond was "a cowboy from the San Simon Valley" and that Dan Tucker "issued Bond a ticket to eternity with his trusty shotgun." P. 9.
33. Pioneer Foundation Interviews {Wayne Whitehill}. Dan Rose alleges that Tucker unfortunately killed two men on this occasion, "I say unfortunate, for they were not outlaws of the real bad-man type—just two drink crazed men spoiling for excitement and licensed, according to their code, to 'play it' to the limit, no matter where their folly led." During his address to the Westerners' International, Pat Humble brings up the possibility that Tucker knew he was going to have trouble with Bond, the leader of a local outlaw band, and challenged him to appear at the depot. Audio tape courtesy T. Humble. That Tucker killed Bond with a shotgun certainly could lead to a reasonable conclusion that Dan Tucker was anticipating a violent episode might occur, and had armed himself accordingly.
34. Wichita *Daily Eagle*, 10-11-1884.
35. Silver City *Enterprise*, 01-23-1903.
36. Ibid., 12-29-1949., "I'll Never Forget." Keough's letter written in 1906 describing the killing of Bond by Tucker preceded the publication of Gillet's remembrances by well over a decade.
37. Stanley, P. 7.
38. Southwest Oral Histories {Sylvester Stenson}. This brand of shotgun should not be confused with the much more valuable and highly sought after Westley Richards & Co. Inc. firearms manufactured in London, England. See, S. P. Fjestad, *Blue Book of Gun Values*. P. 1189.
39. Ibid., Sylvester Stenson reports that Dan Tucker gave the shotgun to his father.
40. Silver City *Enterprise*, 12-12-1884.
41. Ball (S), P. 33
42. The New Southwest and Grant County *Herald*. 01-07-1882. The article refers to Tucker being "sick for some time in Tucson."
43. Ibid., 02-25-1882.
44. Ibid., 03-04-1882.

7

"PUT THE CLAMPS ON DEMING"

Meanwhile over in Arizona Territory, Clara Brown, who served as a part-time correspondent for the San Diego Daily Union, was indeed prophetic when she penned, "a smoldering fire exists, which is liable to burst forth at some unexpected moment."[1] After the McClaury brothers and young Billy Clanton were gunned down near Tombstone's Fremont Street, the feud between the Earps and the "cowboys," Democrats versus Republicans, and the competing newspaper journalists began in earnest. As each tragic event took place, depending on family kinship, economic positioning, or partisan political posturing, the episode was immediately colored to paint the preferred picture.

Wyatt's brother, Virgil, was ambushed by lurking revenge seekers three days after Christmas, 1881, and suffered the rest of his life from wounds inflicted by horrific shotgun blasts.[2] Within three months, another brother, Morgan, was fatally gunned down while leisurely absorbed in a game of billiards at the Tombstone poolroom operated by Bob Hatch.[3] In turn, Wyatt Earp and his crew of western misfits, murdered Frank Stilwell who was "begging for his life" between idle trains at the Tucson station.[4] Of Stilwell's death, one curious onlooker declared "...(he) was shot all over, the worse shot-up man that I ever saw."[5] In Dan Tucker's bailiwick the Deming *Headlight* offered, "The Earp party riddled Frank Stilwell with bullets last.(sic) Murder is the order of the day in Tombstone and Tucson."[6] Arrest warrants were immediately issued for the Earp platoon.[7] Their desire for vengeance yet sated, the Earp gang killed Florentino Cruz in the South Pass of the Dragoon Mountains at Pete Spencer's wood camp.[8] Still in the process of "making his own law," Wyatt fired both barrels of his shotgun into the chest of "Curly" Bill during a ferocious encounter at Iron Springs— at least he claimed he did.[9]

Even to this day, the battle of Earpville rages, with a squad of legend debunkers ready to ambush the creditability of almost any statement made by melodramatic myth-makers. The truth is most probably somewhere inbetween. Be that as it may, history records that Wyatt and his associates fled Arizona Territory ahead of legally authorized murder warrants.

That the factual story of Earp's flight from Arizona Territory has suffered nonsensical scribbling is illustrated by just one excerpt which alleges that during Wyatt's exodus he left a plain trail, "deliberately unconcealed to invite a confrontation."[10] Common sense would recognize that if Wyatt Earp (or anyone else) was "inviting a confrontation," he could have had one at anytime or place of his choosing. The truth of the matter is, for whatever reason, Wyatt opted to flee rather than fight or take his chances with due process by submitting to lawful arrest.

A quick review of just three of the much more balanced interpretations tells the straightforward story—minus most of the hype. Gary L. Roberts weighs in on the historical significance, "So, while it probably made little difference in the course of Arizona history, it has profoundly affected our image of the West."[11] From a law enforcement perspective, Ball concludes, "It was a unique spectacle; a posse of federal lawmen forced from their district."[12] Paula Mark's comment regarding Wyatt's departure is stunningly perceptive, "...Wyatt was kicking the dust of Tombstone from his heels and headed for a more favorable clime about the time the cowboy troubles settled down for good, leaving indefinitely open to debate whether he had been part of the problem or part of the solution."[13]

In their flight to avoid arrest and prosecution, the Earp entourage traveled on horseback to Silver City, before moving farther east, catching a train, and finally alighting in colorful Colorado. One author concludes, the bunch avoided a much quicker and more direct route through Deming because they feared arrest by Dan Tucker.[14] In an additional analysis, Thrapp is decidedly convinced, "In March 1882 the Earp crowd in their hasty exit from Tombstone toward Colorado, rather than take the train through Deming—Tucker's Territory—went on horseback the long way around. Apparently they were reluctant to test Tucker's ability to make the arrests Arizona officials desired."[15]

In a recent article, another writer disagrees, stating the Earp party eventually left Silver City and traveled into Tucker territory, "because the fastest way to the nearest railroad was the trip fifty miles south to Deming."[16] Using this line of reasoning does seem somewhat inconsistent, and clearly devoid of simple logic. If the Earp bunch were really seeking the "fastest" escape route north to Colorado, they would have boarded the train along the track, back in Arizona Territory, by-passed Silver City altogether, and been gone for good!

Elementary reasoning would surely question why the Earp crowd went to Silver City in the first place. Assuredly, it was not the "fastest way to the nearest railroad," since Silver City would be absent any railroad service at all, until May 12, 1883, when Engine No. 1, the "E. G. Shields," of the Silver City, Deming and Pacific Railroad Company, on it's debut run, finally chugged into town nearly a year after Earp stealthily slipped into, and then secretly scrambled out of town.[17] From Silver City, the Earp outfit could have either continued their headlong retreat on foot, astride a horse, sitting in a wagon, crowded into a jostling stagecoach, or—lifelessly reposed in a pine box—but there "weren't" no train! The trip to Silver City was nothing less than a contrived stratagem, carefully calculated to create deception and thwart pursuit.

That the Earp boys were indeed a crafty clan, and purposely intent on leaving a false trail for law-dogs to follow can readily be seen in an extraction from the New Southwest and Grant County *Herald*. The newspaper blurb stated, "Virgil Earp, at Colton, A. T. (sic) has received a letter from his brothers in Illinois. The boys say they left the country for fear of killing some good men. They will take steps to return at an early day."[18] Authentic historical assessment reveals Earp, "Doc" Holliday, and their pals, took no steps in the direction of Arizona Territory to answer the murder charges at "an early day"—*or any other day*!

The Earp party, using false names, over-nighted in Silver City, and then the next day divested themselves of their horses, and caught the next stage bound for Fort Cummings.[19] Writer Casey Tefertiller reports that when the Earp crowd arrived in Silver City they stayed at a private home to avoid registering at a local hotel.[20] One of the several "Doc" Holliday biographers offers commentary, "On April 7, 1882, Doc, the Earps, and the rest of their group surreptitiously arrived in Silver City, New Mexico Territory. They found lodging in a private dwelling under assumed names. Their arrival in New Mexico was not known to the public until well after their departure..."[21] Use of the words *surreptitiously* and *under assumed names* are indeed meaningful. A review of the actual source for this information can be found in a newspaper article:

> Last Saturday evening at 10 o'clock, the Earp Boys' party and Doc Holliday were in Silver City. They went at once to the Exchange Hotel to find a stage agent to make arrangements to leave the next morning on the Deming coach. They slept in a private house up town and took breakfast the next morning in the Broadway restaurant, as they had not registered at any hotel, it was not known they were in town until after their departure. The party came on horseback, and put up at the Elephant Corral. They were all mounted and armed to the teeth. One of the men when asked his name, answered John Smith, and another Bill Snooks. This excited the suspicion of Mr. White, proprietor of the Corral, and the next morning when they offered to sell him their horses, he refused to buy them, fearing to get himself in trouble. They offered six of their horses for $300, but as the horses were worth more than that, this offer was also looked on as unfavorable to them. They finally sold the six horses to Mr. Miller, who is about to start a livery stable here. This done they spoke to Mr. White about hiring a team to take them to Fort Cummings, but he advised them to go by stage, which they decided to do. The

saddles and two horses they failed to sell were left here with Charley Bagsby.[22]

Bartholomew suggests the chameleon-like characters first tried to hire a wagon to take them to Fort Cummings, but were refused.[23] Aside from the newspaper report, common sense seems to validate such an assertion. Indeed it would have taken an exceedingly poor businessman to rent out a team and wagon to a platoon of heavily armed travelers, who were making a one-way trip to some undisclosed destination, and it would have taken a fool to volunteer to drive the outfit for them. Forced to take the stagecoach, the fugitive's itinerary took them "to old Fort Cummings, past Dick Hudson's hotel for 'invalids' at the famous old hot springs by Mowery City,...and then on to the Rio Grande, to Rincon, to take the train north."[24]

Marks mentions, from Fort Cummings the Earp assemblage traveled "...a short distance to Rincon," where they then had the alternative of traveling by train south to El Paso, or north to Albuquerque, Las Vegas, and across the line into Colorado.[25] DeArment advises, after leaving Silver City the Earp coterie "continued by stage to Fort Cummings and Rincon, where they caught the train north to Colorado."[26]

Unquestionably, at the time, the fastest pathway from Silver City to Colorado, would have been riding the stage to Fort Cummings, then a short trip to Nutt Station, the Atchison, Topeka and Santa Fe railroad depot, just east of the military reservation, *and then* to Rincon.[27] Headlong in their flight to avoid *due process*, the wanted ensemble of controversial characters at last made good their flight, and caught northbound rails leading to illegal liberation.

What the fugitives chose to do is fact, why can only be left to supposition. Evidenced by their sneaky behavior, and use of false names, it is only reasonable to believe the legendary Wyatt Earp and the gutsy "Doc" Holliday were cleverly and prudently avoiding confrontation with area lawmen. Deputy Dan Tucker was already well known up and down the rail-line as a fearless peace officer as his exploits had been well publicized.[28] Had he not shot down fleeing suspects; captured Sandy King and "Russian Bill;" exchanged scalding shots with George Brown; punched Charley Gough's ticket; popped Jim Bond smooth out of the saddle; and simply run other "hell raisers" out of town? Deputy Dan Tucker's escapades were repeatedly exacting comments from newspaper reporters up and down the tracks, as well as word of mouth elucidation from "rounders" within and outside the law. DeArment wrote: "The word soon spread all along the border that Dan Tucker had put the clamps on Deming. Lawbreakers and fugitives gave the town a wide berth."[29]

Why Wyatt conspicuously avoided Tucker's bailiwick is moot, and massaging historical facts will not change simple reality—Dan Tucker never had a showdown with the escaping Wyatt Earp.

Again for undisclosed reasons Tucker left home and traveled to California. Upon his return, he once again reported Deming relatively quite and peaceful, noting there were no "desperate characters" currently in the city. He was concerned however, about the number of railroad tramps who were arriving in town, averaging fifteen per day. "The public had little sympathy for them (tramps). Most such characters had little money, few friends, and no political influence. Even courts took a jaundiced view of those who rode the rails, begged from house to house, and made nuisances of themselves."[30] And as Ball reminds, the problem of vagrants only increased as railroads expanded their operations throughout the territories. After grading the rail-bed, hauling cross-ties, and laying track, many laboring men simply drew their last check at terminal junctions—out of a job in a strange, and sometimes wicked end-of-the-line frontier town. Some stayed and found jobs, others became leeches, a few turned law-breaker, and others returned home. For a while there was no shortage of vagrants and hobos.[31] Tucker's vagrant strategy was simple, since Deming was equidistant between Kansas City and San Francisco, Deputy Tucker would simply give them their choice of direction, and then "fire them out."[32]

Generally overlooked in some writings is a signal fact. Even in the nineteenth-century frontier, a litigious atmosphere was pervasive. Lawyers fed on civil lawsuits, plaintiff's hungered for dollar pie, and both scavenged for the scraps which fell from the boardroom conference tables of successful and financially fat corporations. Railroad executives *couldn't* afford to suffer vagrants and tramps. Deputy Sheriff Dan Tucker *wouldn't*!

> Five tramps, who were stealing a ride jumped off a railroad train the other day near Raton; and in doing so one of them was badly hurt. The injured man is now suing the railroad company for damages.[33]

Numerous personal disputes where adjudicated and disposed of by recourse to civil court action. Dan Tucker was no stranger to the court process, and although the exact details are fuzzy, he did file a claim against the estate of one of Shakespeare's leading mining powerhouses, William G. Boyle. Tucker filed a suit (Oct. 20,1880) requesting $511.33. The Probate Judge ordered John Boyle as administrator of the estate to sell shares in the Shakespeare Gold & Silver Mining & Milling Company to pay off numerous claims. Eventually (March 6, 1884) Dan Tucker either voluntarily accepted a offer in compromise, or the court so ordered the settlement, but in either event he was paid $240 by the Boyle estate.[34]

Unlike numerous western heroes, many of whom can be identified with particular political or economic causes, it seems that Dan Tucker simply relished his role as a unbiased peace-keeper. Quite possibly he was pleased with his self-image and maybe there was a degree of ego gratification in having a no nonsense reputation, but it certainly wasn't phony, and it didn't go unnoticed by others. Tucker's achievements were often praised in area newspapers, such as this comment from El Paso: "Deputy Sheriff Tucker at Deming, keeps that town free of rough characters."[35]

While Tucker had been away in California, young Billy Dwenger had been confined in the Grant County jail for murdering his father. He was awaiting delivery to the penitentiary, along with several fellow prisoners, when he escaped lax security and "flew the coop." Immediately the sheriff posted a reward of $200. Seemingly he vaporized or vanished. His whereabouts, at least for a time, would be a true public mystery and serve as political discomfiture for the Sheriff.

When not dealing with troublesome hobos or out looking for escapees, Dan Tucker from time to time had to focus on more serious criminal infractions, such as when a party of tough and scabrous hombres high-jacked a man on a Deming street in broad daylight. Relieved of his entire outfit (team and wagon), the crime victim wailed, attracting the attention of Deputy Dan Tucker, who recovered the stolen property, and then sent the would-be thieves packing, rather than hauling them off to jail.[36] The complainant was no doubt pleased upon the return of his property, the scoundrels thanked their lucky stars for the opportunity to depart Deming, and Dan Tucker made it easy on himself, not encumbered with bothersome prisoners.

With Deming under control, at least temporarily, Dan Tucker traveled to Silver City, and checked into the Southern Hotel.[37] While in town, for whatever reason, Dan sold ¼ interest in his Esperanza quartz mine, located in the Chloride Mining District west of Silver City, to Rufus B. Higbie for $50.00.[38]

In addition to dabbling in mining interests, indications are that Tucker also speculated in real-estate during this time period. He acquired ten lots in the Grant County Townsite Company, at Deming. Most of the city lots were priced between $100.00 and $200.00, but one, at the corner of Chestnut Street and Gold Avenue sold for $1000.00.[39] The boom in town lot real-estate continued to escalate, and in just one week R. E. Comfort sold about fifty individual lots, those on Gold Avenue being some of the most desirable.[40] Another firm, Proctor & Byron, bought 133 lots, and almost before they could turn around, had sold 97, causing a newspaper editor to brag, "how is that for a dull town."[41] Tucker maintained at least minimal financial interests in Grant County real-estate ventures for many years.[42]

Whether or not Tucker remained in the county seat conducting sheriff's duties, or was on a purely personal pleasure trip is undetermined. Undoubtedly, he would soon wish he had stayed in Deming. James Burns, part-time deputy sheriff from the Burro Mountain copper mining community of Paschal came to town. Reportedly, the twenty-two year old Burns side-stepped his normal well-mannered behavior and began drinking heavily—all day. The transplanted Texan finally alighted at Sam Extine's Saloon, and continued with his stuporous spree. Although the truth remains a mystery, Burns either intentionally flourished or inadvertently exposed his six-shooter, a movement quickly detected by Deputy Sheriff Mahony, who was temporarily responsible for Silver City peace keeping duties in the absence of the city marshal, G. W. Moore. Mahony ordered Burns to remove his revolver, despite Burns's protests that he was entitled to carry the weapon, especially in light of his status as a deputy sheriff. Mahony, threatening arrest if his mandate was not complied with, simply departed, presumably to verify Burn's official standing in the often confusing network of sometimes deputies, and to obtain "back up" if it was determined that an arrest was warranted.[43] Burn's personal party lasted all night. The next morning he brazenly toasted the dawn of the new day, August 24, 1882, with more booze.[44]

Burns, in his cups, tried to pick a fight with another patron, and would have succeeded had it not been for the intervention of another deputy sheriff, Billy McClellan. Later that night, Burns fired off a shot, which attracted the attention of City Marshal Moore, who by now had returned to Silver City, and the municipal lawman rushed to the scene in an effort to investigate, and determine just who was shooting up the town. Bystanders advised Marshal Moore that Burns was the culprit, and he could be located inside the Centennial Saloon. The marshal stepped inside the tap house, found Burns seated at a gambling table, and requested Burns accompany him outside. Burns replied he would comply—after his game was finished. Moore retreated. Outside he was joined by deputy McClellan, and the two walked around the block, re-entering the Centennial through a back door. Noticing the officers, Burns jumped up, pulled his six-shooter, backed into a corner, and defied anyone to get his gun. And predictably, Deputy Dan Tucker, who is never too far removed from erupting violence, was also present in the bar; and he, City Marshal Moore, and Deputy McClellan, in unison, pointed their cocked six-shooters at the drunken Burns. John Gilmo, an ex-deputy sheriff, ex-Silver City marshal, prospective bounty hunter and future Arizona Territory prison convict, interjected himself into the disorderliness, talked Burns into surrendering his weapon "for the time being," and there the matter should have ended. Later Burns, in the act of leaving the saloon, asked Gilmo to return his pistol, which Gilmo foolishly relinquished. Informants tracked Burns to the Wolcott & Mills

Saloon and Club House, and soon reported the inebriated deputy was continuing to make contemptuous and vile threats. Moore and McClellan determined to take action, finally located a Justice of the Peace, and obtained a warrant for Burn's arrest. The officers soon discovered Burns had re-entered the Centennial, and was engaged in a heated exchange with none other than the inflexible Dan Tucker, while Frank Thurmond and others of the gambling element looked on. When appraised of the warrant, Burns jerked his six-gun and fired wildly. Dan Tucker, City Marshal Moore, and Billy McClellan fired back, and Burns went down, mortally wounded.[45] At least that's one side of the story!

The other side of the squalid yarn is, "McClellan wished to have Burns put out of the way as he was a witness in a case of horse stealing then pending against him; and the two officers deliberately planned the murder. When Moore and McClellan went to arrest him, they did not show the warrant nor wait for him to pull his revolver but fired at once, riddling him with bullets..."[46] Adding fuel to the fire, McClellan, although a deputy, had a less than favorable reputation in the eyes of many. One who knew him at the time noted, McClellan "was as notorious a horse and cattle thief as ever lived..."[47] Others offered different theories, "The reason that Moore hated Burns was because Burns was aware of a murder that Moore had committed which was not justified. Afraid that Burns would expose him, he framed up a dirty deal on him."[48]

Surely Dan Tucker would have taken exception with headlines such as "Riddling a Rowdy: Three Brave Deputy Sheriffs at Pascal Murder a Drunken Man."[49]

Justice Rilea held a impromptu inquest, the jury adjourned for the night, a decision to be rendered the next day.[50] Upon examination it had been determined that Burns suffered wounds from six shots, including a slight scalp wound, three in the torso, and two in the neck, "either one would necessarily have proved fatal."[51]

Due process demanded some reasonably legal disposition be made upon commission of a possible crime, especially one with easily identifiable perpetrators. Representing the defendants were lawyer G. G. Posey, and noted attorney, Indian fighter, politician, and Mesilla Valley newspaperman, Albert J. Fountain. Arguing for the prosecution was the locally respected attorney and mining speculator H. C. McComas, assisted by W. T. Kendrick and J. M. Wright. The prosecution team argued the defendants were inappropriately charged with manslaughter, when in fact they had committed murder in the first degree. "Mr. Posey argued and "severely criticized Mr. Wright for bringing up public opinion in the case, and in response to Judge McComas's argument, said that every one understood the meaning of manslaughter, and that as Judge Warren Bristol had often said the justices of the peace should not enter into little legal squabbles, but should try to get at the justice in the case without noticing the technicalities of the law."[52]

The finding was made. Tucker's bullet had missed, and Billy McClellan and G. W. Moore had caused Burn's death.[53] A rather fastidious conclusion in light of remarks in a local paper, "The shot had hardly left his (Burns) pistol before Tucker returned the fire, hitting Burns in the left ribs just below the heart."[54] Because of the public esteem credited to Tucker's account, was he being offered a legally acceptable way out? Later, Moore and McClellan waived a preliminary hearing, the case against the pair placed in abeyance, pending the December term of District Court, and "the prosecution decided not to bring any action against Tucker."[55]

Burns had proven to be a very popular man at Paschal, and when news of his death reached there mob mentality took hold. At a meeting of area miners, the decision was made to lynch three lethal lawmen, Tucker, Moore, and Billy McClellan. Someone with a cooler head finally suggested tabling the idea of vigilante justice, in lieu of a monetary subscription, the funds earmarked for prosecuting the three shooters. Common sense prevailed![56] With thoughts of hanging pushed to the back burner, the Paschal crowd began legal maneuvers in earnest, and much like an earlier crowd in Cochise County Arizona, began the process of "shopping" for a sympathetic court. Local Justice of the Peace Nickerson issued arrest warrants, and Grant County Deputy Sheriff Richardson attempted to take Moore and McClellan into custody. Fearing removal to Paschal for a kangaroo court justice and a subsequent lynching, the deputies refused to then allow arrests, but instead went to Central City, turning themselves over to Deputy Sheriff Baldonado, who had molded a guard detail sufficient to forestall any attempt at vigilante reprisal. Under lock and key at Central City, Moore and McClellan were soon joined by Dan Tucker, who after learning that he too was named in the warrants, opted to surrender to legal authority, rather than take to the brush.[57]

Unable to perform his duties as Wells, Fargo express messenger while confined, Dan Tucker was for the moment replaced by Bruce Glasgow on the Silver City to Deming run.[58] Possibly for the right reasons, and certainly with thoughtfulness of future political realities, Sheriff Harvey Whitehill sought City Marshal Moore's resignation as a part-time Grant County deputy sheriff. Moore voluntarily, at least from the public perspective, surrendered his deputy's commission but retained his police position with the city government.[59] The sheriff was less inclined to finesse with his next personnel change. On August 22, 1882, he simply advised Justice of the Peace Givens "to put no more cases in the hands of Deputy Sheriff Wm. McClellan, as he was about to take his commission away from him and appoint someone else in his place."[60] Sheriff Whitehill took no action regarding his friend and trusted employee Dan Tucker, apparently content to gamble that due process would exonerate his esteemed deputy.

The incensed crowd from Paschal arrived at Central City to witness the hearing, but were quickly disarmed by Grant County Sheriff Harvey Whitehill, who feared for the prisoners safety.[61] In their unbridled anger, the threatening crowd had gone so far as to have Deputy Sheriff Mahoney arrested for "complicity in the murder of Burns," but even the prosecution could not overcome a legal barrier—Mahoney was not even present when the shooting took place. He was released.[62] Apparently, the legal scheming had indeed fostered a ominous and frightful atmosphere, the court stenographer Lawrence McCrae fainted, and "the rest of the testimony notes had to be taken in long hand."[63]

Prosecution lawyer John Mulinsbury Wright was contemptibly criticized by the local press for his earlier efforts to have a preliminary hearing held in Paschal, "the home of Burns, where everybody was a friend of the deceased, where money was subscribed for the prosecutions," and where the community had publicly passed resolutions denouncing the accused.[64] The hearing at Central City proceeded.

John W. Gilmo testified City Marshal Moore, with a pistol in hand, had ordered Burns to give up his six-gun, but Burns replied, "Go away, I have done nothing," and then Moore lowered his revolver, only to have Burns jerk his, at the same time stubbornly declaring, "I will not go to jail, I have done nothing." Siding with the city marshal, Dan Tucker had surreptitiously pointed his pistol at Burns, *just in case!* Finally according to his testimony, Gilmo was successful in acquiring the pistol from an inebriated Burns, who "then fell to quarreling with Dan Tucker, because somebody had told him that Tucker had leveled his gun on him during the difficulty with Moore." Gilmo reported he later returned the revolver to Burns, who pledged he was going home, but who in fact came back to the saloon twenty minutes later. Shortly thereafter, in came Moore and Billy McClellan, their pistols drawn, announcing they had "papers' for Burns, and for him to relinquish his revolver. According to Gilmo, Tucker then pulled his six-shooter, and for the second time that evening, pointed it at Burns, admonishing him to surrender his weapon. "As Burns spoke, McClellan shot, Tucker and Moore shooting a moment after at almost the same time." Gilmo further clarified, "that Tucker was about five feet from Burns, and the other defendants about four feet from him..."[65]

A. Stevenson, a gunsmith, swore that McClellan shot when Burns reached toward his waist, "before he had his gun," and that Moore shot four times. J. E. Comerford testified McClellan and Moore entered the Centennial "their revolvers cocked in their hands" and that McClellan fired first, never giving Burns the chance to "surrender or to defend himself." C. H. Munson witnessed the quarrels, the confrontation with Tucker, and declared McClellan fired first, followed by Moore.[66]

C. B. Ely's testimony did not bode well for the defense. Under oath, he declared that after the shooting, McClellan turned over Burn's body, removed his revolver (Burn's) from it's scabbard, and then placed it in Burn's hand. Several days later, according to Ely, Marshal Moore approached him and offered to give him $300 if "he would leave the country without testifying against him, but if he would not do this he would bring some charges against him that would send him to the penitentiary for life."[67]

Naturally the defense challenged Ely, and under cross-examination it was revealed Marshal Moore had "frequently" arrested him, and that Ely had been intoxicated at the time of the thunderous shooting, although sober enough to remember "that the gun was arranged after the lamps were lighted, when fifteen or twenty people were present."[68]

Gambler Frank Thurmond testified he heard McClellan and Moore talking after Burns had refused the initial arrest attempt, saying that if he had been in Moore's place, he would have killed Burns. According to Thurmond, Moore replied "that it was best as it was." Tucker apparently got a pass from Thurmond, in that his testimony did not include reference to any conspiratorial premeditation on Dan's part.[69] Frank was a good man to have on your team. By most accounts he was considered poisonously dangerous, but a straight-talker and a gentleman.[70] Subsequent events confirmed both appraisals.

Nicholas Biddle "knew nothing about the shooting and could not answer the questions asked," and "was asked a number of things by the prosecution, but was dismissed without imparting any information."[71] Whether referring to Biddle's lack of testimony or not, the New Southwest & Grant County *Herald* amusingly reported:

> Among the witnesses subpoenaed by the prosecution of the Burns' murder case was X, who had not seen the affray, being fifty miles from town on the 25th ult., and to whom the trip to Central City would have been a serious inconvenience, so when he saw one of the prosecuting attorneys on the street Wednesday evening he asked him if he could not be excused as he knew no particulars of the crime. He was told he could not. "Well," said X, "I will not go any how." "My dear Sir," said the disciple of Blackstone, "you will have to go, if you do not go voluntarily, I will have you arrested and taken over and probably you will be heavily fined." "Very well then," said X, "I will pay the fine as I do not intend to go and will probably have to pay a second fine for assault and battery at the same time." Upon mature consideration the lawyer decided that as his testimony was not expected to be of very much value, he need not make the trip.[72]

After the hearing the trio of prisoners were removed to Silver City. "No little excitement was caused in town last Saturday evening by the arrival of Tucker, Moore and McClellan from Central City, heavily chained and under a strong guard, Judge Givens having committed them to jail without bail to await the action of the grand jury."[73]

Dan Tucker immediately began the legal steps necessary to bring about his release. His attorney, G. G. Posey filed a petition for *a writ of habeas corpus*.[74] By September 30th, Tucker had been taken to Mesilla.[75] Shortly thereafter, before Judge Warren Bristol, Tucker had a hearing, and was released on a $2000 bond.[76] Moore and McClellan remained in custody.[77] Again one of the prosecutors was lampooned by an apparently unsympathetic and possibly partisan press, "…J. M. Wright, conducted himself, if it is possible, in a more ridiculous manner than at the previous examination."[78]

Tucker immediately resumed duties as shotgun messenger on the Silver City-Deming express, and as a Grant County Deputy Sheriff.[79]

Incensed at what he perceived as a case of wanton injustice, Tucker granted a interview to a local newspaper. "Dan Tucker informs us that in the course of his duty as deputy sheriff he has been obliged to kill eight men in this county, besides several in Lincoln and Doña Ana counties, and the killing of Burns, in which he was implicated, was the first time he was ever put under bonds to await examination."[80] Interestingly, Tucker did not deny that he shot Burns, which can be interpreted two ways. He could seize the opportunity first offered by the coroner's inquest jury, and declare his split-second, short-range shot missed Burns completely, or he could stand his ground with a claim of self-defense. Tucker stood pat!

Whether or not the correspondent even asked the obvious follow-up questions, or perhaps just failed to include the answers in his published piece remains a mystery. Was Tucker actually telling the truth or was he exaggerating? Would Tucker knowingly lie to a local reporter who would have knowledge of actual facts, and expect to get away with an observable overstatement of the truth? As a Grant County Deputy, did Dan track dangerous desperadoes to Lincoln or Doña Ana counties, and there end their misspent and no-account criminal lives? It will be recalled that on at least one occasion Tucker returned with blood-stained horses and no riders. Were the missing horsemen among the dead? Or, was he a deputy even before coming to Silver City? Could he have killed men at Lea's Station on the Jornada del Muerto, or in a smoke filled "sin den" at Leasburg? At one time, could he have been a lieutenant in John Kinney's infamous collection of border bandits, who on at least one occasion were temporarily deputized?

The answers to these questions remain elusive, at least for the time being. Although a great deal of historical sleuthing has thus far been achieved, admittedly with little result on this particular count, sustained interest in the subject may produce further investigation and meaningful clues regarding Tucker's comments to the reporter.

At least one question, however, could now be answered. The mysterious and abrupt disappearance of fugitive Billy Dwenger was at long last resolved. Apparently with sufficient skill and sly undercover acumen, Billy had traveled across the Black Range to Hillsboro and assumed the name of Ned White. For awhile he was employed by N. Galles & Co. in the mines. Reportedly, being "very quite and pleasant in his demeanor," the youthful Dwenger quickly became very popular with the rough hewn set of prospectors and adventurers. After changing jobs a time or two, and saving a portion of his wages, Billy acquired partial interest in a butcher shop. By a stroke of pure luck, but not Billy's, a traveling P. P. Whitehill, on his way to Kingston chanced to stop in Hillsboro, recognized and arrested the fugitive. Returned to confinement at Silver City, Billy's last hope was that his friends efforts at petitioning Territorial Governor Sheldon would prove successful.[81] Clemency chances crumbled, and by the end of January, 1883, Billy Dwenger was safely tucked away, imprisoned at Leavenworth.[82]

While Tucker had naturally been concerned with his personal legal difficulties, and how his involvement in the Burn's shooting would play out on the stage of due process, others were predictably more engrossed in playing southwestern regional politics. Sheriff Harvey Whitehill had decided to dabble in Territorial politics and entered the race for a representative's seat in the New Mexico Territorial Legislature's Ninth Council District, which consisted of Dona Ana, Lincoln, and Grant counties. Patrick Floyd Garrett challenged.[83] Two well-known lawman pitting themselves against each other in a battle over ballots was commonplace, but in this specific case there is indeed a interesting historical irony—a young southwestern outlaw served as the common denominator. One aspirant was the very first officer to apprehend "Billy the Kid," while the opposing candidate was the last.

At the County Commissioner's meeting on November 13th, 1882, the November 2nd election results for Grant County were certified, and the 2865 votes were distributed: H. H. Whitehill 1027; Pat F. Garrett 704; John A. Miller 605; David M. Easton 474; John D. Barncastle 55.[84] When combined with the other two counties comprising the Ninth District, Harvey Howard Whitehill was declared a winner, Garrett a loser. James D. Woods was slated to become sheriff in Grant County with a January, 1883, inaugural.[85]

Certainly both contenders, Whitehill and Garrett, had been encumbered with heavy political baggage. Whitehill, although generally well thought of, was mired with the sticky varnish of having sometimes chosen a set of dubious and debatable deputies. And, contrary to some popular belief, Pat Garrett's reputation did not necessarily meet with universal approval—not with partisan politics factored in.

> The defeat of Pat Garrett is one of the gratifications that roll
> upon us like sea waves upon the bathers of the beach. It is very
> cooling and delightful to think that this great statesman (?)
> whose only claim to the office was that he had been sheriff of
> Lincoln county, and while acting in that capacity had slain an
> outlaw or two. The democracy of this district should learn that
> if they hope to elect their ticket in the future, that they must put
> up men who are qualified for the office. A man may be a good
> sheriff or clerk and yet be wholly unfit for the council.[86]

Leon Metz, in Garrett's defense, reminds us that Pat did not get on the Grant County ballot until late, had almost no popular newspaper support, (the *Rio Grande Republican* had accused him of being illiterate; not true) and many voters were not adequately informed about the lawman's actual record. In an election-day issue the *New Southwest*, published at Silver City, warned the Grant County electorate of the "Doña Ana clique" and challenged voters not to be made "fools" of.[87] Fundamental fairness had not much of a foothold in highly-charged regional and partisan Territorial politics. Much to Garrett's disadvantage, the one county which he did succeed in carrying, Lincoln, was the least populated and had the fewest legal voters.[88] Garrett's biographer crisply closed the chapter on Pat's bid at becoming a Territorial Legislator, "The ex-manhunter took his loss without bitterness."[89]

Historic investigation tends to indicate Dan Tucker's overall health began to deteriorate, especially after the shoot-out with Brown at Benson. A later report will imply Tucker was steadily becoming an alcoholic, and evidence does indicate Tucker was "right at home" and frequently in attendance at barrooms and gambling dens, but area newspapers failed to ever attribute drinking as one of Tucker's ailments.[90] Tucker's state of well-being was usually reported in one sentence bulletins similar to one in an early issue of the Silver City *Enterprise* (1882), "We are pleased to announce that Dan Tucker, who had been quite ill lately, is rapidly recovering and able to get around once more."[91] The illness remains a mystery.

Facts which are not evasive reveal that Dan Tucker was still and always just one-step away from catastrophe. Out of jail and pistol-packin' for Grant County by Halloween, back in Wells, Fargo harness by Thanksgiving, he was nearly murdered by Christmas. It seems Dan entered a "Mexican house" at Deming, which is generally believed to have been a whorehouse, and while there, two women "threw their arms around him." Tucker thinking they were in playful mood, willingly surrendered. Suddenly, he was grabbed from behind, and a masculine hand jerked his Colt revolver-pistol from the scabbard. Urgently, Tucker tried to re-gain possession of his six-shooter, and the skirmish intensified into battle for life itself. In the ensuing "tooth and nail" scrap Dan

Tucker finally got hold of his pistol, and snapped a "blue-whistler" at his antagonist, who luckily ducked at the right time. Unfortunately, one of the señoritas didn't, falling to the floor slightly wounded. Other customers then jumped on Tucker, and the original assailant, now in control of a revolver, shot Dan twice, the first shot sledgehammering the bone in his shoulder, the next bullet inflicting a less serious wound "somewhere about the face." Some "Americans," hearing the shots, rushed to the scene and "prevented Tucker from being massacred."[92]

Another newspaper rather dryly advised, "It would seem that Tucker fell among those unfriendly to him..."[93] The bone crunching shot to his shoulder proved to be quite severe and permanently painful, but after initial treatment, not life threatening, although Dan Tucker was forced to travel to Mariana (near Tucson), Arizona Territory and seek the service of a particular physician.[94]

Could this physician have been the renowned Dr. George Goodfellow, the pre-eminent medical expert for treating gunshot wounds? Goodfellow's biographer, Don Chaput, reveals the good doctor's fame had spread throughout southeastern Arizona Territory, and "he no longer had to seek business—people came to him, or practically begged him to come to them."[95] Regardless, what medical help he received, or where he got it, Dan Tucker suffered the pain and inconvenience.

Surely, Dan Tucker was glad to see 1882 come to an end. As the new year arrived, Dan found himself "quite ill," confined to bed at Deming, but at least not imprisoned, although he was still under a $2000 bond in the pending Burns murder case.[96] The approaching trial set for the April term of court at Las Cruces continued to garner press coverage from time to time, much to Tucker's displeasure.[97]

While Tucker was recuperating from whatever malady (most probably the gunshot wound), his friend and gambling buddy Frank Thurmond was doing rather well, so much so, that he purchased a wholesale liquor business in Deming. The local press congratulated Thurmond on the procurement, wishing him the best, and in remarks similar to those frequently spoken of Dan Tucker, the reporter commented that Frank was "well known in Silver City."[98] Apparently Frank's better half was doing quite well also, "Mrs. Lottie (Deno) Thurmond has sold the Broadway Restaurant to Mr. Andrews, formerly proprietor of the hotel at Santa Rita."[99] This move by Frank may have planted another entrepreneurial seed in the mind of Tucker, but before it could blossom, pressing matters required resolution.

Moore and McClellan were acquitted of the murder charges in the killing of James Burns, and the case against Dan Tucker was dismissed.[100] Beyond doubt all three were much relieved; the whole sour experience had been difficult on them individually, and had tarnished the image of the Grant County Sheriff's Office, and the legal entanglement, at least for one of them, was not quite over. As soon as he was released from custody on the Burns homicide case, Billy McClellan was arrested regarding the rustling of livestock.[101] And, bad luck did not turn to good for Billy. Later, drunk and racing his horse down Silver City's Bullard Street, "at breakneck speed," the ex-deputy fell, striking his head. The fall proved fatal.[102]

Dan Tucker went back on duty at Deming. DeArment suggests Tucker had lost his deputy sheriff's commission as a result of the Burns affair, but this seems not to be the case, even though Harvey Whitehill had been replaced by J. B. Woods as a result of the preceding November election.[103] The El Paso *Lone Star* in a one-liner simply reported, "Dave Tucker is again deputy sheriff at Deming."[104] And the July 21st edition of the *Southwest Sentinel* makes reference to Dan's employment status, "Deming has been well represented here during the past week. Among the visitors were Judge Bristol and Deputy Sheriff Tucker."[105] Possibly as a favor to the incoming Woods, Whitehill had deputized D. L. "Doc" Belt, with a pre-arranged understanding that Belt would be retained after the new sheriff was officially installed in office.[106] Although the major deputies continually traveled throughout the entire county as needed, for the most part, from this point forward "Doc" Belt under the new Sheriff's administration assumed the title of Chief Deputy. Practically speaking, Belt ruled the law enforcement roost in the northern reaches of Grant County, and Dan Tucker to the south.

That something as routine as an a deputy's appointment would prick a outlying editor's commentary is evidenced by a stab at humorous but harmless dueling. The Las Vegas *Optic* taunted, "Silver City has a deputy sheriff named Belt. He goes all around and buckles in front." The Silver City *Enterprise* parried, "If the funny man of the *Optic* ever visits Silver City, Doc will buckle on to and Belt him around town."[107]

Odds-on, Tucker would not have been the majority's choice to fill the position of future son-in-law, but everyone, including the recently elected sheriff, knew Dan was the right man for the job. One old-timer phrased it rather succinctly, "Being deputy sheriff in those days was no weakling's job; nor was it one for a man without nerve. There could be no faltering in the decision to act; no figuring as to whether it was right or wrong to shoot. Having the drop on the other fellow, the order was to shoot and shoot quick; then let the opponent do the thinking."[108] Dan Tucker and "Doc" Belt were such men!

NOTES AND SOURCES

1. Brown, Clara S., *Tombstone from a Woman's Point of View*, edited by Lynn R. Bailey. P. 47.
2. Marks, P. 317.

3. Tefertiller, Casey, *Wyatt Earp—The Life Behind the Legend*. P. 200. Hereafter cited as Tefertiller.

4. Ibid. P. 227.

5. Hand, George, *Whiskey, Six-guns & Red-light Ladies, George Hand's Saloon Diary, Tucson, 1875-1878*. P. 228. Edited by Neil Carmony. Hand's remark does not come from a diary entry on a date implied by the book title, but rather from a tabulation of area deaths which cover a broader time span.

6. Deming *Headlight*, 03-25-1882.

7. Tefertiller, P. 228. Murder warrants were issued for Wyatt and his youngest brother Warren, "Doc" Holliday, Sherman McMasters, and "Turkey Creek" Jack Johnson. Thrapp characterizes Holliday as "dentist, gunmen," Vol. II, P. 671; McMasters as "desperado," Vol. II, P. 921; and Johnson as "lawman, desperado," Vol. II, P. 731.

8. Marks, P. 352. Tefertiller does acknowledge "…Wyatt had stepped beyond the law." P. 235. And "Wyatt Earp was making his own law." P. 241.

9. Gatto, P. 183-193. The author offers some particularly insightful information regarding the alleged shooting of "Curly" Bill, and quite correctly recommends Earp's claim that he killed Bill "should be cautiously considered before writers simply accept it as fact."

10. Boyer, Glenn G., *Wyatt Earp, Family, Friends & Foes*. P. 17.

11. Roberts, Gary L., "The Fremont Street Fiasco," *True West*, July 1988. P. 14. The author, from the historical perspective, correctly articulates that the shoot-out, "marked no watershed in the national epoch" and it, "hardly caused a ripple on the troubled waters of westward expansion."

12. Ball, Larry D., *The United States Marshals of New Mexico & Arizona Territories 1846-1912*. P. 125. Hereafter cited as Ball (M). Also see "The Dark Side of Wyatt Earp," *True West*, February 1999, by Bob Boze Bell. P. 18-24. "He (Wyatt Earp) was indicted for murder in Arizona but he escaped as a fugitive from justice."

13. Marks, P. 365.

14. Bartholowmew, Ed., *Wyatt Earp—The Man and the Myth*. P. 323. Cited as Bartholowmew (II). The author theorizes, "The Earp gang could not take the rail coaches to the east or the west for officers all along the line were watching for them." And, "From a close study of numerous contemporary newspaper accounts, and from other archival material, it is seen that these fugitives were fleeing for their very lives, running from murder indictments, an outraged citizenry, and the realization that Territorial officials and other officers had decided that the time had come to clean house in southern Arizona." P. 321.

15. Thrapp, Vol. III, P. 1443.

16. Hornung, Chuck, "Wyatt Earp's New Mexico Adventures," *Old West*, Summer 1999. P. 17.,

17. Myrick, P. 193. Also see, Berry & Russell, P. 24-25. The Silver City, Deming and Pacific Railroad Company, was organized in March 1882, under the leadership of Edmund G. Shields. Later (1884) the S. C., D. & P would be sold to the Atchison, Topeka and Santa Fe Railroad, and by 1886 the narrow gauge tracks had been widened to the standard width.

18. New Southwest and Grant County *Herald*, 04-29-1882. The Earp and Holliday flight to avoid extradition back to Arizona Territory is a story in and of itself. Suffice to say, assistance from friends and deception proved successful in shielding the fugitives from murder prosecutions in Arizona Territory.

19. Marks, P. 374. Also see Bartholowmew (II) P. 324.

20. Tefertiller, P. 247.

21. Tanner, Karen Holliday., *Doc Holliday, A Family Portrait*. P. 183. Hereafter cited as Tanner.

22. New Southwest and Grant County *Herald*, 04-22-1882. Tanner fails to include the last two sentences of the newspaper account, and her assertion that the Earp/Holliday squad arrived at Silver City on April 7, 1882, seems to be off by a week, at least according to the date the article appeared in the paper. The April 8th edition of the same paper reports, "Deputy Sheriff Tucker, who has been absent in California for some days past, arrived from Deming last night." If one were to accept Tanner's contention, although in conflict with the newspaper report, that the Earp party arrived on April 7th it would place Deputy Dan Tucker and the fugitives in Silver City at the same time, and may indeed be one of the reasons the group did not stay in a hotel or use their real names. Tefertiller who has written the most complete biography of Wyatt Earp to date, correctly places the Earp crowd arriving in Silver City, New Mexico on April 15, 1882. P. 247. Regardless, for whatever reason, Earp bashers, Earp devotees, and unbiased historians seem to all be in agreement that the fleeing felons traveled to Silver City incognito.

23. Bartholowmew (II), P. 324.

24. Ibid. The author fails to address one important question. If the Earp bunch was avoiding Deming because of Deputy Dan Tucker, what measures did they take, if any, to determine his whereabouts, especially in light of the fact he often acted as shotgun messenger on the Silver City to Deming run.

25. Marks, P. 375.

26. DeArment, P. 17.

27. Sherman, P. 162. Nutt Station, the Atchison, Topeka and Santa Fe Railroad depot was established and granted a post office in 1881. The rail line was extended north to Lake Valley in 1884. At the time the Earps were running from the law, April, 1882, Nutt Station was operational.

28. Historical investigation clearly reveals numerous mentions of Dan Tucker's law enforcement exploits and public adulation. Many frontier "heroes" were much more publicized in the twentieth-century, but during the time Tucker was an active Grant County lawman, only a few could lay claim to a legitimate gunfighter reputation equal to his. Thrapp reports, "One early visitor to Deming found that Deputy Tucker had quickly brought order to what had been a wild railroad town. 'He was certainly the right man,' he wrote, 'for if he wanted to arrest a desperado he was sure to either arrest or kill him.' In 1881 Tucker arrested 13 members of the 'cowboy gang' of desperadoes within 20 days and few ever returned to Deming while Tucker was the law there." Vol. III, P. 1443.

29. DeArment, P. 17.

30. Jordan, Philip D., "The Town Marshal Local Arm of the Law," *Arizona and the West*, 16.

31. Ball (S), P. 271.

32. New Southwest and Grant County *Herald*, 04-08-1882.

33. Unger, P. 86. Also see, El Paso *Lone Star*, 01-24-1883.

34. Probate Court Record, Grant County Clerk, Silver City, New Mexico. The records reflect that John Boyle as administrator of the estate wanted to settle eleven claims by offering shares in the Shakespeare Gold & Silver Mining & Milling Company at one dollar per share. Whether anyone accepted this proposal

is unknown. Apparently the legal negations dragged on and Dan Tucker finally received his cash settlement four years after filing suit.

35. El Paso *Lone Star*, 12-03-1881.

36. Ibid., 05-27-1882.

37. Ibid., 07-08-1882.

38. Grant County Mining Records of Deeds, Book 8., P. 389. Grant County Clerk. Silver City, New Mexico.

39. Investigation at the Luna County (Deming) courthouse does not currently show a Chestnut St., but persistence on the part of T. Humble, assisted by Art Roman of the Deming Luna Mimbres Museum, was rewarded when they found a old Deming map in the museum archives which indicated Chestnut St. had been changed to Cedar St. at some undetermined time. Around the turn of the century the Grant County Townsite Co. area was cleared for a city park. Now the area is under Interstate Highway I-10 which cuts through the northern edge of Deming, New Mexico.

40. Silver City *Enterprise*, 01-11-1883.

41. Ibid., 05-11-1883.

42. On April 25, 1892 Tucker sold his last two lots.

43. New Southwest & Grant County *Herald*, 08-26-1882. Founded in 1882, and located approximately fifteen miles southwest of Silver City, Paschal, for a brief period enjoyed success. At one time the community contained a population of a thousand persons and numerous business, in addition to a fifty-ton smelter. "The smelter ran successfully until the plummeting cost of copper, high-price labor, and exorbitant freight costs caused management to close down." Sherman, P. 169.

44. DeArment, P. 17.

45. New Southwest & Grant County *Herald*, 09-02-1882. DeArment reports Burns was gambling with Frank Thurmond, ex-deputy John Gilmo, and deputy Dan Tucker. P. 18.

46. Ibid. Indeed Billy McClellan was under charges for horse theft at the time, but the case was dismissed. "The trial of Wm. McClellan, of Central City, for alleged horse stealing took place before Justice Rilea on Tuesday last. Peter Dillman of the Burro mountains, identified the horse found in McClellans's possession as his property, but McClellan proved by several witnesses that he had bought the horse. The case against McClellan was dismissed, and the animal given to Dillman."

47. Silver City *Enterprise*, 09-19-1902.

48. Rose, 09-22-1931.

49. Prassel, Frank Richard, *The Western Peace Officer—A Legacy of Law and Order*. P. 248. Quoting the 09-02-1882 edition of the Albuquerque Review.

50. New Southwest & Grant County *Herald*, 09-02-1882.

51. Ibid., 08-26-1882.

52. Ibid., 09-02-1882.

53. Ibid., Later testimony would reveal Moore and McClellan were four feet from Burns when the shots were fired, and Tucker was standing five feet away. It is hard to imagine Tucker missing at this distance, but that was the initial determination.

54. Ibid., 08-26-1882. This report credits Tucker firing one shot, McClellan one shot, and Moore four shots, "every shot taking effect."

55. Ibid., 09-02-1882. Also see Grant County Civil and Criminal District Court Cost Book, *Territory vs. Glaudius Moore and William McClellan.*

56. Ibid., Also see DeArment, P. 18. T. Humble reports the citizens of Paschal were extremely upset, demanding a full investigation, and ultimately in deference to public pressure, Sheriff Harvey Whitehill had to revoke McClellan's deputy sheriff's commission, as well as that of Moore who held dual commissions. Moore kept his city marshal commission. Conversation with T. Humble, May 1999. Silver City, New Mexico. DeArment dates the Paschal miners meeting as August 30, 1882.

57. DeArment, P. 19.

58. The New Southwest & Grant County *Herald*, 09-16-1882.

59. Ibid., 09-02-1882.

60. Ibid.

61. Ibid., 09-09-1882.

62. Ibid.

63. Ibid., 10-07-1882.

64. Ibid., 09-09-1882. Also see DeArment, P. 18. "The miners finally drew up and published a resolution condemning the 'cowardly, premeditated killing'."

65. New Southwest & Grant County *Herald*, 09-09-1882.

66. Ibid. Dan Rose asserts that Tucker was in on the killing of Burns from the beginning, "Too cowardly to 'pull off' the killing alone, he (Moore) deputized Bill McClellan, a gambler and a hard case, to help him. Dan Tucker happened to come up from Deming at this time. Drinking heavily and being lured on by Moore to add the life of another bad man to the many he had already taken, Tucker consented to a part in the bloody drama about to be enacted." Silver City *Independent*, 09-22-1931, "Dan Tucker, The Killer."

67. Ibid.

68. Ibid. Indeed there were reports that when the shooting started the lights went out. Wayne Whitehill, a child at the time, but a witness, claims, "...And this fella (Burns) was settin' in a stud horse poker game and all of us kids was there. I was right in there in the door just like that and could see all the whole fun. So this fella went up to this fella and he...I seen him raise up outa his chair in this poker game and then the shootin' took place and all the lights went out, just coal oil lamps and, god, that give me a scare and out I went..." Pioneers Foundation Interviews {Wayne Whitehill}

69. New Southwest & Grant County *Herald*, 09-09-1882.

70. Rose, C., P. 34.

71. Ibid.

72. New Southwest & Grant County *Herald*, 09-09-1882

73. Ibid.

74. Ibid., 09-23-1882. The writ was forwarded to District Court at Mesilla.

75. Ibid., 09-30-1882.

76. Ibid., 10-07-1882.

77. Silver City *Enterprise*, 02-08-1883. "Moore and McClellan are in excellent health, as are all the prisoners in the county jail."

78. Ibid.

79. Ibid.

80. Silver City *Enterprise*, 12-14-1882. At this time, at least to this author's knowledge, this is the only interview Tucker ever granted.

81. New Southwest & Grant County *Herald*, 11-04-1882.

82. El Paso *Lone Star*, 01-20-1883.

83. Metz, Leon C., *Pat Garrett—The Story of a Western Lawman*. P. 96-106. Hereafter cited as Metz (G). Also see, Thrapp, Vol. III, P. 1556.

84. Minutes of the Grant County Commissioner's Court meeting, November 13, 1882. Grant County Clerk's Office. Silver City, New Mexico. And as reported in the Silver City *Enterprise* for 11-16-1882, cited by Unger.

85. Ibid.

86. Silver City *Enterprise*, 11-30-1882 as quoted by Unger. P. 17.

87. *New Southwest*, 11-04-1882.

88. Metz (G), P. 106.

89. Ibid.

90. Silver City *Independent*, 09-22-1931. Seemingly any accusation of Tucker having any problem with alcohol addiction can be traced to this article written by Dan Rose. Indisputably the author was, at least at one time, personally acquainted with Tucker and may very well be correct. There are indeed frequent newspaper mentions of Tucker having health problems, a few articles referring to old wounds, and the remainder failing to make any diagnosis. Undeniably Tucker was repeatedly exposed to the "wilder side of life" and may have succumbed to temptations, but equally evident is the fact that contemporary newspaper accounts fail to mention Tucker being intoxicated on those occasions when he performed some newsworthy act. Tracing Tucker's instances of illness to alcohol abuse, may be true, but it is more speculative than factual.

91. Silver City *Enterprise*, 11-16-1882.

92. Ibid., 12-21-1882. Also see Thrapp, Vol. III, P. 1443 & DeArment, P. 19.

93. The New Southwest and Grant County *Herald*, 12-23-1882.

94. An address to the Grant County Archeological Society, on May 17, 1989 by Pat Humble. Audio tape courtesy of Terry Humble.

95. Chaput, Don, *Dr. Goodfellow, Physician to the Gunfighters, Scholar, and Bon Vivant*. P. 55. Hereafter cited as Chaput.

96. Silver City *Enterprise*, 01-11-1883.

97. Ibid., 02-08-1883 & 03-30-1883. Also see, *Southwest Sentinel*, 03-28-1883 & 03-31-1883.

98. Ibid., 01-11-1883. Frank Thurmond and his wife, Lottie Deno, were to remain in Deming until their deaths. At Deming, Thurmond killed a man, was later cleared of the offense, and eventually became a highly respected speculator, cattleman, and bank vice-president. See Rose, Cynthia. Also see, F. Stanley, P. 18.

99. The New Southwest & Grant County *Herald*, 10-07-1882.

100. *Southwest Sentinel*, 04-07-1883. Also see, DeAarment, P. 19. And Thrapp, Vol. III, P. 1443. Also see, Owen, P. 89, "The press described Fountain's arguments as 'brilliant and forcible' and the verdict as 'not guilty.'"

101. Ibid., 04-11-1883.

102. Ibid., 05-19-1883 & Silver City *Enterprise*, 05-18-1883.

103. DeArment, P. 19., The following newspaper excerpts, made after the Burns trial, clearly indicate Tucker maintained his commission as a deputy sheriff, not only under Whitehill, and Woods, but under Andrew B. Laird as well. *Southwest Sentinel*, 07-18-1883, "Deputy Sheriff Tucker came up from Deming to serve a warrant…" And the 07-21-1883 edition of the same paper advises, "Deming has been well represented here during the past week., Among

the visitors were Judge Bristol and Deputy Sheriff Tucker." Silver City *Enterprise*, 02-01-1884, "Dan'l Tucker deputy sheriff, precinct No. 11, paid $95.00." and the 04-22-1887 edition reports, D. J. Tucker, deputy sheriff was paid $20.20. Laird was sheriff at the time of the 1887 payment.

104. El Paso *Lone Star*, 02-07-1883.
105. *Southwest Sentinel*, 07-21-1883.
106. Silver City *Enterprise*, 01-18-1883.
107. Unger quoting the Silver City *Enterprise*, 02-15-1883. P. 96.
108. Rose, 09-22-1931.

8

"EVEN SUCH A DETERMINED OFFICER AS TUCKER"

By February 1883, cattle rustling and horse theft was at an all time high in southern New Mexico. Especially hard hit were Lincoln, Grant and Doña Ana counties. Area newspapers were lamenting there was "hardly any use in engaging in the stock business," and that the country was a "wasteland."[1] Even rustlers of the semi-literate variety should have been able to read between the lines.

> A large amount of stock has been stolen in Doña Ana county lately and the cattlemen of that section have become thoroughly aroused. If the thieves are caught their chances for escaping from the Mesilla jail will be very slim.[2]

Just a few short weeks after being sworn in, "Doc" Belt operating in the vicinity of Fort Bayard, captured three Mexican horse thieves in the act of disposing of a pair of mules stolen from Joe Hanson, an area railroad contractor.[3] Brazen thieves were even stealing work oxen out of farmer's plowed fields.[4] Jimmy Hughes had a horse shot out from under him by a hard riding posse from Lake Valley, forcing the recalcitrant rustler to abandon stolen livestock in the process, while he made good with his escape.[5] "Doc" Belt arrested John Erskine for stealing a team of horses, and rumors were running rampant that as many as sixty rustlers were hanging out on the Gila.[6] The war against culpable cowboys tinkering with cattle brands, and miscreant Mexican vaqueros casting a "wide loop," was seemingly ceaseless. Dan Tucker, "Doc" Belt, and every other legitimate lawman, were simply overwhelmed. And adding to their frustration was none other than Tucker's former subordinate from years gone by, John Kinney.

After abandoning his interests in the Exchange Saloon at old El Paso, and wearing out his welcome in Lincoln County, John Kinney leeched on to the Santa Fe Railroad town of Rincon on the Rio Grande, fifty miles upstream from Las Cruces and Mesilla. To sometimes gullible visitors and preoccupied travelers, Rincon may have just been another necessary stop on a transcontinental trip, but to locals, those in on the know, it was tagged Kinneyville, headquarters of a loosely organized, but clearly competent gang of cutthroats and cattle rustlers.[7] With reasonably good business wisdom, infused with a liberal dose of conniving criminality, John Kinney simply cut the middlemen out of the stolen livestock trade. Operating his own slaughter house, John Kinney was moderately triumphant in circumventing the occasional gaze of peering lawmen.[8] And as is often the case, greedy customers could slyly wink at violations which afforded them such a "good deal." Soon butcher shops in El Paso and southern New Mexico were "gobbling up" John Kinney's beefsteaks and rump roasts to such an extent that his poor wife and his brother were forced to make regular trips to the bank in El Paso, burdened by bulging bags of cash.[9]

Unbelievably, John Kinney as the "boss man," rode herd over some forty henchman, even having access to a "hidden railroad siding" which allowed him to quickly facilitate movement of stolen live cattle between Chihuahua, Mexico, and Socorro, New Mexico Territory, and vice-versa.[10] With squadrons of cattle driving cowboys, plus the ability to ship both hanging carcasses and "beef on the hoof" in carload lots, John Kinney came to dominate the lucrative traffic in illicit livestock, becoming a piercing thorn in the backside of honest cattleman and overworked lawmen.[11] Increasingly, Kinney began dividing his time between Rincon and his Cottonwood Ranch at Lake Valley, thirty-five miles to the west.[12] The price of success was fame, and with certainty, celebrity status drew attention, resulting in the Silver City *Enterprise* straightforwardly labeling John Kinney "the chief mogul of the gang of rustlers."[13]

Not that it wouldn't have happened anyway, but politicians could ill afford to turn a deaf ear to cattlemen's warranted and persistent complaints.[14] New Mexico Governor Lionel Sheldon "unleashed the hounds," ordering a contingent of territorial militia, commanded by one of Dan Tucker's former defense counsels, Albert J. Fountain, to run the rustling scoundrels to ground.[15] Under his operational orders, Fountain was to have unprecedented power to commandeer railroad cars for his transportation needs, cross-county enforcement jurisdiction, unlimited telegraphic use at territorial expense, and most important, he was allowed to "act in every way upon his own best judgment."[16]

The issue was just the ticket for frontier journalists: "The governor is determined to capture or vanquish this lawless band who have been holding such unterrified sway over the stock raising country of southern New Mexico, driving off stock and committing innumerable depredations at their pleasure for the past few months. It is earnestly hoped that the effort to capture them will be successful, and that if the militia should be unfortunate as to capture them alive, that they will be sent where they will no longer have an opportunity to gratify their weakness for theft or murder."[17] Another reported that the Governor intended to "make New Mexico safe for honest and industrious people, or depopulate the whole d—d Territory."[18]

Thoroughly recognizing the long overdue opportunity to wage war on rustling reprobates, and probably equally aware of the potential for political plaudits, Albert J. Fountain struck—with a vengeance! Issuing strict but precise orders to company commanders, Fountain dispersed his legions. At Rincon, Mariano Cubero and Leonardo Maese were arrested. Farther down the river, Gaspar Montenegro and Juan Bernal were snagged by Company A, led by Eugene Van Patton. Leading Company B, Francisco Salazar rolled over the village of La Mesa, in search of the exceedingly dangerous Doroteo "Tiger" Sains (Saenz), and his brother Mario. Unsuccessful in nabbing the brothers, Egenio Pedraza, "a bold and expert thief," and three others were taken prisoner, but Pedraz was shot down while in the act of *escaping*. Seven fugitives were later captured near Rincon by Van Patton's Company. Across the line in the Lone Star state, Texas Ranger Captain Baylor reported he had scooped up Jose Caballero, Nestor Cubero, and the notorious Doroteo Sains— "come get em!" Fountain did. But on the return train ride back to New Mexico, Doroteo Sains was killed while *escaping*.[19]

According to Ball, when all was said and done, the dragnet snagged more than twenty suspects, and the militiamen killed a total of five outlaws, four of which foolishly tried to *escape*.[20] However, Fountain was not allowed any safe passage from severe criticism concerning his tactics, which to many, smacked of too much militarism. The deaths of bandits, smart enough to steal, but stupid enough to run once caught, raised questions in the minds of not just a few, and some newspaper editors were championing the hypothesis that lawbreakers and law enforcers were peas in the same pod.[21]

Unfortunately for Fountain, and the law-abiding public, the scandalous John Kinney was still on the loose, and was boastfully postulating that the "greaser militia" was fearful of a face to face, shoot-it-out showdown.[22] Despite rancorous rhetoric, intelligent analysis revealed substantial withdrawals from Kinney's bank accounts, and it was patently clear the "King of the Rustlers" was on the run.[23] In fact, he had jogged over to Grant County and his presence was duly recorded, "Capt. J. F. Black, of Shakespeare, is making the Gila a very uncongenial resort for the followers of his highness—Sir John Kinney— and deserves great credit for the same. Mr. Black is not a tenderfoot as the rustlers will observe after he comes in contact with him a few times."[24]

John Kinney finally tripped the snare-wire, and Frank Cartwright, superintendent of the Sierra Mining Company, reported to Fountain that the worrisome outlaw had been seen at Silver City stocking up on groceries and gun fodder, and had afterward hightailed it to the southwest. Fountain immediately telegraphed the info to the Shakepeare Guard's Captain Black, who had been cutting for sign between Lake Valley and Silver City.[25] Black picked up the trail, followed it down the Gila River into Arizona Territory, and without firing a shot captured the pugnacious outlaw seven miles south of Clifton.[26] Black escorted his three prisoners, Kinney, his wife, and Kinney's brother Tom, along with twenty-five head of stolen horses, back to Lordsburg, the nearest railroad station.[27] Of the surrender, the El Paso *Lone Star* sneered, "Notwithstanding all his brag and bluster, he quietly surrendered and begged like a Mormon elder for his captors to spare his life."[28]

At Lordsburg, Kinney's wife and brother were for some never explained reason released, and if the Governor himself had not interceded, John Kinney too would have once again pranced down the outlaw trail. With the disreputable desperado safely, at least for the moment under guard, Albert Fountain arranged for a special train, and quickly spirited the prisoner back to Las Cruces, where the legal wheels were turning, and where inmate security could be assured. Johnny Kinney cringed, remarking, "that he would as soon be sent at once to hell as to be returned to Las Cruces." He went anyway![29]

Nolan reports that one of the posse members who slipped into Arizona and arrested John Kinney was none other than ex-sheriff Harvey Whitehill, who by the time had become quite a successful Grant County cattleman.[30] And as will be learned, it was Harvey Whitehill, along with others, who eventually put up collateral for Kinney's bail bond.[31] Why? As plaguing as the question may be, the aim of this narrative is to focus on Dan Tucker. Certainly, acknowledging a close friendship between Tucker and Whitehill, paired with the fact, Dan definitely was familiar with John Kinney, could easily lead historic observers down a crooked trail of speculation, cluttered with suppositional trash. Without doubt, placing the daring deputy, Dan Tucker, in on the thrilling chase and nabbing of his eminence "Sir John" Kinney, would lend itself well to hustling up a hero. However, there is no proof. In fact, attempting to pinpoint Tucker's whereabouts during the hunt for Kinney cannot be conclusively determined, but so far, the best evidence indicates it could have been detrimental for him to be exhaustively chasing over the country side. A snippet in the Silver City *Enterprise* demonstrates why: "Dan Tucker is again quite ill at Deming."[32]

With the head of the snake pinned to the floor of legality, it was but a short time before militia hunters entered the serpent's den, and once again bagged their prey. Dropped into the sack were such notables as Tom "Tomcat" Coyne, Bob Reese, Pancho Saenz, and unfortunately for Kinney, Margarito Sierra, who "spilled the beans" and turned state's evidence.[33] At Lake Valley, militia action resulted in the capture of "Hurricane" Bill Phillips, Matt Irwin, Bill Leland, aka Butch Hill, John Watts, and Jimmy Hughes, but not surprisingly, the later three attempted *escape* and were gunned down—at least according to one report.[34]

The Silver City *Enterprise* reported, "A band of territorial militia, under command of Major Fountain, about two weeks ago, arrested John Watts and William Dillard, two alleged rustlers at Lake Valley. They were started under a squad of Mexican militia for Nutt station, but when near the Lake were riddled with bullets, and after being shot down were kicked in the head and face. They were then taken a short distance from the road and partly covered with dirt. The squad of militia under whose charge they were, claim that the prisoners made an attempt to escape, when they were shot down."[35]

At nearby Kingston, John Shannon tried to buck the odds and draw to an inside skip, but he too was mortally wounded during the *escape*.[36] As expected, once again newspaper editors cried fair or foul, depending on party affiliation, and the political pot-shooting for a time squashed other news.

While battling scribes were enthralled with self-adulation, dribbling out colorful, but usually biased reports, the Grand Jury returned 132 indictments, against twenty-five defendants. John Kinney was rewarded with seventeen true bills, but in a effort to assure a rock solid case at the time of trial all were dismissed, save one. Charged with theft of cattle from Victoriano Sanches, it took the jury but eight minutes to return a verdict, "guilty as charged." Ultimately sentenced to five years in prison, John Kinney's criminal career came crashing down.[37] And beef prices went up! The El Paso *Lone Star* demonstrated just how fickle and sometimes nonchalant the consuming public could actually be.

> When Kinney was in his glory, beef at Rincon was six-cents a pound: now it is twenty-five and scarce at that.[38]

Dan Tucker could only marvel at the turn of events. On the one hand everyone wanted something done about this particular problem or that, just so long as it didn't affect them—or their pocketbook!

Examination of Grant County Commissioner's records reveal that Dan Tucker maintained his status as a deputy and was apparently reasonably busy. At the beginning of July, 1883, for services performed as a deputy he received $70.00, a not insignificant amount at the time—especially for a lawman of the working variety.[39] Little did he know it then, but he was *fixin'* to once again become involved in a local controversy, not nearly as serious as the Burns affair, but nevertheless one in which he had friends in both camps.

Earlier (May, 1883) at Deming, Doc Kane, became embroiled in a drunken row at a "lodging house kept by two women" with a railroad conductor who went by the sobriquet of Richard "Three-Finger Dick" Tabler. Not taking any guff, Dick got up and "put a head" on Kane. Kane staggered from the scene, appropriated a .44 caliber six-shooter and returned only to find Dick passed out. Noting that nothing that simple should deter a methodically determined man, Doc Kane callously "put the gun within a few feet of his bowels and fired." Completely oblivious, Dick continued with his sleep—permanently![40] Although usually a popular figure at Deming, thanks in large part to his hiring a beautiful female piano player for his saloon, on this occasion Doc Kane found himself in a serious bind.[41] Townsmen were outraged. Deputy Dan Tucker immediately took Kane into custody and "concealed him from a crowd of indignant citizens," who were very much excited over the affair.[42] With an eye directed toward prisoner security, most likely an arrangement was made between Tucker and Kane, wherein the latter would voluntarily turn himself in at the county seat, although such an assertion cannot be irrefutably confirmed by hard evidence. In any event, Kane was released and lit out for the safety of Silver City.[43]

Fermenting alcohol and festering impatience finally gave way to real theatrics and unrestrained macho action. Kane was followed, *days later*, to Silver City by a highly incensed mob with vigilante justice on their minds, and a good stout rope in their hands.[44] The enraged townsmen had gone so far as to charter a special train from the Silver City, Deming & Pacific Railroad. Allegedly, train engineer J. C. Bailey was forced at gunpoint by the "excursion party" to disregard company policy and chug north, minus headlight or whistle blasts.[45]

Upon a reasonably noiseless arrival, about sixty would-be executioners secreted themselves south of Silver City, sending in three or four spies to scope out the situation in town, cautiously followed by another squad of surreptitious soldiers. Several citizens from Silver City became suspicious over the repeated inquires as to Doc Kane's location, and quickly notified Sheriff Woods, who "slunk off home, refusing to take any hand in the proceedings which were soon to follow."[46] The entire mob squad had finally ventured to town, dispersing into small groups to continue their apprehension mission, all carrying rifles or pistols. After eight of the crowd were arrested by a group of citizens led by town marshal Horn, the loud blast of a train whistle caught the attention of remaining invaders, and the race was on as "they hastily beat a retreat for the depot...and they pulled out for Deming."[47] Sheriff Woods was chastised by the local press for his "cowardly action," and railroad management was censured for very nearly becoming "an accessory to the crime."[48]

Kane, out on bail, barely escaped into custody with his life! A blurb, with emphasis added, in the *Southwest Sentinel* not only offers some details of a later attempt to arrest the suspect, but emphasizes the esteem in which Dan Tucker was held: "Deputy Sheriff Tucker came up from Deming to serve a warrant for the arrest of Doc Kane, but the sureties upon the bond of the latter had already surrendered him to the sheriff, and the warrant was consequently inoperative. Had Kane been arrested and taken back to Deming, it is thought he would have been lynched, not withstanding the resistance *of even such a determined officer as Tucker*."[49]

The whole affair was taking on comic proportion, and rival newspaper editors eloquently tried to maintain the moral highroad. In a response to a journalistic gig hurled at Silver City by the Deming *Headlight*, the *Southwest Sentinel* tossed it's own spear:

> The Deming *Headlight* seeks to make light of the movement of a large body of citizens of its town, in chartering a train and moving upon Silver City as vigilantes. The fact is, the affair was a most disgraceful one, and the best men in Deming cannot but so regard it. The mob had ample opportunity to have hung Kane in Deming, and it would have been better for the reputation of the town had they done just that, instead of waiting until the object of their vengeance had escaped to this point, and then attempting to carry their mob law into execution here. Had their plans been carried out Silver City would have had all the disgrace and Deming all the satisfaction. As it is the disgrace of the attempt and the mortification of failure alike attach just where they belong.[50]

Dan Tucker was seemingly in constant motion between Silver City and Deming. The newspaper reported on July 21, 1883, "Deming has been well represented here during the past week. Among the visitors were Judge Bristol and Deputy Sheriff Tucker."[51] And, on September 3rd the Grant County Commissioners received Tucker's account in the amount of $25.00 for "deputy sheriff fees."[52] A lawman's work is seldom done!

Although amounting to nothing more significant than a fractious historical footnote, while Deputy Dan Tucker was busily engaged carrying out his sworn duty, fellow law officers at Silver City were likewise right on the job. In some sort of imprudent melee, Billy the Kid's brother, Joe Antrim, managed to become agitated enough to bop B. W. Tait over the head with his six-shooter. Joe paid a $50 fine.[53]

Back at Deming, man-killer Dan Tucker took on another important law enforcement assignment. Miss Thorn reported that Mrs. A. T. Jones stole a number of napkin-rings from her, while she had been a guest at Silver City's Timmer House. Probably with a butterfly filled stomach, churning with apprehension, and his sweaty hands reassuringly adjusting his gunbelt, Dan Tucker faithfully executed the warrant, and took the petticoat wearing desperado into custody, delivering her to Justice Givens in Silver City. During the hearing Mrs. Jones declared her innocence and begged for understanding. According to her story, she had been nursing Miss Thorn through a illness, and the napkin rings had been given her as security for payment. The recovering patient denied Jones version, and rightfully the newspaper sympathized with the already overburdened court: "The evidence is very conflicting." Fortunately for Mrs. Jones the case was dismissed, fortunately for Miss Thorn the napkin rings were returned, and unfortunately for Tucker—the story made the paper.[54]

Although the reasons are not all together clear, the *Southwest Sentinel*, picking up a story from the Deming *Headlight*, reported that Deputy Sheriff Dan Tucker would resign his position as deputy sheriff.[55] The El Paso *Lone Star* carried the story that Tucker would be engaged in "detective work," and had been replaced as the Deming deputy by "Doc" Gilpin.[56] It didn't take long for the rumor to spread. The next Saturday night, friends, foes, and "probably a few who feared him," whooped it up on the Deming streets and in the local nightspots, shattering peace and quite with "wild Apache yells" and a symphony of "vile cursing" which made the night "hideous." A crowd of rambunctious and boisterous celebrants disarmed Constable Hedgins, and more or less "treed" the town.[57] Where was Dan Tucker? Was he in town? Did he just think the sporting crowd entitled to a few shenanigans? Or, was he thinking of opening his own "joint," and just wanted to let the good times roll, and not spoil anyone's fun? The answers remain a mystery, as does whether or not Tucker actually turned in his resignation; but if he did, he must have changed his mind, since later newspaper accounts continue to make reference to his duties as deputy sheriff, and county commissioner meeting minutes reflect payment of fees for "Deputy Sheriff Dan Tucker."[58]

NOTES AND SOURCES

1. Gibson, A. M., *The Life and Death of Colonel Albert Jennings Fountain.* P. 155. Quoting the February 10, 1883 edition of the El Paso *Lone Star.* Hereafter cited as Gibson.

2. El Paso *Lone Star*, 01-13-1883.

3. Silver City *Enterprise*, 02-15-1883.

4. Gibson, P. 155.

5. Silver City *Enterprise*, 03-01-1883.

6. Ibid., 03-08-1883.

7. Price, P. 207. Also see Owen, P. 129, "Kinney so dominated area affairs of the area that Rincon was commonly called Kinneyville. In fact, he was alleged to have used the depot area at Rincon as a loading corral for shipment of his stolen cattle."

8. Mullin, P. 232.

9. Ibid. The author states Kinney deposited the ill gotten funds in the State National Bank, El Paso, Texas. Price says of the Rincon operation, "It is estimated that during 1883, alone, some ten thousand head of cattle were stolen. The residents of Palomas, Colorado (Rodey), Lake Valley, Leasburg, and Doña Ana were the big losers." P. 211.

10. Price, P. 211.

11. Mullin, P. 232.

12. Ibid.

13. Silver City *Enterprise*, 02-22-1883.

14. Ball (II), P. 54. The author states sixty-six stockmen petitioned New Mexico Governor Sheldon for assistance in dealing with the rustlers.

15. Nolan, Fredrick., "The Life and Crimes of John Kiney—Part 2.," *True West*. October 1996. P. 13. Hereafter cited as Nolan (II)

16. Gibson, P. 115.

17. Silver City *Enterprise*, 02-22-1883.

18. Nolan (II), P. 13. Quoting the Albuquerque Journal.

19. Ibid. And Gibson, P. 116-119. Nolan correctly reports that Sain's name is variously spelled.

20. Ball (II), P. 55.

21. Ibid.

22. Gibson, P. 119.

23. Ibid.

24. Silver City *Enterprise*, 03-15-1883.

25. Gibson, P. 119.

26. Mullin, P. 235.

27. Ibid.

28. Nolan (II), P. 13. Quoting the El Paso *Lone Star*.

29. Ibid., P. 14. Quoting the El Paso *Lone Star*. Also see Mullin, P. 236, who believes Kinney was about to be released by the local Justice of the Peace because "Kinney's name inspired such fear."

30. Ibid.

31. Ibid., The author identifies three bondsmen, Harvey Whitehill, T. J. Williams, and D. M. Reade. Also see Silver City *Enterprise*, 09-24-1886.

32. Silver City *Enterprise*, 01-11-1883.

33. Nolan (II), P. 14.

34. Gibson, P. 123.

35. Silver City *Enterprise*, 0-4-06-1883.

36. Ibid. Also see Owen, P. 136, "Shannon, nevertheless, attempted an escape and was shot and killed, adding to the list of 'escapee' fatalities."

37. Information about the indictment, trial, conviction, and sentence, come from Gibson, Mullin and Nolan. Of the three, Nolan provides the most abundant legal and name-specific material.

38. El Paso *Lone Star*, 04-25-1883.

39. Grant County Commissioner's Court Minutes, July 3, 1883. Grant County Clerk's Office. Silver City, New Mexico.

40. Silver City *Enterprise*, 05-18-1883 as cited by Unger.

41. Stanley, P. 9.

42. *Southwest Sentinel*, 05-191883.

43. Silver City *Enterprise*, 05-18-1883.

44. Interview with T. Humble, May 1999, Silver City, New Mexico. Also see the Silver City *Enterprise*, 05-18-1883. The paper also offers the spelling for the suspect's name as Cain rather than Kane.

45. Unger, P. 9.

46. Silver City *Enterprise*, 07-13-1883.

47. Ibid. Also see El Paso *Lone Star*, 07-18-1883. "A number of the most prominent men of Deming are charged with having been in the party that attempted to lynch Doc Cain (Kane) at Silver City."

48. Ibid. Reportedly the train engineer stated he came into Silver City "without headlight and without ringing the bell."

49. *Southwest Sentinel*, 07-18-1883. T. Humble also advises that several of the lynch mob were arrested in Silver City.

50. Ibid., 07-18-1883.

51. Ibid., 07-21-1883.

52. Minutes of Grant County Commissioner's Court Meeting, 09-03-1883. Grant County Clerk's Office. Silver City, New Mexico.

53. El Paso *Lone Star*, 07-11-1883.

54. *Southwest Sentinel*, 08-01-1883.

55. Ibid., 09-29-1883.

56. El Paso *Lone Star*, 10-06-1883.

57. Silver City *Enterprise*, 10-05-1883.

58. Commissioner Court Minutes for 04-13-1887. Reflecting payment in the amount of $20.20 to "D. J. Tucker, deputy sheriff."

9

"JERKED TO JESUS"

Good times may have been rolling along in downtown Deming, but on November 24th, 1883, fifteen miles to the west, near Gage station, a Southern Pacific locomotive screeched to a grinding stop. During the train's caterwauling slide to avoid a misplaced rail, shots rang out, and train engineer Webster fell dead. The pinging sound heard by fireman, Thomas North, turned out to be other shots striking hard steel, fired at him—he ducked—and fortunately bullets ricocheting in the cab failed to find their mark, as a terrified railroad man scurried for cover. In a flash, the train brakeman, Thomas Scott, sized up what was happening, and slyly slid from the train, heading for Gage station, five miles away.[1]

At the now still train, heavily armed robbers successfully looted the express car of eight hundred dollars and appropriated what money frightened passengers had failed to hide. The traveler's efforts at secretly stashing personal treasure were stunningly successfully, exhorting congratulatory remarks from the *Southwest Sentinel*:

> The alacrity exhibited by some of the passengers in secreting their valuables is said to have been wonderful...Watches, rings and other valuables were dropped in the water coolers, in the coal boxes, behind the hot water pipes, in pillow boxes, and in fact in every conceivable place in the coaches and sleeping car. One man went so far as to attempt to secrete himself in the linens in the sleeping car.[2]

Scooping up their plunder, the four desperadoes, one of whom was thought to be black, beat a hasty retreat.[3]

Successful in his attempt to evade the robbers, a fatigued and footsore brakeman stumbled into Gage station and sounded the alarm. The telegraph wire hummed! Amid rumors, speculation, and hopeful guesses at just who the suspects might be, Dan Tucker organized a posse at Deming which departed the next day, but as the newspaper correctly surmised "the desperadoes had too far a start and were too well mounted."[4] Tucker stayed on the trail, or at least kept looking for a promising trail, but much to his displeasure there was no development of consequential clues, or encouraging investigative leads, and the investigation appeared stagnated, in spite of a $2200.00 reward offered for the capture of each of the yet unidentified fleeing suspects. Day after day the search continued.

Wells, Fargo & Co. detective James B. Hume and Southern Pacific Railroad detective Len Harris were sent to the area to assist in the investigation. Hume, in an effort to reinflate a seemingly forlorn and flat investigation, reassured the public, and any potential informants who might be listening, "...rewards offered by the railroad company and the express company still stand and hold good, and the amounts offered will be paid to any party or parties who may capture the robbers."[5] And for the moment, it seemed to Hume and Harris that they were butting their heads against a Silver City stone wall, "the officers here being occupied attending court...and they being unwilling to confide their business to strangers."[6]

Indeed, when subpoenaed, an appearance at court was highly advised. "Dr. W. K. Perkins, of Deming, languisheth in the county jail on the charge of contempt of court." The good doctor had failed to show up for the Doc Kane trial, offering that he had merely confused the court dates, but his excuse was useless. Placed in jail in lieu of $1000 bail, Dr. Perkins probably fumed when he picked up the Silver City *Enterprise* and read, "the way of a witness is truly hard in New Mexico."[7] Deputy Dan Tucker chose to make his appearance! "D. Tucker arrived in town Tuesday as a witness in the Kane case. 'Tuck' returned last week from the chase after the train robbers."[8]

It may be somewhat difficult to believe Tucker's pursuit of homicidal train robbers was at the moment reined in, but reality reveals it was not an exception to the rule. Dan Tucker's presence at court, along with the other officers, was demanded! Ball directs his attention to this case in particular, "The sheriff's office labored mightily to deliver all court process in order to make the session successful. Other important tasks had to be set aside. On 4 January 1884, the Silver City *Enterprise* noted that Sheriff James Woods had suspended the investigation of a train robbery. He and his staff were 'occupied attending court.' Wells Fargo detectives, who were anxious to continue the search for clues, were very upset with the sheriff."[9] Tucker's attendance was required for the trial of Doc Kane. Tucker testified, but ultimately the jury acquitted Kane.[10]

According to at least one source, Harvey Whitehill, the now ex-sheriff of Grant County was approached by Wells, Fargo and Company representatives and asked to "assume the almost hopeless task of running down the train-robbing cowboys."[11] Others simply believed Whitehill joined the chase for a percentage of substantial bounty money being offered. In either event, clue cards were soon to be dealt investigating officers, which in effect would net them a "full house."

Officers learned on the day of the robbery, two unknown cowboys had visited the hay camp of A. C. Eaton near Gage Station, and each told a story which contradicted the other, arousing enough suspicion for especial attention. Three weeks later, at Silver City, the mule one of the cowboys had been riding was seen, and ultimately traced back to make the identification of a previous owner, Frank Taggert, who had been "running" with A. Mitchell "Mitch" Lee, and Christopher "Kit" Joy. The trio had been "hanging out" around Duck Creek where a black cowboy, George Washington Cleveland, was employed.[12] This quartet's description matched that of the train robbers.[13]

This information took on added significance when incorporated with other facts. Namely, Harvey Whitehill in a return trip to the crime scene, located a copy of a Kansas newspaper which was caught in the brush. It was indeed a critical clue, because "it was addressed to a storekeeper in Gage who recognized it. Moreover, he recalled wrapping some food in it for a 'Negro' cowboy the morning of the holdup."[14] At last, with at least viable suspects in their sights, lawmen began looking for the foursome. Much to the disgust of investigators, it was soon learned friends of the cowboys were secreting them, except for George Cleveland, who it was reported had decamped for Socorro, New Mexico Territory. One editor pled, "Hunt them down, ranchmen and cowboys. They are your enemies, the enemies of law and order, and deprived an honest, hard-working man of his life, leaving his wife and children in destitute circumstances. Do not protect such villains by informing them of the movement of the officers."[15]

Angrily some cowboys fired back with a missive of their own, aimed at the local editor. Speaking of Lee and Joy, the letter acknowledged the pair "passed through our range but did not stop at any of our camps," and the letter continued by censuring accusing officers of "making charges against our honesty and integrity."[16]

Harvey Whitehill headed for Socorro. After some surreptitious sleuthing, Whitehill was successful in locating Cleveland's then current place of employment, a local restaurant. The determined manhunter began surveillance, his diligence paying off with the capture of Cleveland, albeit at the point of an "eared back" six-shooter. Belligerent, Cleveland demanded to know why he was being arrested. Whitehill replied, "You know, for shooting the train engineer."[17] Cleveland folded. Terrified, he blurted, "It wasn't me, it was Mitch Lee that killed him!"[18] Thinking the other three already in custody, Cleveland confessed the crime's details to Whitehill on the train trip back to Silver City, and unknowingly furnished important leads which would aid in leading lawmen to where the remaining outlaws were hiding.[19] Little did he know it then, but George Washington Cleveland had just signed his own death warrant. Upon his arrival back at the county seat, Cleveland was dumbfounded when he was inadvertently appraised that his partners in crime were not in custody, nor had they been.[20]

At St. Johns, Arizona Territory, Harvey Whitehill, accompanied by others, arrested twenty-two year old Frank Taggart, who had a "large mouth, which, while in conversation is always wreathed in smiles."[21] In all probability his smile faded when he was later identified by Southern Pacific Conductor Zack Vail, as one of the murdering train robbing gang.[22] Mitch Lee and Kit Joy were arrested, after a law enforcement ruse, in a line cabin north of the San Francisco River, near Horse Springs.[23] All the fugitives were now in jail, awaiting trial, which as everyone knew would "certainly" lead to their conviction.[24]

While southwestern New Mexico Territory lawmen had been actively engaged in the criminal investigation and pursuit of man-slaying train robbers, events further to the west in Cochise County, Arizona Territory were soon to steal the headlines. A mournful episode, dubbed the "Bisbee Massacre" in the historical retelling, would be noted as the most significant single event in the "history of outlawry" for the Queen of the Copper Camps.[25] And although it is usually innocently overlooked, Deputy Dan Tucker was to play a not insignificant role in that story.

There being no banks in early Bisbee, the major mercantile firm known as the Goldwater and Castaneda Store handled the payroll for the Copper Queen Mine, as well cashing checks, storing valuables, and extending credit to the area miners and other citizens. Such being the case, and with monthly shipments of hard cash regularly coming in from Tucson just in time for payday, it was relatively simple for a criminal mind to deduce that the store's safe contained rich reward, and should be "easy pickings." At least so thought five masked desperadoes on December 8, 1883.

Two outlaws armed with repeating rifles and with revolvers tucked in their waistbands, remained outside, while the other three dashed inside to scoop up the loot.[26] When advised by others that a robbery was in progress, citizen James Krigbaum took cover, sighted in on the outside outlaws, and blasted away with the only weapon he had, a pistol. Unfortunately he missed, but one of his shots burned a graze mark across the back of one of the crook's coat. Hearing gunshots, John Tappiner and Joseph Bright stepped out from the Bon Ton Saloon. Tappiner was gunned down by a bullet tearing open his forehead, and Bright luckily hightailed it for safety. Exiting Joe May's Saloon to inquire as to the source of all the hubbub, a man named Howard was mortally gunned down, as was D. Tom Smith when he exited onto the street from a local restaurant.[27] When expectant mother Mrs. Annie Roberts looked out the open doorway of her café, she was fatally struck by rifle fire. Likewise, J. A. Nolly was killed as he rushed to investigate.[28] In just a few short minutes, five innocent bystanders were wantonly killed by the Bisbee bandits.[29]

Inside the store, excited brigands hastily discovered the payroll had not yet arrived, and the safe only contained approximately $600.00 in cash, and a gold watch belonging to William Clancey.[30] Grabbing the paltry reward, the five guttersnipes fled. Arizona historian Lynn Bailey reports that Deputy Sheriff Billy Daniels, assisted by Horace C. Stillman, John Reynolds and a now rifle toting James Krigbaum, all shot at the fleeing suspects but with no apparent effect.[31]

Over in Grant County the editor of the Silver City *Enterprise* added his two cents and said the crooks "possessed swaggering desperado habits so familiar to the people of the west."[32] And of the outlaws' departure he passionately scribbled, "The crimson-handed villains" rode off and were followed by lawmen and "a volunteer party of true-blue men."[33] Deputy Sheriff Dan Tucker was on the lookout in his bailiwick!

Preparations were made during the night, and the next morning a posse led by deputy Billy Daniels took off after the homicidal robbers. One of the temporary deputies was John Heith, a recent arrival to the area, and the operator of a newly opened Bisbee dance hall.[34] Two other members of the posse were former Cochise County Sheriff John H. Behan, and the incumbent Jerome L. Ward, at least according to one author.[35]

While tracking the desperate fugitives, Heith seemingly was trying to misdirect the posse away from the suspected escape path, a point noted by more than one! Soon Heith and another separated themselves from the main posse, obstensibly still following a suspicious trail.

The main squadron of lawmen finally stopped at the ranch of Luben Pardu, who advised that five men had recently been by, divided what appeared to be cash, split up, and rode off in several different directions. Of special interest to the posse was Pardu's acknowledgment that he had seen the men, one week before, accompanied by a sixth man, who acted as the band's leader. Pardu named the conspirators.[36] They were, Dan "Big Dan" Dowd, Owen W. "Red" Sample, James "Tex" Howard, William Delaney, Daniel "York" Kelly, and the leader was reported to be none other than local ballroom owner, John Heith.[37] The decision was made to capture the "bird in hand," and continue looking for those in the "bush."

Barthlowmew claims it was John Behan and Sheriff Ward who arrested Heith, while Fred Dodge asserts it was his fellow colleague and part-time Cochise County deputy Sy Bryant who performed the deed; but in any event, Heith was delivered to the county jail in Tombstone.[38] Heith refused to talk, or give away the others' escape plans, but quite naturally, an inflamed public demanded action, and the search advanced. Doing their part in the schemes to capture the killers, the Copper Queen Mining Company funded the publication of "Wanted" flyers describing the outlaws and the stolen watch, plus assisted in distributing the posters throughout Arizona and New Mexico Territories, as well as the northern Mexican states.[39]

There are several versions of the next arrest, but they each have a common denominator—Deming's Dan Tucker. Bailey advises that Daniel "York" Kelly had made it as far east as Deming, and was in the barber shop getting a shave, when the barber recognized him from the wanted circular, and notified the local lawman, who forthwith took the wanted outlaw into custody.[40] Fred Dodge reported, "Capt. J. B. Hume, Special Officer for Wells Fargo and Co., was at Deming, New Mexico when the Bisbee holdup took place—and he noticed a man had come into town and acted very suspicious. The descriptions had gone out by wire and Hume was sure that this man answered the description of one of the men. Tucker, Special Officer for the Southern Pacific R. R., was a Deputy Sheriff of Grant County, New Mexico and a friend of Hume's. Hume went to Tucker and told him about the man and they then watched him a little and thought that they would arrest him, thereby preventing him from getting away. They done this and Hume questioned him and become certain that he was one of the men and Hume wired the Sheriff at Tombstone and Ward got him—he was York Kelly."[41] Breakenridge succinctly reports, "Special Officer Tucker captured York Kelly at Deming, New Mexico."[42] Bartholomew, as well as a local newspaper report, indicate that Kelly was "disguised as a tramp" when arrested at Deming.[43] And according to Ball, when Kelly was arrested in Deming, he was in possession of an "incriminating hat" which was later turned over to Sheriff Jerome Ward of Cochise County.[44] Admittedly, between the stories some minor details are at variance, but uniformly Deputy Dan Tucker is credited with arresting Daniel "York" Kelly at Deming.

Interesting indeed is Breakenridge's remark that Dan Tucker was a "Special Officer," which in the vernacular of the times can easily be interpreted to mean Dan Tucker was, at least occasionally, employed in the capacity of a railroad express messenger guard, or often given responsibility for protecting the considerable railroad assets amassed at Deming. By the time of Kelly's arrest, stagecoach operator Ed Marriage had reallocated the seventy-four horses used on the Silver City to Deming run and had shut down the operation. He couldn't compete with the railroad, which by now had connected the two cities, much to the traveling public's delight.[45] Two contemporary penmen make the same assertion as Breakenridge, but they differ as to Tucker's employer. Fred Dodge advises Dan Tucker was employed by Grant County as a deputy, and was also a "Special Officer for the Southern Pacific R. R."[46] In the version offered by Dan Rose, because he had been wounded in a Deming gun-fight, Dan Tucker was suffering from "a bullet which broke his rib under his right arm and lodged in the skin of his back," and was in need of an "easy riding" job, which he found by providing security for the Santa Fe Railroad.[47] In either case, it is not unreasonable to believe that after his stagecoach riding days, Dan Tucker from time to time rode the rails protecting Wells, Fargo express, or patrolled and protected the considerable railroad property located at Deming.

Regardless which railroad contributed to Tucker's monetary pot, evidence clearly reveals the title of deputy sheriff was still appropriate, as revealed under the caption "Fees of Sheriff, Deputy Sheriffs and Constables" in the February 1, 1884, edition of the Silver City *Enterprise*. Payments were made to Sheriff James B. Woods, and Deputy Sheriffs D. L. Belt, H. A. Logne, R. Bledsoe, R. Hadden, G. D. Gilpin, Dan'l Tucker, and H. E. Muse.[48]

Continuing with the Bisbee story, "Red" Sample and "Tex" Howard were captured by a posse near Clifton, Arizona Territory. Sample had foolishly given an ex-lover the watch stolen in the Bisbee robbery, and it indeed proved to be an expensive gift, and a conclusive clue, when it was recovered and identified by investigating lawmen, as was the bullet-burned coat he was wearing. The two were returned to Tombstone and thrown in jail with Heith and Kelly. Meanwhile in Mexico, Cochise County Deputy Billy Daniels, finally located and arrested "Big Dan" Dowd, and also subsequently took custody of William Delaney, who had been arrested by local Mexican authorities in Minas Prietas, Sonora.[49] With all of the fugitives behind bars, preparation for trial got underway.

Heith managed to have his trial sliced off from the others. On February 19, 1884, in the face of overwhelming evidence, the other five were convicted of murder in the first degree, and sentenced to be "hanged by the neck until dead."[50] On February 21st, Heith was convicted of second-degree murder, and sentenced to life in the Yuma Territorial Prison.[51] The townspeople were appalled. A group of vigilantes, named after a popular rifle caliber, calling themselves "Forty-five Sixty," defiantly overcame absolutely no resistance from area lawmen, seized Heith, and hung him from a Tombstone telegraph pole.[52] Even across the line over in Silver City, Heith was characterized as "...undoubtedly the worst man that ever came to Arizona or New Mexico...He died as he had lived, with a hardness of heart that showed no fear of the hereafter."[53]

Of Heith's death, using wording supplied by the renowned Dr. George Goodfellow, a coroner's jury reported, "We the jury, find that John Heath came to his death from emphysema of the lungs, a disease very common at high altitudes. In this case the disease was superinduced by strangulation, self-inflicted or otherwise."[54] The finding met with public approval.

The remaining quintet of incarcerated high-jackers idled away their time behind bars until March 28, 1884, when they stood on the scaffold, donned black hoods, and awaited their "Final Launch Into Eternity."[55] Standing on the gallows, all protested their innocence. As the noose was lowered over Dowd's head, he remarked, 'This is a regular choking machine', and York Kelly's final words were "Let her go," and so ended the lives of the Bisbee Bandits, none of which "showed any signs of weakening, being game to the last."[56]

Meanwhile, back in New Mexico Territory it had been anything but quite. Headlines heralded the story, "A BREAK FOR LIBERTY!" On

March 4, 1884, the four Gage train robbers, "Kit" Joy, Mitch Lee, Frank Taggart, and George Cleveland broke out of the Grant County jail, accompanied by convicted murderer Carlos Chavez, and accused horse thief Charles Spencer.[57] The escapees had overpowered jailer F. C. Cantley, guard Steve Wilson, and night watchman, Nick Ware. During the escape, Mitch Lee was heard to remark that "they would do away with the negro Cleveland before they were many miles from town."[58] Seizing weapons from the jail, (a shotgun, .44 caliber rifle, and four six-shooters) the fleeing prisoners eventually made it to the Elephant Corral and appropriated the requisite number of horses. The doomed George Cleveland chose a "bucker," was soon thrown to the ground, and forced to re-mount behind one of the others. The chase was on![59]

A short distance out on the Fort Bayard road the outlaws were overtaken by a posse that was steadily being reinforced. Frantic in their attempt to elude capture, the outlaws took to the brush on foot. The ranks of the posse swelled, eventually permitting a charge to higher ground, from which a withering fusillade was initiated, resulting in the killing of Cleveland and the critical wounding of Mitch Lee. Taggart and Spencer, out of ammunition, forthwith surrendered, while "Kit" Joy made good his escape through the heavy underbrush, but not before successfully ambushing part-time posseman, and full time Singer sewing machine salesman Joseph N. Lafferr, who was instantly killed.[60] During the dangerous but fruitless search for Joy, the body of Chaves was found, the top of his head blown off.[61]

Other accounts of the daring flight from justice, and resultant shoot-out, indicate Cleveland was actually murdered by his comrades in crime. In his remembrances, Wayne Whitehill emphatically reports that "Kit" Joy shot George Washington Cleveland "right in the forehead," because "they blamed him for the whole thing these other fellas did…"[62] Another author simply remarks, "Out about three miles the robbers made a stand to fight. The first thing they did was to shoot George Washington between the eyes."[63] At this late date, whether Cleveland was killed by his cohorts, or met his demise due to a posseman's bullet cannot conclusively be determined, but one thing is for sure, his admissions to Sheriff Harvey Whitehill had been extraordinarily damaging to the other three, and they knew it!

A local newspaperman, who was along on the adventure reported the next development, "It was here determined without a dissenting voice that Mitch Lee and Frank Taggart should, by request, attend a neck-tie party and a vote should be taken as to what disposition should be made of Spencer…The crowd, which was increasing rapidly, was about evenly divided as to Spencer's fate, and it was decided to return him to jail."[64]

Sensing the end was indeed near, Frank Taggart admitted he was guilty of robbing the train, but that it was Mitch Lee who had murdered the engineer, against the wishes of the other robbers. A fearful and exasperated Lee, at last blurted out, "Well, by God! I did kill him."[65] When the wagon rolled from under a convenient limb, the two were "jerked to Jesus," the gravely wounded Lee dying almost immediately, and it was reported, "Taggart died hard of strangulation—a throat disease that is becoming extremely common among their ilk in this section."[66]

For the next several weeks "Kit" Joy led a hand to mouth existence, hiding in the Gila River country, his familiar stomping ground. There were conflicting reports, as some implied Joy was existing on commissary provided by those friendly to him, and others indicated the desperately wanted fugitive was obtaining his "eats" from behind double barreled muzzles of the shotgun he filched during the jailbreak.[67] But in the end it made little difference, "Kit" Joy, who could have fled to parts unknown, chose to stay in well-known surroundings, and ultimately was brought down by a supposed friend, the bullet shattering his left leg below the knee, breaking both bones. At Silver City the leg was amputated, before Joy was transported to Hillsboro, Sierra County, for trial.[68]

At trial the evidence against Joy was overwhelming. The eye-witness testimony of express messenger Thomas Hodgkins, baggage master William White, and postal clerk W. O. Swan was not ambiguous—each identified Joy as the "man that came into the car and went through the express matter."[69] Robert Ferguson swore he saw Joy the evening before the robbery at Eaton's hay camp, and that Joy even asked him about the train schedule. Other witnesses contributed to the overall effectiveness of the prosecution's case through both direct and circumstantial evidence. In the end, Joy was convicted of murder in the second degree, but escaped Dan Tucker placing the hangman's noose around his neck, because it could not be shown he was the one who actually killed train engineer Webster, and that the murder had not actually been premeditated. Joy was sentenced to life in prison.[70]

NOTES AND SOURCES

1. Kildare, P. 27. The accounts of the Gage train robbery are numerous. For a complete narrative refer to all sources as cited. Gage, was a Southern Pacific railroad stop 20 miles west of Deming. For a time a small community including stores and a school existed. See Julyan, P. 142.

2. *Southwest Sentinel*, 11-28-1883.

3. Silver City *Enterprise*, 11-30-1883. Theopolis (sometimes spelled Theophilus) C. Webster was the train engineer's full name. The newspaper incorrectly states there were five train robbers, but in fact it was but four.

4. Ibid. Bronson advises that posses from Lordsburg and Silver City also took to the field. P. 163. There is also a report in the 11-28-1883 edition of the *Southwest Sentinel* which says of the pursuit, "A special train consisting of one

flat car and two emigrant sleepers was made up as soon as possible and started for the scene of the robbery with about fifty well armed men." Tucker is not mentioned in this article.

5. Dillon, *Wells, Fargo Detective, A Biography of James B. Hume*. P. 218. Hereafter cited as Dillon.

6. Silver City *Enterprise*, 01-04-1884.

7. Ibid., 08-24-1883. Also see, Jail Register.

8. Ibid., 12-14-1883.

9. Ball (S), P. 93.

10. Silver City *Enterprise*, 12-14-1883.

11. Kildare, P. 27.

12. Silver City *Enterprise*, 12-04-1884. This newspaper account misspells the names of the suspects, but there is no question as to their true identity. Also see Thrapp, Vol. II, P. 747 for Joy; P. 830 for Lee; Vol. III, P. 1397 for Taggart. And Hertzog, alphabetical listings by last names.

13. Kildare, P. 28.

14. Ibid. A story in the 12-04-1884 edition of the Silver City *Enterprise* reports the newspaper was a copy of the Placer *Herald*, a California paper, and that Hume telegraphed the publisher, and received word back that "Johnnie Ross, Keg Saloon, Silver City" was a subscriber. Ball (S) reports it was a Kansas newspaper. P. 189. In any event the newspaper turned out to be a significant clue which ultimately led to the arrest of George Washington Cleaveland.

15. Silver City *Enterprise*, 01-04-1884.

16. Ibid. 01-18-1884. The letter was signed by Lyons and Campbell foreman, G. P. Lyda, and cowboys, J. B. Harris, Charles R. Harris, V. E. Bustchen, N. Henderson, J. H. Nickelvain, and H. O. Peck.

17. Kildare, P. 28.

18. Ibid.

19. Ibid. The 12-04-1884 edition of the Silver City *Enterprise* reports Cleveland gave a written confession.

20. Pioneers Foundation Interview {Wayne Whitehill}.

21. Silver City *Enterprise*, 01-18-1884. Also see, *Southwest Sentinel*, 01-19-1884. "Ex-Sheriff Whitehill, accompanied by John Gilmore (Gilmo), brought in the second of the Gage train robbers last Monday. His name is Frank Taggart, and after much difficulty, Whitehill and his companion succeeded in capturing him in the western part of Socorro county near the Arizona line."

22. Ibid.

23. Kildare, P. 28. Horse Springs is located about 28 miles southwest of Datil, New Mexico. The springs were named by soldiers traveling from old Fort Tularosas to Socorro when they lost a horse, later recovering it at the springs. See Julyan, P. 170

24. Register of Prisoners Confined in the Grant County Jail.

25. Bailey, Lynn R., *Bisbee—Queen of the Copper Camps*. P. 88. Hereafter cited as Bailey.

26. Ibid. Bartholomew identifies the outlaws who remained outside as Bill Delaney and Dan Dowd. And the three that went in the store as Red Sample, York Kelly, and Tex Howard. P. 146.

27. Ibid. Bailey identifies D. Tom Smith as a "stage driver and deputy peace officer from New Mexico…"

28. Ibid. Bartholomew refers to "Mrs. R. H. Roberts" and identifies Nolly by the initial J. R. rather than J. A. as reported by Bailey. P. 147.

29. Ibid. The author reports that Nolly died a few days after he was shot.

30. Ibid. Bartholomew places the loss at $1000.00. P. 147

31. Ibid. P. 89. Bartholomew indicates one of Billy Daniel's shots hit Red Sample in the leg.

32. Silver City *Enterprise*, 12-14-1883.

33. Ibid. The report stated that the Cochise County lawmen were Bob Hatch and Si Bryant.

34. Bailey, P. 89.

35. Bartholomew, P. 148.

36. Bailey, P. 89.

37. Breakenridge, P. 324. Brown advises oftentimes Heith's name is spelled phonetically as Heath.

38. Bartholowmew, P. 148. And, Dodge, Fred., *Under Cover for Wells Fargo*. Edited by Carolyn Lake. P. 48. Hereafter cited as Dodge.

39. Bailey, P. 90.

40. Ibid. The author does not name any officer by name. Most other accounts of Kelly's arrest do in fact name Dan Tucker as the arresting officer.

41. Dodge, P. 53. Dodge's assertion that Hume was in southern New Mexico Territory at the time is absolutely correct. Also see, Dillon, P. 217-218.

42. Breakenridge, P. 326.

43. Bartholomew, P. 148. Also see, Martin, Douglas D., *Tombstone's Epitaph*. P. 239. Hereafter cited as Martin. Raine reports Kelly arrested "on a train near Lordsburg, New Mexico, by Anton Mazzanovich, assisted by two other citizens." P. 115.

44. Ball (S), P. 189. DeArment comments that "Tucker and Hume arranged for the return of Kelly to Cochise County..." P. 19.

45. Unger, quoting the Silver City *Enterprise* of 05-11-1883, "Ed Marriage has withdrawn his stage line between Silver City & Deming." P. 175. And the 03-1883 edition, "Seventy-four head of horses are used on Marriage's stage line between Silver City and Deming."

46. Dodge, P. 53. Also see Gustafson, P. 10. "...Tucker served as a special officer for the Southern Pacific Railroad."

47. Rose, Silver City *Enterprise*, 09-22-1931. DeArment reports Tucker was employed by the Southern Pacific Railroad. P. 19.

48. Silver City *Enterprise*, 02-01-1884.

49. Bailey, P. 90.

50. Ibid. Also see Brown, P. 327. And Martin, P. 239.

51. Brown, P. 327.

52. Bailey, P.

53. Silver City *Enterprise*, 02-29-1884

54. Chaput, P. 60.

55. Martin, P. 237. Ball (S) describes the construction of the gallows as "six-by-eight-inch timbers. The platform was eight by sixteen feet and stood eight feet above the ground in order to accommodate the condemned men's fall. The deck could hold twenty-five spectators. The cross beam to which the ropes were tied rested eight feet above the platform. The trapdoors under the feet of Dowd and his partners in crime were supported by triggers, or bolts. When

Sheriff Jerome Ward dropped a heavy weight, to which the triggers were tied by a rope, all the bolts were simultaneously pulled." P. 149.

56. Silver City *Enterprise*, 04-04-1884.

57. Kildare, P. 28. Also see Silver City *Enterprise*, 03-14-1884.

58. Silver City *Enterprise*, 03-14-1884. Charles Spencer one of the escapees, who was indeed fortunate not to have been killed by possemen's bullets or the lynch mob's rope, was eventually tried, found guilty of horse theft, and sentenced to five years in the penitentiary.

59. Ibid. Bronson says that Cleveland's horse was killed by gunfire before the escapees got out of town, but "one of his pals stopped and picked him up." P. 165. The itemized list of stolen armament is reported in the Silver City *Enterprise*, 03-14-1884.

60. Ailman, P. 71. Lundwall reports that Joseph N. Lafferr, who sold and repaired sewing machines, was one of Silver City's most respected citizens, took an active part in civic affairs, a member of the school board, and the father of five children. P. 169. Also see Silver City *Enterprise*, 01-04-1883 and 04-20-1883, for mentions of Laffer.

61. Kildare, P. 28. The author identifies the deceased posse member as Joseph N. Laferand.

62. Pioneers Foundation Interview {Wayne Whitehill}.

63. Nelson, P. 44. In this account the night watchman is identified as Charley Cantley, and the deceased Lafferr as LeFur.

64. Silver City *Enterprise*, 03-14-1884.

65. Ibid.

66. Ibid. Later the Silver City *Enterprise* offered justification, "The *Enterprise* is not an advocate of lynch law, and yet we are forced to the conclusion that there are sections of the country in which justice cannot, or will not be had in any other manner."

67. Ibid. 03-21-1884 & 03-28-1884. Also see Nelson, P. 44.

68. Ibid. 03-28-1884. Nelson reports, "Joy escaped and returned to a friend's place on the Gila. He hid there for three weeks, but as soon as Joy was off his guard, the friend shot him in the leg." P. 44.

69. Ibid., 11-28-1884.

70. Ibid.

10

"NO ARMS EXCEPT SIX-SHOOTERS"

As one year gave way to the next Grant County settled up with Tucker for services rendered as deputy sheriff in Precinct 11.[1] While some may not have condoned certain aspects of Tucker's personal behavior, and others perhaps questioned his affinity toward the sporting crowd, it seems no one had the slightest doubt regarding his law enforcement integrity. In April, 1884, Grant County Commissioner Holgate appointed Tucker deputy cattle inspector, a job of considerable responsibility, but more importantly a indication of public confidence, especially in light of the dominance cattle culture influence had on local affairs.[2] One respected historian indelibly places his brand on frontier reality, "Tempers sometimes exploded over ownership of livestock during roundups. Cowboys quarreled. Fugitives sought food, sanctuary, or companionship on isolated ranches. The sheriffs of counties in which cattle ranges existed were eventually constrained to post deputies in those wilderness spots."[3]

Probably desirous of fulfilling the fantasy of any dedicated drinking man, but yet retaining his Grant County titles as deputy sheriff and cattle inspector, Dan Tucker opened a saloon across from the Deming depot, "just west of Thompson's Rialto." Dan christened his new barroom the Eclipse, and local news commentators quickly predicted the business would be a success, based largely on the fact, "Tucker has so many friends."[4] Maybe Tucker had failed to take note of an earlier news bulletin, "Three saloons have failed at Deming during the past few days."[5]

Many of those friends must have been saddened when they thumbed through the newspaper and learned Dan Tucker was "stricken down with a fit...resulting from an old wound. The doctors apprehend nothing serious."[6] Not all of Tucker's scrapes, bruises, and battle scars can be authoritatively documented, but at least up until this point it is reasonable to allow; he had his hands burned by the blast of a revolver in a row with drunken soldiers from Fort Cummings; received bullet wounds to the leg and abdomen in the shoot-out in Benson, Arizona Territory; had a bullet break a rib on his right side, which was still lodged in his back; and had suffered a shoulder shattering shot, as well as a face wound, during the fight in a Deming whorehouse. Taken in total, Tucker's scorecard for personal bodily damage makes the characterization "he wasn't quarrelsome, just a nice even tempered man," somewhat suspect.[7] Yet, historical scrutiny does seem to fundamentally support the conjecture, "Everybody liked Dan Tucker."[8]

Tucker had so many friends in fact, he represented the Deming delegation to the Grant County Democratic Convention at Silver City in September of 1884.[9] And although it cannot be confirmed with documentation, it is only reasonable to suspect that Dan Tucker later joined these friends in the frantic search for two and a half-year old Willie Williams. The toddler was reported missing by his mother, and immediately scouting parties were combing the town, desperate to locate the boy before he was run over by a train, stabbed by fangs from a rattlesnake, disappeared into a open well, or fell into evil hands, red or white! All day and well into the evening the exhaustive search continued, to no avail. The next morning, "every saddle horse and vehicle was brought into requisition" and the hunt began again. Finally, the trail of "little feet" was picked up by J. S. Allard, and with cautious anticipation the track was followed south of town toward the Florida Mountains. Darkness came and went, but the search continued, and after thirty-two hours, nine miles from Deming, little Willie Williams was at last located "lying down and crying." Although badly sunburned and sore-footed, the wandering youngster was soon returned to his distressed mother with "sincere congratulations from all her neighbors, and in fact from all the people of the city."[10]

Dan Tucker no doubt was thankful little Willie had made it through two desert nights unharmed, but for sure, his relief gave way to uncertain apprehension when realizing he just might have to arrest a friend. The Silver City *Enterprise* carried the story.

> If Deming is not a sensational town it is nothing. Without a weekly sensation the people are morose and sulky, and consider that the angel that hovers in the look-out chair is not on duty. On Wednesday night Dan Baxter, we learn, aggravated Frank Thurmond into a quarrel which resulted in Baxter's getting badly cut in the abdomen. We did not learn the particulars farther than that Baxter threw a billiard ball at Thurmond and provoked the trouble. Frank Thurmond has always been known as an inoffensive citizen here, while Baxter had the reputation of being very quarrelsome. Dan Baxter, the man cut by Frank Thurmond last week in a quarrel at Deming, died at that place on Tuesday night, from the effects of his injury. The affair is a very unfortunate one and the friends of both parties very much regret the occurrence. The newspapers published there for the purpose, we suppose, of disseminating news at the request of the friends of the parties, suppress the matter, not giving even the facts connected with the affair. Both men are well known in Silver City and throughout the territory and the facts would be of

general interest and would not necessarily prejudice any fair minded person.[11]

The degree of Tucker's participation in Frank Thurmond's temporary legal troubles is not a matter of record. Suffice to say, pleas of self-defense, or maybe just the fact Baxter had it coming carried the day, but because of being forced into the killing of Baxter, Frank decided to give up gambling and concentrate his efforts on land speculation, mining, and cattle ranching.[12] Dan Tucker remained in law enforcement harness at Deming, continuing to maintain a reasonable balance of control over the conglomerate gathering of cowboys, miners, railroaders, transits, sports, and a heaping helping of unadulterated hellions.

Meanwhile back at the mine, the Old Man Mine to be specific, just ten miles west of Silver City, the firewater was once again flowing freely, making some of the men feel forty-feet tall and bullet proof—but they weren't. The budding community around the mine was named Fleming, in honor of the owner Jack Fleming. The silver mining locale and it's sister neighborhood, Penrose, were "caught up by the throbbing pulse of prosperity" and could smugly boast of saloons, a blacksmith, a boarding house, general merchandise stores, and a bakery.[13]

Fleming's first murder was that of black baker John Woods, an apparent robbery victim who was found dead in his cook-tent, a gunshot wound to the head. There were no lawmen assigned to Fleming, and the criminal homicide was never really competently investigated, nor solved.[14] But just a short two months later, James Hunter, under the influence, found himself embroiled in a heated exchange in front of the Parlor Saloon. As is naturally the case, one thing led to another, and James O'Connell interjected himself into the mess by jerking his "double-action revolver" and conking it over Hunter's head for the first lick, and on the second wallop the six-shooter discharged, the bullet inflicting a "ugly" wound over the left eye of an already sore headed disputant.[15] O'Connell was immediately captured by citizens, taken to Silver City, but for some unknown reason turned loose.[16] Full well realizing administrative error would soon probably be corrected, O'Connell caught the south bound train for Deming.

It was too late. Joe Henry filed a formal complaint, a warrant was issued and Deputy Dan Tucker at Deming was notified by telegraph. Somewhere north of the Deming Depot, Deputy Dan Tucker surreptitiously boarded the train, located O'Connell, and with not too much fanfare "ordered him to throw up his hands." Tucker escorted the prisoner back to Silver City, lodged him in the Grant County Jail, and headed home to Deming.[17]

In September of 1885, Dan Tucker made the trip over to Tombstone, Arizona Territory, taking into custody a "dangerous and desperate man," C. A. Tucker (no relation), aka "Italy." The prisoner was charged with stealing sixty-five head of cattle owned by the Stevens and Upcher brand. "Italy" had sneakily, but not necessarily skillfully, altered the bovine's brand from PPP to BBB. The rustler, who had become a fugitive with a $500.00 price on his head, had been arrested in Tombstone by Cochise County deputies "Hairlip" Charlie Smith and Sy Bryant. With the assistance of his attorneys, "Italy" was attempting to "escape through the technicalities of the law."[18] But, Tucker arrived in Tombstone soon enough after the proper receipt of lawful extradition papers, or maybe not; but in any event he took custody of the prisoner and delivered him to justice in Deming across the territorial line.[19]

Although there is a paucity of actual evidence to indicate Dan Tucker had ever officially tied the matrimonial knot, the 1885 special territorial census records reveal he was cohabiting with a woman named Maria, who identified herself as his wife.[20] Interestingly, these same records disclose the Tuckers' operated a rooming house, because as many as sixteen males are listed after their name, and are named as being "boarders." All were reported as single males, and their occupations covered the gamut of what would be expected in a southwestern frontier community, such as, railroad men, miners, teamsters, clerks, and cowboys.[21] This pattern of diversified income fits with Dan Tucker's personal frontier portfolio. Obviously, Tucker was acutely aware that income from the county government was sporadic at best, and his financial experience with city bureaucracy had left him with a sour taste. What is known during the time period of Tucker's residency in Grant County indicates he had diverse revenues from law enforcement fees; mining ventures; shotgun messenger wages; income for railroad security assignments; real-estate transactions; cattle inspector commissions; and as the owner of a saloon. All possibly supplemented by an undetermined degree of gambling. Dan Tucker soon added another to the list.

"Deputy Sheriff Tucker, of Deming has been appointed deputy U. S. Marshal for Grant county."[22] Undoubtedly, Tucker's appointment as a member of the federal law enforcement team was based on two, possibly three factors. First, and foremost, Tucker was a Democrat! As the political party of the U. S. President changed, so changed the U. S. Marshals. When the country's top job was filled by Grover Cleveland, a Democratic, political patronage rewards quite naturally followed, and on June 8, 1885, Don Romulo Martinez, former Santa Fe County Sheriff and local political powerhouse, was appointed United States Marshal for New Mexico Territory.[23] Martinez would be expected to fill the ranks of deputy marshalships' from a pool of fellow Democrats. Secondly, Dan Tucker had a reputation of absolute fearlessness; and, unlike some other frontier brothers of the badge, he was never accused, suspected, or implicated in any criminal collusion with criminals. Lastly, the fact he had a non-anglo wife helped endear him to the Hispano community, a wise political calculation on the part of Marshal Martinez.[24]

From a practical viewpoint, Dan Tucker had been performing hazardous duty for years, now with the new appointment as a federal lawman, he at least would be allowed more liberal compensation for his efforts. Fully recognizing the immense geographical areas of New Mexico and Arizona Territories, the United States Congress had doubled the fees for mileage chalked up by overworked deputy marshals. Deputy U. S. Marshal Dan Tucker could expect $.12 per mile, less a slight percentage legally retained for administrative purposes by Martinez. Dan Tucker would be given other allowances in connection with the exercise of this new federal law enforcement appointment.[25]

In addition to duties already familiar to Tucker, such as tracking down fugitives and making arrests, acceptance of the new title opened a much larger law enforcement umbrella of responsibility. Deputy U. S. Marshal Dan Tucker now found himself embroiled in investigations relating to trafficking liquor to Indians, conniving land fraud schemes, theft of the U. S. mail, violations of the Edmunds Act (polygamy), and a code book filled plumb full of other federal statutes he had previously ignored. Coupled with the hard-core enforcement duties were the seemingly incessant appearances as a servant of the U. S. District Court, and the corresponding service of both civil and criminal process. Occasionally cases go to trial, and trials require witnesses and juries. Because of the expansive distances involved in his bailiwick of New Mexico Territory, just locating people with potential testimony, or those chosen to sit in judgment was a headache of migraine proportion. But on the other side of the coin, a healthy income could be derived from the fees associated with laboring for a busy court, one with a crowded docket.[26]

When Dan Tucker pinned on the deputy U. S. Marshal badge it didn't necessarily mean he discarded his local star. Cross-deputization was commonplace. "It made sense for a sheriff or deputy sheriff to be vested with federal authority. When they rode into the hinterland to serve court process, they could serve federal as well as territorial court papers on the same route."[27] Certainly it was a practical solution to a existent problem in early territorial days, but cross-deputization does sometimes create confusion for later day writers. Profiling Dan Tucker is no exception. After his federal appointment, in some newspaper accounts Tucker is occasionally referred to as a deputy U. S. Marshal, but still at other times he is characterized as a deputy sheriff. Adding to the confusion can be comments such as "Dan Tucker, formerly deputy sheriff here…," which seems to imply Tucker held no law enforcement commission. Apparently, in this instance the local editor erred, inaccurately assuming that acceptance of one commission automatically voided the other. From the best evidence thus far reviewed, it appears that from his very first days in Grant County, until his departure from

New Mexico Territory, Dan Tucker was always vested in some form or fashion with official law enforcement authority.

One of New Mexico's finest, Dee Harkey, explains just how prevalent cross-deputization was, "I said I had six sets of duties. I was sheriff J. D. Walkers's deputy and United States deputy marshal, from the time I went over and talked to the Phoenix bunch about behaving themselves...I had been elected constable and then I was made cattle inspector for the Cattle Raisers' Association of Texas, and the same for the Cattle Sanitary Board of New Mexico, and to complete the list I was appointed town marshal...That was maybe one way of getting cooperation between the various officers, or offices, but I had more than a full-time job."[28] Certainly most southwestern lawmen didn't horde official titles, but assuredly it was not at all uncommon to have one badge pinned over the heart, and another tucked in a trouser pocket— one that could be proudly exhibited when jurisdictional necessity demanded. One brand of border raiders could have cared less which badge Tucker was wearing or what governmental entity it symbolized.

During the first part of November, 1885, Josanie captained a band of a dozen hostile Chiricahuas from across the international line in a blistering raid into New Mexico Territory.[29] Riding with characteristic speed and stealth the marauders neatly maneuvered into the picturesque Florida Mountains overlooking Deming. Rendezvousing with a like detachment of daring clansmen, the two guerrilla fighting squads collaborated.[30]

Apparently oblivious to the Apache incursion, Dan Tucker and William Graham embarked on a prospecting mission in the vicinity of Zuni siding, eleven miles east of Deming and directly north of the Floridas. Whether the trip was planned for serious pick and shovel work, or was just a reconnaissance, is undetermined. Perhaps the pair traversed the flat tabled landscape in their buckboard as they drank from a sloshing jug passed back and forth—perhaps not? For sure though it is known, neither had exercised sensible judgment—both had left their rifles at home. They were attacked by fast charging warriors and the race was on![31]

Realizing their already wearied team would never reach Deming, and armed only with six-shooters, Tucker and Graham beat a hasty retreat for the only usable source of fortification within miles, a sidetracked boxcar at Zuni. Pell-mell the two fugitives slapped reins and cracked the whip over the backs of frightened mules, cajoling the team into high-gear. Quickly glancing over his shoulder Dan Tucker began mentally calculating, could he and Graham reach cover before seven Apache attackers rode them down. Surely Dan prayed none of the hounding horde would have foresight enough to pull-up, take a steadily braced shot, and tumble one of the mules in a jumble of harness and wagon wreckage. A pedestrian would have no chance![32]

Luckily, before the heaving mules gave way to utter exhaustion, Tucker and partner reached the finish line, not a tautly stretched blue ribbon, but rock solid rails which brought not only short-term safety, but psychological comfort. Jerking back on the wagon brake, hanging on to a section of sweaty leather reins, Tucker and Graham anxiously scrambled under the abandoned boxcar, unlimbered six-shooters, and made ready their defense. Practicality prompted the Apaches to make a sliding stop. Josanie's raiders reconnoitered—just shy of revolver range. Stunningly skilled at uncompassionate and wholly relentless warfare, Chiricahua warriors quickly accessed fighting options. Dislodging pale-face adversaries was possible, but like reaching into a rattler's den, it could only be done suffering the bite. Keeping defenders pinned down until flesh fell from their bones was not pragmatic; a locomotive was sure to come by, or possibly a gaunt patrol operating out of Ft.Cummings. It was a standoff! Common sense dictated but one course—kill these two burrowing rats...on the next trip. The Indians scooted off to the east before zigzagging back to the west.[33]

Something had to be done about Chiricahua Apache incursions. Adopting a time-tried, although not necessarily successful Mexican solution, the Grant County Commissioners pounced on a proposal. If Wells, Fargo & Co., the Southern Pacific and the Santa Fe Railorads could post rewards, why not local government? The motion passed.[34]

$250 REWARD

> The above reward will be paid by the Board of County Commissioners of Grant county to any citizen of said county for each and every hostile, renegade Apache killed by such citizen, on presentation to said board of the scalp of such Indians. By order of the board.
>
> E. STINE, Clerk.[35]

Undoubtedly, in the final analysis, posting of a bounty for Apache scalps was much more an act of symbolism than a genuine solution. In fact it was really nothing new. Back in March, 1880, many of Silver City's elite businessmen and prominent residents had subscribed money for "the head of any Indian that is connected with the band of Fiends who are murdering our fellow citizens."[36] Without doubt, the crisis was bona fide, but there is no evidence that Grant County citizens actually rushed off into the hinterland with thoughts of ripping hair from bleeding skulls.

Despite the sporadic Apache ambush or a chance encounter with some "pure quill" bad hombre, not a few immigrants found Deming delightful. There was a certain magnetic charm in casting a gaze through brilliantly clear atmosphere to some distant point where horizon and sky fused and then melted into memory, interrupted only by "great black mountains, in lumps and in ranges" which rose up "suddenly out of the flat, and look as if they had been accidentally left by some range of mountains which had moved away."[37]

In 1885, life in Deming offered much more than an occasional adventure with Indians. While a few "top and bottom men" were still operating; the Deming Y. M. C. A. was trying to acquire some prime real-estate; Deming and Silver City frequently geared up for a rousing baseball game; subscriptions were being solicited to fund a public library; the Deming Glee Club was organized; telephone lines were being strung; Willie Lockhart was bitten by a vicious dog; the Odd Fellows and Masons searched for a suitable cemetery location; music teacher Louis Runge was tuning pianos and hoping to discover a talented child prodigy; School Principal Thomas Brown volunteered to teach through the summer free of charge; and a census taker discovered there were no unmarried women over eighteen at Deming.[38] Deming offered more than bullets and beer.

When he had arrived in Deming, in 1881, C. M. Chase learned from others that Silver City was "really one of the pleasantest, best ordered little cities in the territory, although situated in the midst of the wildest and most reckless surroundings...and that the town was "indebted to Sheriff Whitehill and his deputies for its good order and safety as a place of abode."[39] Of first-hand observation at Deming, Chase remarked, the climate was "delightful" and because the city was being touted as the "future railroad center of New Mexico," he thought real-estate investment might earn high dividends, commenting, "If I knew it, and the credit system was in vogue, I should invest."[40] Dan Tucker had invested in southern Grant County property, was happy to be alive, and glad to be at Deming!

As do criminal investigations, historic inquiries occasion minor mysteries. In June (1886) the Silver City *Enterprise* reported, "Rumors of expected bloodshed at the Indian Springs ranch, caused Judge Masterson to telegraph to Dan Tucker, deputy sheriff of Sierra county, at Lake Valley, to go out and command the peace..."[41] The intriguing news blurb was not carried in the columns normally citing local or territorial news, but appeared sandwiched between items of national note, which seems to indicate the *Enterprise* simply "picked up" and reported a story written elsewhere. The reference to "expected bloodshed," for this narrative will have to remain unexplored, simply due to a paucity of evidence. Of particular note is the allusion to Tucker being a deputy sheriff of Sierra County. Either a distant and somewhat errant reporter simply made a understandable mistake, or Dan Tucker had garnered another commission.

The latter assertion is plausible, and especially likely as evidenced in strikingly comparable circumstances. Several years later, and also a Deming resident, prominent southwest lawman George A. Scarborough held multi-county deputyships. Popularly known to history as the man who killed the man (John Selman), who killed the man (John Wesley Hardin), Scarborough led an exhilarating life, contumaciously stood his ground, and came through all but the last of his many eye-popping adventures. His biographer explains how Scarborough was cross-deputized, "He now returned to his home Deming and took work as a cattle detective for the Grant County Cattlemen's Association. With the help of this organization, which worked in concert with similar ranchers' associations in New Mexico and Arizona territories, he eventually was issued deputy-sheriff papers for Grant, Sierra, Doña Ana, and Socorro counties in New Mexico..."[42]

Certainly Dan Tucker had not given up his official Grant County law enforcement commission, as evidenced by the County Commissioner's meeting eleven months later when he was paid $20.20 for services rendered as a deputy sheriff.[43]

Edward Pennington, former editor of the Deming *Headlight*, writing of the town's early days noted, "Dan Tucker and Dr. Gilpin were the first peace officers, and when business was dull used to go gunning for each other, then everybody else hid out."[44]

Indeed the author is correct in his assertion that G. D. "Doc" Gilpin also held a deputy's commission, in addition to his regular job of managing Dick Hudson's Deming corral, and his employment with Grant County is confirmed by review of courthouse records indicating County Commissioner's paid him fees for such service.[45] Just how effective a peace officer "Doc" Gilpin was is yet to be discovered, but for certain he put Dan Tucker in the shade when the analysis finally came down to who could get the drunkest. On one occasion, "while in a maudlin state of intoxication" Gilpin simply entered a private residence, told the lady of the house to get out, took off his clothes, crawled into her bed and retired for the night. Later his wife embarrassingly rushed to the scene, awakened him from a deep foul-breath slumber, and belligerently carted him off so he could rest his pounding head on the right pillow. The Silver City *Enterprise* remarked with appropriate disdain, "Model deputy sheriff, this fellow."[46] On another occasion, in a fight, "Doc" Gilpin was "badly pummeled" by his adversary.[47]

Pennington's suggestion that Dan Tucker and "Doc" Gilpin went "gunning for each other" has not been proved, but he was right on target when he stated that Gilpin "went gunning one afternoon" and ran up against Charley Roberts by *mistake*. Roberts killed him.[48] And as was often the case in sporting circles, Charley too soon played his last hand. An El Paso newspaper confirmed both killings, "C. H. Roberts a saloon man of Deming was shot and killed on the night of the 14th, at Deming, by Tom Little. Roberts is the man who killed Gilpin last April in the same place."[49]

In November of 1886, Deming voters ventured out, going to the polls and electing Dan Tucker constable.[50] One fact remains signal in the historic investigation of this particular southwestern lawman. Despite what a proclivity toward frequenting barrooms and bordellos, Dan Tucker seemingly always remained popular with the general populace.

One who was definitely a believer was Miss Millie Davenport. Millie had reopened the Gem theater in Silver City, and by most accounts was running a velvety smooth operation, albeit a dash of credit was indispensably required. Technically a theater, but in reality performances were zeroed in for masculine entertainment. To such rousing classics as Tra-ra-raboom-der-ray, a "galaxy of pretty women in bespangled tights of every hue," kicked, danced, and sang risqué songs that "captivated the large male audience."[51] So much fun was to be had at the Gem, that a local constable was thrown from a balcony box-seat and had the stuffings knocked out of him. He landed hard and for a time couldn't "understand nor speak." Later, after recovering his senses, to a Silver City *Enterprise* reporter the humiliated lawman vehemently denied being drunk at the time of the mid-air somersault.[52] But after a time, Millie's financial backers were not all that pleased by the ribald joviality, and not just a few insisted on reimbursement, or at a minimum, some return for their investment. Millie Davenport skipped! Dan Tucker, at Deming, was laying in the gap, and upon the train's arrival with the fleeing passenger, he took the damsel in tow, practiced some "earnest solicitation" and she without delay "remitted by wire" settling up on her "little bills."[53] The local press loved it, creditors rejoiced, Millie skeedaddled, and Dan Tucker's stock once again rose appreciably.

Maybe part of Dan's popularity is based on the simplest of facts: he would tackle assignments others thought distasteful and shied away from. Like the case of P. J. O'Donnell. O'Donnell, "killed a man at Central City because the latter had been in company with an abandoned woman whom O'Donnell claimed for his own."[54] The deceased, a Sergeant Bowman, was a United States soldier, and had been shot through the neck, "the ball taking a horizontal course, passing back of the carotid artery."[55] Two of Bowman's fellow soldiers gladly offered testimony evidencing premeditation; however, O'Donnell claimed the incident a tragic accident. The jury bought the soldiers' story! Convicted of murder, O'Donnell was scheduled to hang, despite considerable efforts on the part of his lawyers and friends to gain clemency from the Territorial Governor. The debate was raging, not particularly about O'Donnell's guilt or innocence—clearly he had shot Bowman—but rather the broader issue of capital punishment in general. A newspaper editorialized in favor of the death penalty, "It would be practical evidence to pistol fiends that life must not be taken by them. If the sentences be commuted to imprisonment what guarantee have the people that the villains un-hung may not ere long be pardoned by some governor?"[56] Unquestionably, at least for some of the area's citizens, the spectacle of public hangings was wearing thin. Trying a tactic of appeasement, and a poorly disguised effort designed to avoid confrontation, Grant County Sheriff Andrew B. Laird announced if O'Donnell was to hang, it would not be in public, or as the newspaper reported, "The ceremony would be conducted strictly in the quite."[57] With Laird's general reluctance about death's details, Dan Tucker volunteered to perform the duties of Chief Executioner, and the local newspaper reported he was "getting the hemp in readiness, oiling and stretching the rope that is to send a fellow mortal hence."[58]

Dan Tucker had in the past taken his place on the gallows and discharged his official duty, but his willingness to volunteer for this assignment speaks to his general law enforcement philosophy. As a lawman, Dan Tucker believed there was a well defined line drawn between right and wrong, which could only be crossed at risk of supreme peril. If one chose to run he would shoot him, if one opted to fight he would shoot him, if one even threatened to do either he just might shoot him, and if one were actually convicted in a legitimate court of law, he would personally stand beside him, adjust the hangman's knot, wait until the last moment—then kick open the trapdoor.

NOTES AND SOURCES

1. Silver City *Enterprise*, 02-01-1884.

2. Ibid., 04-25-1884. At a later date, the killer of John Selman, and noted frontier lawman George Scarborough served the Grant County Cattlemen's Association. See P. 189, *George Scarborough—The Life and Death of a Lawman on the Closing Frontier*, by Robert K. DeArment. Hereafter cited as DeArment (S).

3. Ball (S), P. 33.

4. *Southwest Sentinel*, 05-31-1884.

5. El Paso *Lone Star*, 05-26-1883.

6. Ibid., 05-31-1884.

7. Pioneer Foundation Interviews {Wayne Whitehill}.

8. Ibid.

9. *Southwest Sentinel*, 09-27-1884.

10. Silver City *Enterprise*, 11-14-1884

11. Rose, C., quoting 08-19-1884 edition of Silver City *Enterprise*. P. 79-80. Also see Grant County Civil and Criminal District Court Cost Book, Territory vs. Frank Thurmond. Thurmond was "no-billed" by the Grand Jury.

12. Ibid.

13. Sherman, P. 84.

14. Ibid.

15. Silver City *Enterprise*, 12-12-1884.

16. Ibid.

17. Ibid. Also see, Jail Register.

18. Bartholomew, P. 38-40. Also see Silver City *Enterprise*, 09-04-1885.

19. Ibid. Bartholomew states "Italy" was returned to New Mexico by Jeff Milton and Sheriff Charles Russell from Socorro, New Mexico Territory. The newspaper account clearly reports "Sheriff Tucker arrived in Deming yesterday with Tucker, alias "Italy," the party who stole sixty-five head of Stevens & Upshers's P P P brand of cattle last year." These two accounts do not irrevocably collide. In all probability, in a effort to get "Italy" back into New Mexico Territory as quickly as possible, before anything could legally interfere, Dan Tucker brought the prisoner back as far as Deming, to be picked up by Milton and Russell.

20. 1885 Territorial Census, Deming Group, Page 58, Lines 26 &27. Tucker is listed as married, born in Canada, both parents born in Canada. Maria Tucker is listed as being born in Mexico, parents born in Mexico. A check of county records for official documents relating to Tucker's marriage has proved futile. It would appear, at least at this time, Tucker and Maria were living in a "common law" relationship in regards to territorial statutory law, but could have been married in the "eyes of the church" during a religious ceremony, a not uncommon practice at the time for Latinos or in unions where one of the partners was of the Catholic faith. Religious custom often took precedent over simple civil law.

21. Ibid.

22. El Paso *Lone Star*, 10-03-1885.

23. Ball (M), P. 136.

24. Ball (S), P. 31-32. "A wise personnel policy took into account minorities and other groups in the county."

25. Ball (M), P. 157-158.

26. Ibid. P. 135-163. See Ball (M), chapter The New Mexico Marshalcy, 1882-96, which covers the wide range of enforcement activities and civil responsibilities of territorial U. S. Marshals' and their deputies.

27. Ball, P. 34.

28. Harkey, P. 72-73. Harkey's reference is not to Phoenix, Arizona, but rather to Phenix, New Mexico Territory, then a wild and wide-open town just outside of Carlsbad.

29. Thrapp, Dan L., *The Conquest of Apacheria*. P. 324. In some accounts Josanie is referred to as Ulzana.

30. Ibid. The second band of Chiricahuas numbered sixteen.

31. *Southwest Sentinel*, 11-17-1885. Also see Silver City *Enterprise*, 11-13-1885.

32. Ibid.

33. Ibid. It cannot be said with certainty that Josanie was involved in the attack on Tucker and Graham, but the timing and location fit with the untiring Apache's movements as later tracked by historians. Probability would suggest the raiders were indeed a detachment of Josanie's platoon.

34. Grant County Commissioner's Court minutes, 01-04-1886. Grant County Clerk. Silver City, New Mexico.

35. Silver City *Enterprise*, 10-22-1886.

36. Grant County *Herald*, 03-23-1880.

37. Chase, P. 123.

38. El Paso *Lone Star*, 07-11-1885; 07-22-1885; 08-05-1885; 09-09-1885; 08-01-1885; 07-18-1885; 07-15-1885;

39. Chase, P. 124.

40. Ibid., P. 128.

41. Silver City *Enterprise*, 06-11-1886. The Indian Springs Cattle Co. was located north of Cookes Peak, ten-miles southwest of Lake Valley, Sierra County, New Mexico Territory.

42. DeArment (S), P. 189. The author advises that the deputy sheriff commissions carried no compensation, but did enable him to "...make arrests over a wide sweep of territory...an area more than two hundred miles north to sought and almost three hundred miles east to west."

43. Silver City *Enterprise*, 04-22-1887.

44. Pennington.

45. Grant County Commissioner's minutes, 01-07-1884. Grant County Clerk's Office. Silver City, New Mexico. Also see Gustafson, P. 9. And see, Grant County *Herald*, 03-12-1881.

46. Silver City *Enterprise*, 10-31-84.

47. Ibid. 12-14-1882.

48. Pennington.

49. El Paso *Lone Star*, 09-19-1885.

50. Silver City *Enterprise*, 11-05-1886. Deming voters also chose Fred H. Smith as Justice of the Peace. Also see, Silver City *Enterprise*, 08-12-1887, "The following accounts were received from constables as to fines charged to their accounts having been received by them to-wit: G. W. Gillard, precinct 1; J. D. Skillen, precinct 2; Dan Tucker, precinct 11."

51. Silver City *Enterprise*, 06-11-1953.

52. Ibid., 03-11-1887

53. Ibid.

54. Ibid., 04-29-1887.

55. Ibid., 12-11-1885. As quoted by William H. Mullane, This Is Silver City, New Mexico 1885-1886-1887. Vol. II. P. 44. Also present and a witness to the shooting was Salome Gonzalez, a "woman whose name was well known throughout Grant County."

56. Ibid. This article is in regards to the cases of four separate individuals throughout the territory who were scheduled to be hung. The editor was championing the death penalty for all four. Also see, Jail Register.

57. Ibid.

58. Ibid.

11

"THE TWO GREATEST CIVILIZERS, DAN TUCKER AND HIS SHOTGUN!"

Toward the end of May, 1887, in his capacity as a Deputy United States Marshal, Dan Tucker scooted over to Lordsburg with a bench warrant from the United States circuit court at Santa Fe. Tucker was seeking the whereabouts of William McVeigh who was "wanted to give testimony in a mail robbing case."[1] Whether or not Tucker actually located McVeigh is undetermined, but as subsequent events reveal, a spate of train robberies would put travelers riding southwestern rails, and not just a few newspapermen, into state of panic. Dan Tucker focused his intuitive investigative skills on culling innocent vagabonds from the pack of freewheeling spirits operating along the miles and miles of southwestern rails, and concentrated on identifying viable train robbing suspects. Stopping trains, rifling through mail pouches, stealing express sacks, and frisking terrified passengers was a serious crime. Much more so than some itinerant cowboy turning a wandering Mexican steer into the boss's heard. Public interest in the latter act might be casually dismissed with a sly wink—train robbery was not!

At the August meeting of the Grant County Commissioners, Dan Tucker, as Constable for precinct 11, submitted and settled with the county in the amount of $42.00 for "fines charged to their (the constables) accounts."[2] At the same commissioner's meeting the sheriff was given the following mandate:

> You are hereby commanded in accordance with the laws of the territory in such case made and provided, to collect all territorial, county, school, penitentiary, capitol building, county funding, territorial funding, and poll taxes levied on the citizens of said county, and non-resident property owners whose property may have been assessed in your county, and all taxes assessed upon property within your county as appears from the tax lists of said county for the year 1887, being the foresaid county for the previous years: and also that you collect all interest due on delinquent taxes as provided by the laws of this territory.[3]

Fortunately, at least from Tucker's viewpoint, he was not overly concerned with the sheriff's tax-collecting headaches. He may have had a brief respite from the more glamorous side of the law enforcement profession, but as quick as the flip of a coin, Dan Tucker was enmeshed in a dusty whirlwind of simply trying to sort-out facts and separate "wheat from the chaff" in the confusing case of who wore the badge, and who wore the mask?

During early August, 1887, masked outlaws again robbed a west-bound Southern Pacific passenger train near Pantano, Arizona Territory.[4] Throwing open a switch the high-jackers disabled the locomotive, and eventually were successful in dynamiting doors off of the express car. The bandits made off with $3500 in their pockets, and a instant $1000 reward on their heads. Two Yuma Indian trailers' were successful in following the escape path for a while, but torrential downpours finally forced the posse to abandon the chase—all clues washed away.[5]

Some witnesses claimed as had been the case in an earlier robbery that there were seven wrongdoers, however, others were thoroughly convinced there were but two. Reports that the outlaws had been hiding in a secret cave whistled through the air and blew through the barrooms. Speculation, comment, and guesswork accompanied the news that a bag containing 600 "Mexican dollars" had been found, presumably discarded by the crooks because the loot was too heavy to carry.[6] With reward posted for the capture, anybody and everybody became suspect. A three-ring circus atmosphere prevailed, at least in some circles, but everyone readily agreed an arrest needed to be made. Actual evidence didn't have to be compelling—not when reward money was the prize!

A private detective had followed one of the suspected highwaymen, Charley Small, to Deming and decided to have him arrested. The private-eye employed ex-part-time deputy Johnny Gilmo, who as will be recalled played a central role in the James Burns shooting affair, to arrest Charley Small. Gilmo was not an officer at the time, but nevertheless, for the promise of reward money attempted to take Small into custody. Charley Small's reputation was not exactly the best, and many knew him to be a rustler and rascal. Fresh out of jail at Tombstone, and normally inebriated, on this trip the cowboy was sober, or at least reasonably so. Regardless, Small refused to submit to Gilmo's ad hoc arrest, drew his gun, thrust it under the cash-wanna-be policeman's nose, and backed him into a corner. "A serious difficulty might have occurred, but Constable Dan Tucker fortunately arrived upon the scene."[7]

Charley Small wisely concluded that he best not make a desperate play in view of Tucker's gun. Blessed with common sense on this occasion, the "suspected robber submitted to arrest without any further ado."[8] While Constable Dan Tucker was making investigation into the peculiar affair, Gilmo "skipped" for Mexico, just 30 miles to the south. Tucker "then got out a warrant for Gilmo."[9] Continuing with his efforts to untangle the baffling web of jumbled misinformation, Tucker determined there was no evidence against Small, whatsoever, and turned him loose. Small then went to the depot, and boarded the train for Silver City. Much to his surprise, and indignation, a second private-eye boarded the coach and demanded his arrest. Charley Small belligerently refused to submit, and stated that he "would not surrender to anyone but an officer of the law, and that he was tired of being arrested, and did not propose to surrender, but that if the detective wanted him very bad he could telegraph to the sheriff to make the arrest when the train arrived at Silver City."[10] The detective retreated! Small advanced! No request of the sheriff was made, but the newspaper editorialized.

> These detectives are fast becoming the laughing stock of the entire country. They have made seven or eight arrests, and have in every instance turned their men loose. One poor fellow was brought all the way from Los Angeles to Tucson, and turned loose without a dollar, and left to make his way back to the coast as best he could. Such action on the part of the detectives is unbecoming on the part of Pinkerton's men, and is calculated to make a strong feeling against them. They should have some evidence in hand before making their arrests, or give the job up and go home.[11]

Maybe the newspaperman would have sung a slightly different tune, had he a fortune-teller's crystal-ball. Then again, maybe not.

According to at least one account, Charley Small was later involved in the robbery of a Mexican Central express train near Mapula, Chihuahua, Mexico. The outlaws were later run down by authorities, and one "Doc" Hines confessed, naming Charley Small as the outlaw band's leader. And although the newspaper editor predicted the end of Charley Small and his "villainous gang" because robbing trains in Mexico was a death penalty case, apparently *Lady Luck* in some form or fashion stayed Charley's date with a Mexican firing-squad.[12]

Several years later in southwest Texas, at Del Rio, Texas Rangers arrested a Charles Small for smuggling, deposited him in jail, and probably were not too much surprised to learn the incarceration was of short duration. Later, further to the west in the Trans-Pecos country near Judge Roy Bean's stomping grounds at Langtry, Charley Small emerged as the leader of a gang of rustlers. On July 22, 1893, with the amber current flowing through his veins, Charley Small picked a fight with Texas Rangers Lewis and Musgrave. He came up short! Ranger D. L. Musgarave's report to the Adjutant General at headquarters in Austin read, "This morning we were fired on by Chas Small a noted desperate character and he was killed by me."[13]

Putting the *maybes* aside, and returning to less thrilling but nonetheless relevant material, historian Larry Ball succinctly captures societal and frontier political reality, "Electioneering and political maneuvering became a consuming passion in the southwestern territories."[14] Long before the era of instant news coverage and telecommunication marvels, frontier society, especially in the

Territories, was paying much more attention to items of interests regarding local happenings, rather than engrossing themselves in National affairs where they had little or no voice. Politics at the county level was usually partisan, occasionally comical, sometimes volatile, irrefutably indispensable, and always fascinating.

Naturally as frontier boundaries shrunk, and demographic shifts populated once uninhabited and isolated regions, there was need for local government. In New Mexico Territory, as well as elsewhere in the frontier west, county building "was a favorite sport of budding politicians."[15] Interesting for sure, are the versions of how this county or that one was born. Conspiratorial copy flourishes as writers sometimes impugn character and salaciously affix sinister motive to what in the final analysis simply boiled down to politics as usual. Understandable from a purely practical perspective were the desires of citizens to bring self-government closer to home. Traveling fifty, or in some cases over a hundred miles, to the county seat for the purpose of sitting on a jury, filing a claim, transferring real-estate title, or a flood of other legally mandated reasons was just plain unacceptable. Carving out new counties was the natural byproduct. And as geographical lines were readjusted, hopeful spirits scrambled for political patronage appointments. Germane for purposes of the Dan Tucker narrative is awareness that upon formation of a new county, the Territorial Governor selected the first slate of office-holders, to be followed usually two years later by local elections whereby a supposedly informed electorate could then make their selections. Then as now, incumbency carried considerable political leverage.

Although he had been out of office for a few years, Harvey Whitehill had tried once again to secure the office of Grant County Sheriff in the November elections of 1886. Whitehill faced a uphill battle, and local editor's predictions did not bode well for the ex-sheriff. One said, "…his time is so occupied, growing pumpkins and nursing babies that it would be only a pity to bring him out to be slaughtered by the most popular candidate in the field—Laird."[16] Another simply revealed what was quickly becoming a safe political bet, "It is now doubtful if Harvey will get there."[17] Much of the agitation over Whitehill's political bid centered around his previous and overly friendly relationship with Dan Tucker's old cohort from the Salt War days. The Silver City *Enterprise* explained:

> There are very few stockmen in Grant county, who have been here for any length of time who have not suffered more or less from the depredations of the notorious John Kinney and his gang of rustlers. There was a time when this prince of rustlers shipped his stolen dressed beef in carload lots from Rincon to El Paso where it was disposed of by men no better than himself to the people of that and other towns. Things were run

in a high and reckless manner then, but thanks to Governor Sheldon's much abused militia, Kinney was arrested at Lordsburg and taken to Las Cruces for trial. Everybody knew he was guilty—in fact he did not deny it himself, and yet the Hon. H. H. Whitehill, the present democratic candidate for sheriff of Grant County, went on his bond, and it is but in keeping with the act to presume that he did all else in his power to secure the acquittal of the rustler....Whitehill has always acknowledged that Kinney was the most notorious rustler in the country, and we are of the opinion that he can give no other reason for going on his bond than that of friendship.[18]

In the end, Harvey Whitehill didn't disappoint political pundits, but Dan Tucker seemed to come through the rough and tumble political scuffing unscathed.

Andrew B. Laird was rewarded with the title of Grant County Sheriff.[19] That Dan Tucker continued at least as a part-time deputy is concretely confirmed by the report on the April, 1887, Commissioner's meeting carried in the Silver City *Enterprise*, "The following bills against the county were examined, found correct and approved, and the clerk ordered to issue warrants for the same to wit; D. J. Tucker, deputy sheriff...$20.20"[20]

Whether or not Tucker actually took part in the proposal is undetermined, but Whitehill's failure to recapture the political plum persuaded some of his Deming buddies to promote a "scheme to cut loose from Grant County."[21] It was more or less taken for granted that once the new county was surveyed and christened Logan, or by some accounts Florida, Harvey Whitehill would receive appointment as the first sheriff.[22] Logically, if the plotter's machinations had borne fruit a whole bushel of new plums of the political variety would have been ripe for harvest. And with almost unqualified certainty, if the plan had succeeded Dan Tucker's political law enforcement future would have been even more firmly secured. For Whitehill it was a devastating loss and unsmiling miscalculation! The idea of Logan County fizzled.

In July, 1887, the Territorial Governor commuted the death sentence of P. J. O'Donnell to life imprisonment.[23] Tucker could now quit "oiling and stretching the rope."Clearly, some citizens were growing weary of public executions and occasional outbursts of vigilante justice. Like it or not, times were changing on the frontier. Too fast for some, not fast enough for others. Dan Tucker seemed perfectly content with the *status quo*.

Despite the proclivity exhibited by many frontier lawmen, Dan Tucker never suffered from yearning to move on to a lawman's job in a larger town. He never aspired to become a county sheriff. Looking back, a few might chastise Dan Tucker for a lack of ambition, but more than likely he simply chose to play out his hand at a familiar table—gambling on peaceful satisfaction rather than fondling his ego by trying to hustle-up the top job. Dan Tucker was unreservedly at ease letting others own the acclaim—and the headaches!

Soon, Tucker would be obliged to arrest a "dangerous rustler," Dave Thurman.[24] Through the authority vested in his position as a Deputy United States Marshal, and his concurrent deputy sheriff status, often confusing county-line jurisdictional barriers had melted away. Dan Tucker forthrightly delivered Thurman to jail at the thriving community of Hillsboro.[25] The story was reported throughout the area.

"The services of Deputy Sheriff Dan Tucker were called into requisition Saturday to head off one Dave Thurman..."[26]

DeArment amplifies details of the unique little story, as extracted from pages of the Deming *Headlight*. "In October 1887 Tucker made an unusual arrest, nabbing a wanted fugitive walking beside the track while he himself was aboard a moving train. Tucker had been asked to apprehend one Dave Thurman, under bond for horse stealing in Sierra County, who had skipped out. 'The officer expected to overtake the flyer between here and El Paso, but missed him. Returning homeward Sunday, Dan, from the engine cab, espied his man plodding alongside the track.' Tucker had the engineer slow down the train, 'and before Mr. Thurman realized the situation, he had to make a choice between a bullet and surrender. He chose the latter, and is now safe in the Hillsboro jail."[27]

Although it may not have been Dan Tucker's final police action, the arrest of outlaw Thurman is the last law enforcement deed of currently identified record. From here on out, Tucker was on the downhill slide—at least according to one report.

Dan Rose, who as previously mentioned when a young man had actually known Dan Tucker, provided what very well may be an accurate reason for Tucker's apparent decline, although accepting his conclusions at face value allows for many unanswered questions. But, its all we have! Rose claims: "By 1884, Dan Tucker had become a hard drinker; that is, while he was never really drunk and 'off his feet', he was 'loaded' all the time. Whiskey had made him less and less the man he was of old—cool in judgment, quick in decision and always within the law. Now his face was bloated; his clear blue eyes blurred and red; his slow drawn pleasant smile a definite sneer...Dan Tucker became more and more irresponsible and was finally forced to resign as an officer."[28] Clearly the author's assertion is erroneous regarding the time-frame, for there is a wealth of primary source material documenting Tucker's dual law enforcement positions and the noteworthy role he played in New Mexico Territorial police affairs, well after the 1884 date used by Rose.

Contrary to Rose's assertion, Wayne Whitehill, who also personally knew Dan Tucker, simply declared, "...he wasn't a drinker or anything like that...He wasn't quarrelsome, just a nice even tempered man."[29] One of the remembrances is flawed.

Rose's allegations at this late date can neither be confirmed or refuted. Melodramatically, Rose attempts psychoanalysis, "Perhaps he was haunted by the ghosts of the men he had killed, and was trying to shut them out of his mind by the spell of liquor. At any rate, to those who had known him so long and admired his bravery, it was evident that he was on the down grade, and that his effective discipline of the bad man was gone."[30]

There is no evidence that Dan Tucker was a drunk! There is a plethora of evidence illustrating that Dan Tucker was no teetotaler! Like most historical controversies, the truth probably lays buried somewhere inbetween.

Old newspaper accounts clearly establish that Dan Tucker suffered considerable illness, some of which no doubt was the result of gunshot wounds. And just as unassailable is notation that none of the newspaper reports or other sources mention alcohol as the cause for any of Tucker's ailments, or even as a contributing factor. Whether Dan Tucker was physically or psychologically disabled by drink, struggled with health troubles as a result of battle scars, or was just plain sick, the evidence reveals sometime during 1888 he moved to California.[31] And that's all it reveals!

During Dan Tucker's four year absence Harvey Whitehill once again was elected Grant County Sheriff, beating out incumbent Andrew B. Laird by just 17 votes in the 1888 battle for ballots. The apprehension over Apache raids for the most part subsided. Silver City flourished, Deming and Lordsburg remained important railway stops, and Shakespeare hung on. Miners continued to search for elusive pots filled with gold. Cattleman began overstocking the natural-grass ranges. Train robbers robbed, cattle rustlers rustled, and drunken cowhands occasionally cussed and caroused. But in spite of it all, mothers scolded, nurtured, and nourished—and in the end—civilization took foothold in old Grant County.

In April, 1892, Dan Tucker returned to southwestern New Mexico Territory for a visit. The Lordsburg *Liberal* reported:

> Last Sunday many of the Lordsburg old timers were surprised to see ex-Deputy Sheriff Dan Tucker get off the train. Tucker says he has been away for a good while and is mighty glad to get back and intends to stay in the county the balance of his days. During the early days in Grant county, when it was in the transition state, when the rustlers and bad men were giving way to the peaceable citizens, Dan Tucker and his shot gun were two of the greatest civilizers in the county. Dan had a way when he had a warrant for a bad man of killing the man and then reading the warrant, that was only equaled by Bat

> Masterson in his best days. He was a valuable citizen in those days and it is to be hoped that he will be equally valuable in other ways.[32]

His arrival was also reported in the Silver City *Enterprise* in a story picked up from the Deming Advance.

> Dan Tucker, an old timer and probably the best known man in Grant county, who has been in California the past four years, returned to Deming Monday. Mr. Tucker is but little changed in appearance and that little is for the better. His many friends in Deming were smiling over his return and appeared as pleased to see him as a little boy is to get a new top.[33]

Another bulletin seemingly contradicted the report that Tucker had changed little in physical outward show. For sure, and unarguably, Dan Tucker had lived a hard life, and with that understanding in mind the following bulletin does seem somewhat believable.

> Dan Tucker, one of the best peace officers Grant county ever had, returned recently from California, and has been in Silver City during the present week, renewing acquaintances with old friends. He has grown so fleshy that his friends hardly knew him.[34]

Although the first newspaper account clearly states Dan Tucker intended on staying in the county for "the balance of his days," the evidence indicates otherwise. It is known that on this trip Dan Tucker divested himself of his last remaining Grant County real estate holdings, selling two Deming lots on April 25, 1892.[35] Quite an exhaustive effort was made throughout Grant County, Deming, and Lordsburg to determine if Dan Tucker did indeed stay in the area for the remainder of his life. The results were negative.[36]

Just how long Tucker remained in Grant County is undetermined, but once again Rose serves as the primary source for the generally accepted version that Dan returned to California. He reported, "He (Tucker) afterward went to Los Angeles and from there to San Bernardino, California, where he died in the county hospital."[37] Wayne Whitehill simply remarks, "He went out to San Bernadino and died, I think."[38] Writer C. A. Gustafson, a Deming resident, simply says, "Tucker died in a county hospital in San Bernardino."[39] Pat Humble remarks that Dan Tucker stayed in California "about a year and a half" before he died.[40] And there for the most part, is where the final curtain is drawn on the saga of Dan Tucker.

The research staff at the San Bernadino County Library was not successful in a concentrated effort to locate additional information on Dan Tucker's later life in California. There was no death certificate, no voter registration, no court cases, no burial and removal permits, and no probate or property records which could offer a clue into Tucker's disappearance from historic pages.[41] Similarly, investigation by the California Room staff at the San Bernardino Public Library failed to produce conclusive primary source leads into Dan Tucker's last days, nor did their examination of city directories for the time period.[42] All known area cemeteries were contacted, each graciously reviewed their interment records, but none could offer positive results regarding Dan Tucker, nor could the San Bernardino Historical & Pioneer Society.[43]

During the time-frame Dan Tucker would have been in San Bernardino, the county hospital was known as the California Hospital for the Insane and Inebriates.[44] Today it is known simply as Patton State Hospital. If Dan Rose is correct in asserting that Dan Tucker died in the county hospital, (absent other intelligence there is little reason to doubt him), this would be the institution where the ex-lawman spent his final days. Shouldn't there then be death or cemetery records available for historic inspection?

California statutes require the records at Patton State Hospital (and all other state hospitals) to be maintained as confidential![45] Gary Gleason, Director, Health Information Management, Patton State Hospital, reported that although a death certificate should have been filed with San Bernardino County when a hospital patient died, in truth, during the early days, oftentimes this was not properly done, and record keeping in and of itself was sloppy and left much to be desired. Obviously, the next reasonable and logical question would be, if a patient died at the institution what happened to the remains? In response to the probe, Gleason with noticeable, yet unexplained reluctance, finally acknowledged that some of the deceased hospital patients were buried "on site" in unmarked graves.[46] Certainly this can be construed to offer a reasonable explanation as to why Dan Tucker's name does not appear in the archival files of area cemeteries, although it falls far short of being historically irrefutable. Sadly, at least from the historic perspective, Gleason hesitantly admitted that a modern golf course now covers the area where deceased patient's remains were discarded and buried.

Unquestionably it would be much preferred to offer the reader categorical certainty (death certificate, etc.) regarding Dan Tucker's final exit from the frontier stage but, at least for now, this is where the chronological story must end.

NOTES AND SOURCES

1. Silver City *Enterprise*, 05-20-1887.
2. Silver City *Enterprise*, 08-12-1887.

3. Ibid.

4. Ibid. Pantano, Arizona was a Southern Pacific Railroad station 18 miles west of Benson. See, Barnes, Will C., *Arizona Place Names*. P. 316. Curiously, two months earlier the train had been robbed at the same location. By the same outlaws?

5. Ibid.

6. Ibid., 08-19-1887.

7. Silver City *Enterprise*, 09-16-1887.

8. Ibid.

9. Ibid.

10. Ibid.

11. Ibid.

12. Silver City *Enterprise*, 01-20-1888. As quoted by Mullane, William H., *This is Silver City, 1888, 1889, 1890—Volume III*. P. 2.

13. Wilkins, P. 314-316.

14. Ball (S), P. 55.

15. Ibid., P. 71.

16. Silver City *Enterprise*, 08-20-1886.

17. Ibid., 09-24-1886, picking up a story from the Albuquerque Democrat.

18. Silver City *Enterprise*, 09-24-1886.

19. Grant County Commissioner's Court minutes, 01-06-1887. Grant County Clerk's Office. Silver City, New Mexico.

20. Silver City *Enterprise*, 04-22-1887.

21. Ball (S), P. 71.

22. Luna County Historical Society, *The History of Luna County*. P. 6. Also see Twitchell, Vol. III, P. 306. At the time the proposals to create a new county fizzled due in large part to the resistance of political powers in Silver City. However, in 1901 Luna County was created, taking in the southeastern portion of Grant County, including Deming. Edward Pennington, ex-newspaper editor and subsequent Deming Postmaster played a significant role in creation of the new county.

23. Silver City *Enterprise*, 07-15-1887.

24. Thrapp, Vol. III, P. 1443.

25. Ibid.

26. Silver City *Enterprise*, 10-07-1887.

27. DeArment, P. 19.

28. Silver City *Independent*, 09-22-1931. "Dan Tucker, The Killer," by Dan Rose.

29. Pioneers Foundation Interviews {Wayne Whitehill}.

30. Silver City *Independent*, 09-22-1931. Rose

31. Thrapp, Vol. III, P. 1443. DeArment, P. 19. Rose, Silver City *Independent*, 09-22-1931. Remarks of Wayne Whitehill as found in Blachly citation. And newspaper accounts listed below.

32. Silver City *Enterprise*, 04-15-1892. Picking up a story from the Lordsburg *Liberal*.

33. Silver City *Enterprise*, 04-15-1892. Picking up a story from the Deming Advance.

34. Silver City *Enterprise*, 04-29-1892.

35. Record of Deeds, Book 23, P. 546. Grant County Clerk's Office. Silver City, New Mexico.

36. Correspondence to the author from Terry Humble, 07-10-1999. In searching for meaningful clues as to the possible location of Dan Tucker's grave all known area cemetery indexes were consulted. Additionally the city hall staffs at Silver City, Deming, and Lordsburg replied in the negative. Certainly responses in the negative cannot be irrefutably used to claim that nowhere in Grant, Luna, or Hidalgo counties could one ever find Dan Tucker's grave-site. But, failure to find his place of interment in New Mexico, coupled with what appears to be a reasonable assertion that he died at a specific location in California tilts reasonableness toward the latter conclusion.

37. Rose

38. Pioneer Foundation Interviews {Wayne Whitehill}.

39. Gustafson, P. 10.

40. Address to the Silver City Westerners Corral, by Pat Humble on April 19, 1983. Audio tape courtesy T. Humble.

41. Correspondence to the author from Nannette Bricker-Barrett, San Bernardino County Library—Reference Center, San Bernardino, California, June 3, 1999.

42. Correspondence to the author from Sue Payne, San Bernardino Public Library—California Room. San Bernardino, California, June 16, 1999.

43. Telephone calls by author.

44. Knopsnyder, Karen. *At the Foot of the Mountains—A History of Patton State Hospital.*

45. Payne to the author as cited.

46. Telephone interview with Gary Gleason, Director of Health Information Management, Patton State Hospital, San Bernardino, California. August 12, 1999.

12

"IN EVERY VILLAGE AND ON EVERY TRAIN"

Tombstone is commonly dubbed "the town too tough to die," and as such, over time has inched toward first place on a list of frontier towns consecrated as a model for rip-roaring Western adventure. novelettes and movie-scripts. Historic truth, however, reveals Tombstone for years lay on her deathbed feebly gasping for breath, until twentieth-century writers charitably inflated her collapsed lungs. That the initial resuscitation has been partly paid for with bogus historical currency is generally not disputed by conscientious commentators.

By contrast, Silver City, which Berry and Russell so aptly describe as being "built to last," on her own merit has withstood Apache assaults, floods, slumps in the mining economy, outlawry and general rowdiness, and surprisingly little historic attention. Silver City's purposeful efforts directed toward stability insured endurance. Community commitment to maintaining alignment with changing times, rather than a singular reliance on old West sensationalism, guaranteed Silver City's municipal immortality. Unlike Tombstone, Silver City has never relied on tourist's enchantment with the frontier west. But, if emphasis on recorded violence is requisite in substantiating a western town's credentials, Silver City, indeed the whole of old Grant County, could lay legitimate claim to the highest historic accolades.

In *The Texas Border And Some Borderliners*, Casey whimsically comments that in some southwestern communities "the only legitimate industry was coffin making," but then on a more serious note says of Silver City specifically, along with several other western towns— Tombstone excluded—that the boroughs "were tough almost to the limit of human endurance." Some Grant County inhabitants lived at razor's edge, and it is in that context that Dan Tucker's story has been told.

Law enforcement was Dan Tucker's vocation. Unlike many Western officers who spun back-in-forth across the line cleaving honesty from hooliganism, Dan Tucker personally preserved legal equilibrium. While in New Mexico Territory, almost from the beginning, Dan Tucker could claim positive affiliation with the forces of judicial authority. Under three county sheriffs he served with distinction, and on two occasions answered Silver City's call for a town marshal. Although his employment guarding Wells, Fargo & Co. express was not technically law enforcement, the assignment is indication of an ever cynical public's trust in his probity—as was his later election to precinct constable. Unquestionably, he had the confidence of area ranchers when named

160

brand inspector for Grant County cattlemen. Toward the end of his chosen enforcement career he was bestowed with the coveted political plum of Deputy United States Marshal.

Prior to counting coffins buried in boot-hill cemeteries, and making the inescapable comparisons between competing frontier gunfighters, a cursory scrutiny must be directed toward three factors which offer fodder for less than precise subjective analysis—reputation, willingness, and ability.

Clearly missing from the record is evidence that Dan Tucker was repeatedly involved in pugilistic encounters. Seemingly he lived by an old cowboy adage, "If God had wanted men to fight like cats and dogs, he'd given em' claws and paws." A prize fighter, Dan Tucker was not. Dan Tucker was a gunman! Owing to his physical size, which as will be recalled was "5' 7" and of slight build," Dan Tucker was forced to rely on a reputation of fearless aggression when need be, capped off by unfettered willingness to shoot to kill. A man-killing reputation, if backed by truth, could prove beneficial to a Territorial lawman whereas bombastic bluff could get him killed.

And although it cannot be proved, there indeed seems the possibility someone prompted Dan Tucker to "get control early on." To be sure, Tucker was entangled in violent episodes throughout his badge-wearing career, but historical review does seem to suggest there were two periods when Tucker definitively asserted himself. First, when he initially accepted employment as a deputy sheriff in 1877, and secondly, when he was more-or-less permanently reassigned to the Deming area in 1881. On both occasions, from the very beginning he "grabbed the bull by the horns" and made sure everyone knew it. Was it a purposeful plan to forestall human owl-hoots from getting the upper hand? Did a couple of "siftings for the coroner" serve as effective deterrence? For sure, in both communities he quickly established a reputation!

Numerous accounts penned by nineteenth-century personalities, those actually on the scene and in a position to know, make reference to Dan Tucker's intrepid reputation. James H. Cook, ranchman and writer, in *Fifty Years on the Old Frontier*, recognized Tucker as having "the reputation of being one of the bravest of the many gun-fighters of the southwest borderlands." O. W. Williams, author of *Pioneer Surveyor— Frontier Lawyer*, simply characterizes Tucker as "the deadliest deputy Grant County ever had." The author of *The Editor's Run in Colorado and New Mexico*, C. M. Chase, advocated, "What is needed in southern New Mexico is one or two such officers (Dan Tucker) in every village, and traveling on every train." Express company operative, Fred Dodge, favorably mentions Tucker in *Under Cover for Wells Fargo*, as does Billy Breakenridge in *Helldorado—Bringing Law to the Mesquite*. Former southwestern lawman, James B. Gillett, in his autobiography *Six Years With The Texas Rangers*, most casually remarks, "Subsequently

Bond was killed at Deming by Deputy Sheriff Dan Tucker in an attempted arrest." In faraway Wichita, Kansas, Dan Tucker's skill with firearms was acclaimed in the October 11, 1884 edition of the *Daily Eagle*. Add the columns of local southwestern black on white newsprint and it is not difficult to discern Dan Tucker's reputation as a gunman on the side of the law.

Eleven authenticated fights involving gunplay can be attributed to Dan Tucker. Probability points to others, as enumerated by contemporaries.

If it were not such a historical distortion, the rapture relating to the quick-draw would be charming. In truth, there was no book of gunfighting etiquette. The fight was sudden, furiously fast, revoltingly raw. A casual contest it was not. The winner was rewarded with life— not a lollipop. A miss by an inch, might just as well have been by a mile, as characterized by remarks of the renowned U. S. Border Patrol shootist Bill Jordan, "Speed's fine, but accuracy's final!" Was Dan Tucker fast on the draw? Of the numerous Tucker escapades the one coming closest to answering the question concerning his leather-slapping speed would be the shoot-out with George Brown in Arizona Territory. On that occasion Tucker came out second best, and was indeed most fortunate to have lived through the ordeal.

In judging Dan Tucker's skill with a six-shooter there are but three recorded examples dealing specifically with his firearms proficiency. The newspaper article alluding to Tucker's gun-handling superbness in perfecting the "border roll" or the "road agents spin" is one. Another is a claim that Dan Tucker, while mounted, "put all five bullets in the little ol' tree, and never stopped his horse." Lastly, the less than well-documented assertion that Dan Tucker killed a fleeing felon at a distance of eighty-four steps. Of the killing there is little room for doubt. Regarding the distance, it was either one hell-of-a-good shot, or a damned lucky one, but in either event—effective!

And, one can only guess concerning the fight at the Deming whorehouse whether Tucker's shot missed it's intended target, or was his aim dead sure when the bullet connected with a conspiring courtesan? By all accounts, Tucker opted for buckshot when he blasted Bond out of the saddle. Just how good of a shot was Dan Tucker? Candidly, since he died sans his boots, apparently the answer should very well be—*good enough*!

Mentioned in the first chapter is the invariable demand to count marks carved into the illusory notch-sticks of frontier lawmen and outlaws, in much the same way plains Indian raiders counted coups. Presumably, those whose tally is highest are touted as the best. This method of measurement may prove accurate in the case of war-bonnet warriors charging onto the field of battle, but in accessing the contributions of early gunmen, maybe most is not necessarily synonymous with best. Undeniably, "Killin'" Jim Miller widowed more than a few western women, but normally his technique was that of a bushwhacker, firing his death delivering gunshots from concealment. The "Border Boss" Captain John Hughes of the Texas Rangers in his distinguished career killed but three men, not even coming close to Miller's score. Was Miller then the better man? A high number of killings on the part of the outlaw, stagecoach robber, and the psychotic, simply denote criminality and wanton disregard. Certainly in the case of frontier lawmen, there would be nothing to write of and no captivation of the public's imagination if everyone they arrested meekly surrendered and was carted off to jail. The old saying "no news is good news," does not apply in a journalistic or historic context. From a practical perspective there is indeed enchantment and attraction attached with dramatic events, and tradition assuredly compels concentration on these rousing components when reporting on the lives of frontier peace officers. The story of Dan Tucker is no exception.

In making a dispassionate comparative analysis of Dan Tucker's stature as a Western gunman, and then undertaking the unavoidable, yet, understandable urge to rate and rank him against other gun-fighting masters, necessitates adoption of a single standard for reference. In this particular case study, Bill O'Neal's informative, authoritative, and easily accessible *Encyclopedia of Western Gunfighters* will serve as that standard.

In decisive efforts to "get it right," author O'Neal analytically subdivided violent gunfights into three distinct categories. From his compilation the following information may be gleaned concerning an individual shootist: the number of persons he killed; the number of gunfights he was actually involved in; and, the number of scenarios in which he was involved and possibly killed someone, or assisted someone else in killing their mutual adversary. In making assessment of Dan Tucker's entanglement in these types of scenarios, the standard of proof will simply be probable cause, that is, as legally defined, "reasonable grounds to believe."

As gentle reminder, review of Tucker's own one sentence statement to a frontier editor regarding the number of people he claimed to have killed is not inappropriate. On December 14, 1882, the Silver City *Enterprise* reported:

> Dan Tucker informs us that in the course of his duty as deputy sheriff he has been obliged to kill eight men in this county, besides several in Lincoln and Doña Ana counties, and the killing of Burns, in which he was implicated, was the first time he was ever put under bonds to await examination.

There is no record that Tucker killed anyone after making this simple yet intriguing declaration to the Silver City newsman, although he was not quite through with shoot-outs. Dan Tucker is laying claim to eight persons he *killed in the line of duty* as a deputy for Grant County. The reader must accept or reject Tucker's statement, but it does seem somewhat unreasonable to believe he knowingly fabricated a lie for a reporter whose next question could have very well been, "who have you been *obliged* to kill, and why were you *obliged* to kill them?" Simple logic would suggest the newsman already had those answers. There are, however, evidentiary pieces that can be utilized in reconciling Dan Tucker's tally book with collateral contemporary data.

The search for dead desperadoes in Lincoln and Doña Ana counties which can be credited to Tucker's account is still a mystery, and the search for clues has thus far proved futile. Hopefully, with publication of this narrative interest in Dan Tucker will be piqued, and additional evidence will come forth that may make the story whole.

For the purpose of tabulating Dan Tucker's scorecard, an abbreviated recap of those escapades punctuated by gunfire is revealing.

Possibly there were others, as will be later explored, but the first victim in this narrative to fall silent before Dan Tucker's smoking six-gun was Atanacio Bencomo, who resisted arrest and was shot by an apparently agitated deputy bent on making sure everyone knew he was going to maintain order. Bencomo's death at the hands of Tucker was reported in the Grant County *Herald*.

Dan Tucker's next gunplay was when he shot Fort Bayard soldier Tom Robinson in the hand. Certainly there is no reason to discount this newspaper report, which was penned by a former soldier who was personally acquainted with both Tucker and Robinson. The tally remains at one killed, but two instances of gunplay.

The next person to be "stopped by a ball from Tucker's pistol" was Juan Garcia, who had possibly lunged at Dan Tucker with a drawn knife, but who had definitely disemboweled Belmudes. The incident was covered by local news hounds, and was subsequently reported by "old-timers" who actually witnessed deputy Tucker in action on this occasion. Two killed. The third example of gunplay.

Seventeen months after our subject's second victim died, the Grant County *Herald* simply reported, Deputy Dan Tucker "charged with killing a man who resisted arrest" had a hearing and the death was ruled "justifiable homicide." The deceased was not named, but it is reasonable to believe that he was the frying pan throwing and rock chunking "Mexican who went haywire" as reported in several different accounts. Tucker tallied his third killing, and fourth shooting incident.

During December, 1879, Carpio Rodriquez, in the act of resisting lawful arrest, jerked his revolver and purposefully but foolishly slipped the hammer, firing at Dan Tucker, perforating only his clothing. The tally remains at three killed. The fifth involvement in a gunplay.

Historian David Johnson quoting the New Southwest and Grant County *Herald*, which was reporting what was becoming a familiar story, briefly acknowledges Deputy Dan Tucker's killing of Charley Hugo, "who had been deporting himself in a riotous manner and who resisted arrest." Deming outlaws surly took note. Four miscreants were now pushing up daisies thanks to Tucker, and for the sixth time he found himself involved in a shooting.

Once again at Deming, Deputy Dan Tucker boldly confronted five drunken soldiers stationed at Fort Cummings. And as reported in the New Southwest and Grant County *Herald*, one of the bluecoats unlimbered his long-barreled U. S. Army Colt and popped a cap just as Tucker grabbed for the weapon. The bullet missed, but flame from the exploding hog-leg seared his hands. Still four marks on the notch-stick. Seven instances of gunplay.

In Arizona Territory, at Benson, George Brown for whatever reason twice shoots and seriously wounds Dan Tucker, who got off two wild shots. The story was carried in the Tombstone *Epitaph* and mentioned in the El Paso *Lone Star*. Four sleeping in the pine box. Eight six-shooting nightmares.

Next, San Simon cowboy and ex-Texas Ranger Jim Bond, horseback and deep in his saddle, creates a row in front of, or by some accounts, actually inside the Harvey House Restaurant at the Deming depot. When Tucker attempts to make the arrest, Bond "monkey-fingers" his gun, and Dan blasts him out of the saddle with a charge of buckshot from a doubled-barreled scattergun. Numerous accounts attests to the validity of the basic story which quickly was embellished in the folkloric retelling. The new score, five killed, and the count jumps to nine recorded instances of gunplay.

Not yet quite through, deputy Dan Tucker, along with Silver City policeman Moore and Grant County deputy Billy McClellan, combine and shoot James Burns, sloshed in sour-mash, in an area saloon. Conformation abounds. Tucker's hard-core count remains at five criminals killed, but now he has assissted in the killing of a sixth.

Still later at Deming, Dan Tucker, intent on amorous adventure, tumbles into the quagmire of whorehouse intrigue. Customarily ready for trouble, but in this case taken unawares, Dan Tucker is forced to scrap tooth and nail, struggling for his life, finally busting loose with his six-shooter and slightly wounding a "fair Cyprian," before some man's bullet thuds into his shoulder and slams him to the floor. None were killed in the "Red-Light Shoot-out," but Tucker marked another shooting onto his tally page—the eleventh and the last—that we know of.

Subjecting the shooting synopsis to the standard of reasonable belief, the almost complete tabulation of Dan Tucker's shooting scrapes discloses that he killed five men in singular shoot-outs, assisted in killing another, and was personally involved in eleven shooting battles. The obvious question is, why do these figures not square with the eight in Grant County that Tucker claimed he was *obliged* to kill? Was Dan Tucker lying?

There is a reasonable explanation for the inconsistency, but it must be addressed in two-parts. First, when Dan Tucker assumed credit for killing eight men in Grant County it was at a time he was formally charged, along with others, of killing James Burns. Tucker was out on bail and thoroughly miffed that he had actually been required to post bond prior to the official examination, a legality invoked for the first time in regards to his killings—hence the interview. Tucker never denied he shot Burns. Dan Tucker, as nearly anyone would, simply acknowledged his part in the Burns killing, rationalizing, maybe with merit, that it was wholly justified. In Tucker's mind, Burn's name was added to the list of persons he had been obliged kill. He was making no distinction between kills and assists. Add one to the fatality column—new tally—six.

Secondly, as will be recalled, Dan Rose, a Silver City resident at the time, reported Tucker killed two horse thieves during a scorching shoot-out at an area saloon. There is absolutely no reason to discount Rose's account, but since it stood alone, unsupported by news accounts, it fell short of the discretionary inclusion on the tally-sheet made for the current analysis. Add these two deceased hombres to the scoreboard, as Dan Tucker probably did, and an assertion of eight killed in Grant County is reasonably reconciled.

There are other accounts that Tucker killed outlaws or livestock rustlers out in the field, absent any witnesses. If true, Dan Tucker could ill afford to publicly offer admissions to what might have been styled vigilante style justice to some, murder to others—and he didn't! These accounts were not addressed in this assessment of Dan Tucker's shooting engagements, not that they were erroneously false, but simply because the allegations failed to meet the test of reasonable belief minus supporting corroboration. True though the allegations may be, or perhaps not, the shrouded mystery only added to the Tucker mystique at the time.

Final conclusions must be left to the reader. Certainly, if Burn's name is transferred from the assist column to the confirmed killed column, six killings can be attributed to Tucker using the reasonable belief standard. Others could be added, dependent upon the weight given Tucker for truthfulness, and to the degree of credit given to selected contemporary commentators.

Dan Tucker had a demonstrated record as a Western gunman. This gives rise to the inescapable question, how would he have fared in a shoot-out with other well-known gunman of the frontier era? Although tempting, reality dictates the foolishness of concocting hypothetical gun-battles and warping factual variables to fit preconceived notions.

Conjecture as to what might have happened is best left to the novelists and scriptwriters.

There is, however, room for an appropriate comparison if the same standard is applicable to all players. In light of how some journalists have popularized certain frontier personalities, the comparison is interesting. How does Dan Tucker rank as a Western gunman?

Utilizing O'Neal's research as that standard offers some conclusions. Dan Tucker does not rank at the top with, say, Jim Miller who reportedly killed twelve men. But Miller was an outlaw, not a lawman. With the lower number of six authenticated killings, Dan Tucker rates in the same league with the more popularly known "Wild Bill" Hickok, Uncle John Selman, and Dallas Stoudenmire, just ahead of other notables like Billy the Kid and "Long-haired" Jim Courtright. Possibly surprising to some, would be the substantial gap between Dan Tucker's actual record and the much lower scores given such an extraordinary conglomerate of Westerners as "Doc" Holliday, Pat Garrett, Bat Masterson, and Wyatt Earp.

From what can be learned about Dan Tucker there seems a certain unjustness in not just accepting his word that he "killed eight men in Grant County, besides several others in Lincoln and Doña Anna counties." However, a pledge of reasonableness and historic constancy oblige mention of his claim, but for comparative purposes the lower number must be used in the absence of corroborative evidence. Were it not the case, Dan Tucker's name would be ratcheted even further forward on the roster reserved for legitimate Western gunmen. Good lawman, or bad, it is reasonable to avow that Dan Tucker was a frontier figure worthy of historic recognition.

How about Tucker's victims and opponents? Jim Bond was an ex-Texas Ranger, but the others had varying skills as gunmen and none were famous. Searching for truthful answers along this line of reasoning may prove strikingly insightful. Rare indeed are bona fide gunfights between combatants of national name. Contemporarily, if a frontier figure was willing, and did extinguish another human's existence, the act of killing itself was inversely worthy of notation. Not until the twentieth-century did the hustling up of Western champions peak, and journalists intent on commercialization well knew a hero needed a dragon to slay.

Despite commonly held perceptions, the victims at the "O. K. Corral," the McClaury brothers and young Billy Clanton, had never before even been arrested, much less involved in a shooting affray. And although most factual accounts concur that Tom McClaury was unarmed when he was killed, Wyatt Earp and his brothers are touted by many as premium examples of the gun-fighting frontier lawman. Leon Metz, however, hammers out historic truth, "...not one of the participants could boast a national reputation as a gunfighter..." And although it might shatter certain preconceived images, Joseph Rosa reminds the reader of reality, "Evenly matched opponents generally killed each other, but few gunfights took place between experts." That Billy the Kid was a killer is not subject to debate, but the efforts to justify his shooting of a local sheriff, while at the same time acknowledging he was hiding behind an adobe corral wall when he pulled the trigger, are diverting as well a deceptive. Who was Dave Tutt before "Wild Bill" Hickok made him a fatal footnote for history books? Notwithstanding screenplay suggestion and movie-made misnomer, biographer Jack Burrows illuminates the fact that an egregious outlaw named John Ringo killed but one person—himself!

The fact Dan Tucker killed is indisputable, and just as incontestable is recognition that his public condoned the virulent measures. Clearly Dan Tucker was the right man, at the right place, for the right time. Had he arrived on the scene twenty-years later, there seems little doubt his tendency to shoot first would have handicapped him with an enlightened populace. Had he tried the same techniques still later, he probably would have been imprisoned or hanged.

During the El Paso Salt War, when the Texas sheriff frantically sought aid from New Mexicans, Dan Tucker was presented with sterling opportunity to exhibit true Western gallantry, ethnocentric evenhandedness, and leadership. He failed in his executive ability to maintain discipline. No evidence has thus far been developed to document Dan Tucker personally participated in the "fearful excesses and felonies;" nevertheless, his captaincy carried unambiguous responsibility, and in meeting that challenge he fell far short of the mark. Had his career ended with this single tragic episode his place on parchment pages could insignificantly be stamped—"botched and bungled." But it didn't. There is no evidence to suggest Tucker ever sought or considered redemption for his actions, but his subsequent performance clearly demonstrated a commitment to lawfulness. In the end, the scales of justice are indisputably tilted in Tucker's favor.

Although not blessed with natural leadership genius, Dan Tucker staked out his enforcement domain, and then defended it with daring defiance and audacity. Whether any of this courage was derived from a pull on the bottle is guesswork, but unlike so many a Western "hero" who never fought unless surrounded by cronies, Tucker never depended on others to impregnate his reservoir of raw nerve. Dan Tucker can aptly be described as a *lone wolf*—fiercely independent, self-reliant, and dangerous.

That Dan Tucker sought pleasure with hard-drinkers, trollops, and gamblers is clear. Evidence suggests he could carouse, drink, gamble, and play in the same league with the best of em'—most of the time. Someone might even imply Dan Tucker was a "sporting man" due to an observable fondness for barrooms, bordellos asnd gambling tables, but in reality this proclivity was recreational rather than vocational.

Was Dan Tucker a hero? That question will have to be answered by the particular reader. Evidence does not indicate Tucker's positive entanglement in any spectacular historic happening of momentous proportion. Tucker simply did his job—everyday! But so did the soldiers, cowboys, merchants, miners, ranchers, railroaders, teamsters, doctors, newspapermen, lawyers, and—their wives and daughters. All made their mark!

Can we assess Dan Tucker's personal contributions to southwestern fact and folklore? The professional historian might with merit argue that Dan Tucker played but a minor role in the overall scheme of southwestern frontier development, while a cadre of grass-root historians, those specializing in biography of Western gunmen, might surrender to the temptation of seating Dan Tucker on an undeserved throne, along with a number of others whose primary fame is that they killed someone. Did Dan Tucker's fearsome reputation in and of itself serve as meaningful disincentive for bandits and outlaws? There is no statistical or other method to measure what didn't happen, therefore, that question is hard to answer. Throughout Dan Tucker's story are the acknowledged instances when deterrence as a crime prevention measure failed. These occurrences we have tallied. Taken as a whole, however, it is reasonable to say that Dan Tucker, while not always triumphant, added a much needed stabilizing presence during a dangerous and wearisome test of New Mexico Territory's resolve to carve "civilization" out of an untamed wilderness.

So then how should we best characterize Dan Tucker when appraising his effectiveness as a frontier lawman, or in passing judgment on his membership in the man-killing fraternity?

Simply this way: Dan Tucker was the "real deal!"

Silver City early 1890s. Broadway Street looking west. The Grant County Courthouse and jail is at the west end of Broadway. Courtesy Silver City Museum.

Silver City 1880. Intersection of Broadway and Main Street.The two-story Grant County Herald *office building shows over the tops of the other buildings and through the trees. The* Herald *documented portions of Dan Tucker's violent career.* Courtesy Silver City Museum.

Basement jail in the old Grant County Courthouse, built in 1883. Dan Tucker brought his prisoners here. Courtesy Silver City Museum.

Fort Bayard, New Mexico, circa 1885. Dan Tucker·had several confrontations with rowdy cavalry troopers in Grant County. Courtesy Silver City Museum.

Harvey Howard Whitehill, longtime sheriff of Grant County, New Mexico. He hired Dan Tucker as deputy sheriff in 1877. Courtesy Silver City Museum.

The hanging of Charles Williams and a black man named Gaines, near Silver City in the spring of 1880. Dan Tucker was the hangman. Courtesy Silver City Museum.

Centennial Saloon, Silver City, where Dan Tucker shot a drunken James Burns in August 1882. Courtesy Silver City Museum.

Palace Saloon, Central City, New Mexico. Like Dan Tucker, the men in the photo appear to be members of the "sporting crowd." Courtesy Silver City Museum.

The Silver City to Deming stage, here pictured at the northwest corner of Main and Broadway, 1882. Dan Tucker sometimes rode shotgun on this stage before the railroad rendered it obsolete. Courtesy Silver City Museum.

Judge Hamilton C. McComas. He is known in western history as the victim of the Apache Chato's raid; he also unsuccessfully prosecuted Dan Tucker for murder. Courtesy Silver City Museum

Deming, New Mexico, circa 1885. The building to the right of the Rialto is Dan Tucker's Eclipse Restaurant and Saloon. Courtesy Deming-Luna-Mimbres Museum.

Railroad Depot, Deming, New Mexico, where Dan Tucker, armed with a shotgun, shot Jim Bond off his horse. Courtesy Arizona Historical Society.

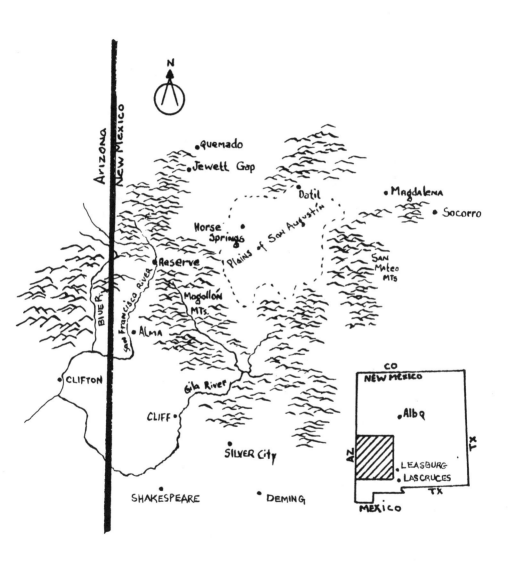

Non-Published Reports and Documents:

Pioneer Foundation Interviews, Zimmerman Library—Center for Southwest Research, University of New Mexico, Albuquerque.

Southwest Oral Histories, Western New Mexico University, Silver City.

The Letters of O. W. Williams. Center for American History, University of Texas. Austin.

Master's Thesis, Conrad Neagle, University of New Mexico. Albuquerque. 1943.

Audio Tapes of Pat Humble's public speaking engagements. 1983 and 1989.

Master's Thesis, Charles Ward, University of Texas. Austin. 1933.

Report of Adjutant General, State of Texas. 1878.

U. S. House of Representatives, Executive Document No. 93, 45th Congress, 2nd Session, 1878.

Muster and Payroll, Texas Rangers, Frontier Battalion, 1877-1878. Texas State Archives and Library Commission, Austin

Unpublished Typescript Edward Pennington's. Personal collection of Wayne B. Humphrey. Deming.

Unpublished Typescript H. E. Muse. Silver City Museum Archives. Silver City.

Unpublished Typescript David Truesdale Silver City Museum Archives. Silver City

Unpublished Typescript Dr. Jeffery Brown. Deming Luna Mimbres Museum Archives. Deming.

United States Census Records.

Grant County Commissioner's Minutes. Grant County Clerk. Silver City.

Grant County Probate Records. Grant County Clerk. Silver City.

Grant County Mining and Deed Records. Grant County Clerk. . Silver City

Journals & Periodicals:

Ball, Larry D. "Militia Posses: The Territorial Militia In Civil Law Enforcement in New Mexico Territory, 1877-1883," *New Mexico Historical Review*, Vol. 55, No. 1, Jan. 1980.

___. "Frontier Sheriffs At Work," *The Journal of Arizona History*, No. 27.

Bell, Bob Boze. "The Dark Side of Wyatt Earp," *True West*. Feb. 1999.

Blachly, Lou. "I'll Never Forget," A Silver City *Enterprise* series. Oct., Nov. and Dec. 1949. (interview of Wayne W. Whitehill.)

Daly, H. W. "The Geronimo Campaign," *Arizona Historical Review*, No. 3, July 1930.

DeArment, R. K. "Deadly Deputy," *True West*, November 1991.

Greever, William S. "Railway Development in the Southwest," *New Mexico Historical Review*, Vol. 32. 1957.

Gustafson, C. A. "Dan Tucker, Deming's Lethal Lawman," *Destination Deming, 1999 Luna County Visitors Guide.*

Hill, Janaloo. "The Sad Fate of Russian Bill. Why Was He Hanged?"

___. "Yours Until Death, William Grounds," *True West*, April 1973.

Hill, Rita. "Mysteries Set With Diamonds," *True West*, September-October, 1980.

Hornung, Chuck. "Wyatt Earp's New Mexico Adventure, *Old West*, Summer 1999.

___. "Wyatt Earp and Doc Holliday in Las Vegas, New Mexico," *True West*, May 1999.

Humble, Terrence M. "The Pinder-Slip Mining Claim Dispute of Santa Rita, New Mexico, 1881-1912. *Mining History Journal.* 1996

Jordan, Philip D. "The Town Marshal: Local Arm of the Law," *Arizona and the West*, 16.

Kildare, Maurice. "Saga of the Gallant Sheriff," *The West*, August. 1968.

Marsan, Joan. "Shakespeare—The Town That Refuses To Give Up The Ghost," *New Mexico Magazine*, February 1998.

Metz, Leon C. "Gunslingers And The Art of Gunfighting," *Wild West*. April 1998.

Meyers, Lee. "Military Establishments in Southwestern New Mexico: Stepping Stones to Settlement," *New Mexico Historical Review*. XLIII: 1, 1968.

Muir, Emma M. "The First Militia," *New Mexico Magazine*, October, 1952.

___. "The Stage to Shakespeare," *New Mexico Magazine*, July 1948.

___. "The Great Diamond Swindle," *New Mexico Magazine*, August 1948.

___. "Bonanza Days at Shakespeare," *New Mexico Magazine*, September 1948.

___. "Shakespeare Becomes a Ghost Town," *New Mexico Magazine*, October 1948.

Mullin, Robert N. "Here Lies John Kinney," *Journal of Arizona History*, No. 14, Autumn 1973.

Naegle, Conrad K. "The Rebellion of Grant County, New Mexico in 1876," *Arizona and the West*, No. 10, Autumn 1968.

Nolan, Fredrick. "Boss Rustler—The Life and Crimes of John Kinney," *True West*, September and October 1996.

___. "The Horse Thief War," *Old West*, Summer 1994.

Phelps, Frederick. "Frederick E. Phelps: A Soldier's Memoirs," *New Mexico Historical Review* {edited by Frank D. Reeve}.

Rasch, Phillip J. "Six Shooter and Three Shooter Smith," *Quarterly of the National Association and Center for Outlaw and Lawman History*. Vol. IX, Number 4, Spring. 1985.

Roberts, Gary L. "The Fremont Street Fiasco," *True West*. July 1988.

Russell, Sharman. "Russian Bill: the True Story of an Outlaw," *Journal of the West*, 23, April 1984.

Theisen, Lee Scott {Editor}. "Frank Warner Angel's Notes on New Mexico Territory," *Arizona and the West*, 18, Winter 1976.

Thrapp, Dan. "Shakespeare's Lively Ghosts," *Westways*, March 1961.

Wallace, William S. "Stagecoaching in Territorial New Mexico," *New Mexico Historical Review*, Vol. XXXII, 1957.
Wallace, W. Swilling. "Short-line Staging in New Mexico," *New Mexico Historical Review*, Vol. XXVI, No. 2, April 1951.
White, Marjorie. "Stage Stop," *Frontier Times*, April-May 1964.

Books:

Adams, Ramon F. *Six-Guns and Saddle Leather*. Dover Publications Inc. Mineola. New York. 1998.
Ailman, H. B. *Pioneering in Territorial Silver City*. University of New Mexico Press. Albuquerque. 1983. {Lundwall, Helen J., editor}.
Austerman, Wayne. *Sharps Rifles and Spanish Mules, The San Antonio—El Paso Mail, 1851-1881*. Texas A & M University. College Station. 1985.
Bailey, Lynn R. *Bisbee—Queen of the Copper Camps*. Westernlore Press. Tucson. 1983.
Ball, Larry D. *The United States Marshals of New Mexico & Arizona Territories 1846-1912*. University of New Mexico Press. Albuquerque. 1978.
___. *Desert Lawmen—The High Sheriffs of New Mexico and Arizona 1846-1912*. University of New Mexico Press. Albuquerque. 1992.
Barnes, Will C. *Arizona Place Names*. University of Arizona. Tucson. 1988.
Bartholomew, Ed. *Wyatt Earp, The Man and The Myth*. Frontier Book Company, Toyahvale, Texas. 1964.
___. *Western Hard-Cases or, Gunfighters Named Smith*. Frontier Book Company, Ruidoso. 1960.
Berry, Susan and Sharman Apt Russell. *Built to Last, An Architectural History Of Silver City, New Mexico*. Silver City Museum Society. Silver City. 1995.
Billington, Monroe. *New Mexico's Buffalo Soldiers, 1866-1900*. University Press of Colorado. Niwot, Colorado. 1991.
Bourke, John G. *On The Border With Crook*. Charles Scribner's Sons. New York. 1891.
Boyd, Frances A. *Cavalry Life in Tent and Field*. University of Nebraska Press. Lincoln. 1982.
Breakenridge, Wm. {edited by Brown, Richard M.}. *Helldorado, Bringing Law to the Mesquite*. R. R. Donnelley & Sons Co., Chicago. 1982.
Boyer, Glenn G. *Wyatt Earp—Family, Friends & Foes*. Historical Research Assc., Rodeo, New Mexico. 1997.
Bronson, Edgar B. *The Red Blooded Heroes of the Frontier*. Grosset & Dunlap. New York. 1910.
Brown, Clara S. *Tombstone from a Woman's Point of View*. Westernlore Press. Tucson. 1998. {Bailey, Lynn R., editor}
Brown, Richard M. *No Duty To Retreat—Violence and Values in American History and Society*. University of Oklahoma Press. Norman and Lincoln. 1994.

{Editor}. *Helldorado, Bringing Law to the Mesquite.* The Lakeside Press. R. R. Donnelley & Sons Co. Chicago. 1982.

Burrows, Jack. *John Ringo—The Gunfighter Who Never Was.* The University of Arizona. Tucson. 1987.

Casey, Robert J. *The Texas Border and Some Borderliners.* Bobbs-Merrill Co. Inc. New York. 1950.

Cashion, Ty. *A Texas Frontier—The Clear Fork Country and Fort Griffin, 1849-1887.* University of Oklahoma Press. Norman. 1996.

Chaput, Don. *Dr. Goodfellow, Physician to the Gunfighters, Scholars, And Bon Vivant.* Westernlore Press. Tucson. 1996.

Chase, C. M. *The Editor's Run in New Mexico and Colorado.* Frontier Book Co., Fort Davis, Texas. 1968.

Clum, John. *Apache Days and Tombstone Nights—John Clum's Autobiography.* High-Lonesome Books. Silver City. 1997. {Carmony, Neil B., editor}.

Clum, Woodworth. *Apache Agent, The Story of John P. Clum.* The University of Nebraska Press. Lincoln. 1936.

Cook, James H. *Fifty Years on the Old Frontier.* University of Oklahoma. Norman. 1980.

Cunningham, Eugene. *Triggernometry—A Gallery of Gunfighters.* The Caxton Printers, Ltd. Caldwell, Idaho. 1941.

DeArment Robert K. *Knights of the Green Cloth, The Saga of the Frontier Gamblers.* University of Oklahoma Press. Norman. 1982.

George Scarborough. *The Life and Death of a Lawman on the Closing Frontier.* University of Oklahoma Press. Norman. 1992.

Dillon, Richard. *Wells, Fargo Detective, A Biography of James B. Hume,* University of Nevada Press. Reno. 1986.

Dixon, David. *Hero of Beecher Island—The Life and Military Career of George A. Forsyth.*

Dodge, Fred. {edited by Lake, Carolyn}. *Under Cover for Wells Fargo.* University of Oklahoma Press. Norman. 1998 (Reprint)

Douglas, C. L. *Famous Texas Feuds.* State House Press. Austin. 1988.

Dykes, J. C. with Kemp, Ben W. *Cow Dust and Saddle Leather.* University of Oklahoma. Norman. 1968.

Edwards, Harold L. *Goodbye Billy the Kid.* Creative Publishing. College Station 1995.

Erwin, Richard. *The Truth About Wyatt Earp.* The O. K. Press. Carpinteria. CA. 1993.

Ferris, Robert G. {Editor}. *Soldier and Brave—Historical Places Associated With Indian Affairs and the Indian Wars in the Trans-Mississippi West.* National Park Service. Washington, D. C. 1971.

Fjestad, S. P. *Blue Book of Gun Values.* Blue Book Publications, Minneapolis. 1998

Frazer, Robert W. *Forts of the West—Military Forts and Presidios and Posts Commonly Called Forts West of the Mississippi River to 1898.* University of Oklahoma Press. Norman and London. 1972.

French, William. *Recollections of a Western Ranchman.* High-Lonesome Books. Silver City. 1997.

Gatto, Steve. *Wyatt Earp—A Biography of a Western Lawman.* San Simon Publishing Co. Tucson. 1997.

Gibson, A. M. *The Life and Death of Colonel Albert Jennings Fountain.* University of Oklahoma Press. Norman. 1986.

Giese, Dale F. *Forts of New Mexico.* Phelps Dodge Corporation. Silver City. 1995.

Gillett, James B. *Six Years With the Texas Rangers—1875 to 1881.* University of Nebraska Press. Lincoln and London. 1976.

Hand, George. *Whiskey, Six-guns & Red-light Ladies, George Hand's Saloon Diary, Tucson, 1875-1878.* High-Lonsesome Books. Silver City. 1994. {Carmony, Neil, editor}

Harkey, Dee. *Mean As Hell, The Life of a New Mexico Lawman.* Ancient City Press. Santa Fe. 1989.

Hertzog, Peter. *Outlaws of New Mexico.* Sunstone Press. Santa Fe. 1984.

Hill, Rita & Janaloo. *Shakespear Cemetery—Resting Place of our Pioneers. Privately Published.* Lordsburg, NM, no date.

Hillard, George. *Adios Hachita—Stories of a New Mexico Town.* High-Lonesome Books. Silver City. 1998.

Hoover, H. A. *Tales From The Bloated Goat—Early Days in Mogollon.* Texas Western Press. High-Lonesome Books reprint. Silver City. 1995.

Horan, James D. *The Gunfighters.* Gramercy Books. New York. 1994,

Horgan, Paul. *Great River—The Rio Grande in North American History.* Two Volumes. Rinehart & Company, Inc. New York. 1954.

Johnson, David. *John Ringo.* Barbed Wire Press. Stillwater. 1996.

Jones, Fayette A. *New Mexico Mines and Minterals.* The New Mexican Printing Co. 1904.

Julyan, Robert. *The Place Names of New Mexico.* University of New Mexico Press. Albuquerque. 1996.

Kemp, Ben W. with Dykes, J. C. *Cow Dust and Saddle Leather.* University of Oklahoma. Norman 1968.

Keleher, William A. *The Fabulous Frontier.* Rydal Press. Santa Fe. 1946.

Knopsnyder, Karen. *At the Foot of the Mountains, A History of Patton State Hospital.* Publisher not listed. Circa 1984.

L'Aloge, Bob. *Riders Along the Rio Grande.* RCS Press. Distributed By Yucca Tree Press. Las Cruces. 1992.

___. *Knights of the Sixgun.* Yucca Tree Press. Las Cruces. 1991.

Lavash, Donald R. *Wilson & The Kid.* Early West. College Station. 1990.

Leckie. *The Buffalo Soldiers, A Narrative of the Negro Cavalry In The West.* University of Oklahoma. Norman. 1967.

Lekson, Stephen H. *Nana's Raid—Apache Warfare in Southern New Mexico, 1881.* Texas Western Press. El Paso. 1987.

Lummis, Charles. *Dateline Fort Bowie.* University of Oklahoma Press. Norman. 1979. {Thrapp, Dan L., editor}.

Luna County. *The History of Luna County.* Luna County Historical Society, Inc. Deming, NM. 1978.

McDaniel, Ruel. *Vinegarroon—The Saga of Judge Roy Bean,"Law West of The Pecos."* Southern Publishers. Kingsport, TN. 1936.

McGaw, Wm. C. *Savage Scene, The Life and Times of Jsmes Kirker.* Hastings House. NY. 1972.

McKanna Jr., Clare. *Homicide, Race, and Justice in the American West, 1880-1920.* University of Arizona Press. Tucson. 1997.

McKenna, James. *Black Range Tales*, Rio Grande Press. Glorieta. 1936.

Marks, Paula M. *And Die in the West.* William Morrow. New York. 1989.

Martin, Douglas. *Tombstone's Epitaph.* University of New Mexico Press. Albuquerque. 1951.

Matthews, Sallie R. *Interwoven, A Pioneer Chronicle.* Texas A & M Press. College Station. 1936.

Metz, Leon C. Border, *The U. S.-Mexico Line.* Mangan Books. El Paso. 1989.

___. *The Shooters.* Mangan Books. El Paso. 1976.

___. *John Wesley Hardin—Dark Angel of Texas.* Mangan Books. El Paso. 1996.

___. *Pat Garrett—The Story of a Western Lawman.* University of Oklahoma Press. Norman. 1974.

Miller, Darlis A. *Soldiers and Settlers, Military Supply in the Southwest 1861-1885.* University of New Mexico Press. Albuquerque. 1989.

Miller, Nyle H. with Joseph W. Snell. *Great Gunfighters of the Kansas Cowtowns, 1867-1886.* University of Nebraska. Lincoln. 1963.

Moore, John M. *Moore's Who is Who in New Mexico.* Moore's Who is Who Publications. Los Angles. 1962.

Myres, S. D, {editor}. *Pioneer Surveyor—Frontier Lawyer, the Personal Narrative of O. W. Williams, 1877-1902.* Texas Western College Press. El Paso. 1966.

Myrick, David. F. *New Mexico's Railroads, A Historical Survey.* University Of New Mexico Press. Albuquerque. 1970.

Mullane, William H. {Editor}. *This Is Silver City, 1888, 1889, 1890—Volume III.* Silver City *Enterprise.* Silver City. 1965

___. *Indian Raids as Reported in the Silver City Enterprise, 1882-1886.* Silver City *Enterprise.* Silver City. 1968.

Nash, Jay Robert. *Encyclopedia of Western Lawmen & Outlaws.* Da Capo Press. New York 1994.

Nelson, Susan & Ed. *The Silver City Book I, "Wild and Wooly Days."* Silver Star Publications. Silver City. 1978.

Nolan, Frederick. *The Lincoln County War—A Documentary History.* University of Oklahoma. Norman and London. 1992.

___. *The West of Billy the Kid*. University of Oklahoma Press. Norman 1998.

O'Neal, Bill. *Encyclopedia of Western Gun-Fighters*. University Of Oklahoma Press. Norman. 1979.

___. *Fighting Men of the Indian Wars*. Barbed Wire Press. Stillwater. 1991.

Prassel, Frank R. *The Western Peace Officer—A Legacy of Law and Order*. University of Oklahoma Press. Norman. 1981.

Price, Paxton P. *Pioneers of the Mesilla Valley*. Yucca Tree Press, Las Cruces. 1995.

Raht, Carlysle G. *The Romance of Davis Mountains and Big Bend Country*. The Rahtbooks Company. Odessa. 1963.

Raine, Wm. M. *Famous Sheriffs & Western Outlaws*. Garden City Publishing Co. New York. 1929.

Rasch, Phillip J. *Trailing Billy the Kid*. Outlaw-Lawman Research Series published for National Association for Outlaw and Lawman History in Affiliation with the University of Wyoming. Laramie. 1995. A collection of articles.

___. *Gunsmoke In Lincoln County*. Outlaw-Lawman Research Series published for National Association for Outlaw and Lawman History in Affiliation with the University of Wyoming. Laramie. 1997. A Collection of articles.

___. *Warriors of Lincoln County*. Outlaw-Lawman Research Series published for National Association for Outlaw and Lawman History in Affiliation with the University of Wyoming. Laramie. 1998. A collection of articles.

Rister, Carl Coke. *Fort Griffin—On The Texas Frontier*. University of Oklahoma Press. Norman. 1956.

Robinson III, Chas. *The Frontier World of Fort Griffin*. Arthur Clark Co. Spokane. 1992.

Rosa, Joseph G. *The Gunfighter—Man or Myth?*. University of Oklahoma Press, Norman. 1982.

Rose, Cynthia. *Lottie Deno—Gambling Queen of Hearts*. Clear Light Publishing. Santa Fe. 1994.

Russell, Sharman A. and Susan Berry. *Built to Last, An Architectural History of Silver City New Mexico*. Silver City Museum Society. Silver City. 1995.

Sherman, James E. and Barbara H. *Ghost Towns and Mining Camps of New Mexico*. University of Oklahoma Press. Norman. 1975.

Simmons, Marc. *Massacre on the Lordsburg Road*. Texas A & M University Press, College Station. 1997.

___. *Ranchers, Ramblers and Renegades*. Ancient City Press. Santa Fe. 1984.

Sonnichsen, C. L. *The Story of Roy Bean, Law West of the Pecos*. The Devin-Adair Company. New York. 1958.

___. *The El Paso Salt War*, Carl Hertzog and the Texas Western Press, El Paso. 1961.

___. *Tularosa—Last of the Frontier West*. University of New Mexico Press edition. Albuquerque. 1980.

Stanley, F. *Longhair Jim Courtright—Two Gun Marshal of Fort Worth*. World Press, Inc., Denver. 1957.

___. *The Shakespeare New Mexico Story.* Albuquerque. Oct. 1961.

___. *The Deming New Mexico Story.* Pantex, Texas. Oct. 1962.

Tanner, Karen. *Doc Holliday, A Family Portrait.* University of Oklahoma Press. Norman. 1998.

Tefertiller, Casey. *Wyatt Earp—The Life Behind the Legend.* John Wiley and Sons. New York and world wide. 1997.

Thrapp, Dan L. *Encyclopedia of Frontier Biography.* Three volumes. University of Nebraska Press. Lincoln and London. 1988.

___. *The Conquest of Apacheria.* University of Oklahoma Press. Norman. 1967.

Unger, Patti, {editor}. *True Tales.* Volume One—Articles Originally Published In the Silver City *Enterprise.* SunDog Publishing. Silver City. 1991.

Ungnade, Herbert E. *Guide to the New Mexico Mountains.* University of New Mexico Press. Albuquerque. Tenth edition. 1995.

Webb, Walter P. *The Texas Rangers—A Century of Frontier Defense.* University of Texas Press, Austin. 1965.

Weddle, Jerry. *Antrim is My Stepfather's Name.* The Arizona Historical Society. Tucson. 1993.

Wilkins, Frederick. *The Law Comes to Texas, The Texas Rangers, 1870—1901.* State House Press. Austin. 1999.

Williams, O. W. *Pioneer Surveyor—Frontier Lawyer, The Personal Narrative of O. W. Williams, 1877-1902.* Texas Western College Press. El Paso. 1966.

Woodard, Bruce A. *Diamonds in the Salt.* Pruett Press. Boulder. 1967.

Worcester, Donald. *The Apaches—Eagles of the Southwest.* University Of Oklahoma Press. Norman. 1979.

Newspapers:

El Paso *Daily Times*

Deming *Headlight*

Southwest Sentinel

El Paso *Lone Star*

Lordsburg *Liberal*

Silver City *Tribune*

Galveston *Daily News*

Silver City *Independent*

The Daily Southwest

Las Vegas *Optic*

Silver City *Enterprise*

Mesilla *Independent*

Las Vegas *Gazette*

Grant County *Herald*

Santa Fe *New Mexican*

Las Cruces *Borderer*

Tombstone *Epitaph*

Rio Grande Republican

Wichita *Daily Eagle*

New Southwest & Grant Co. Herald

Allard, J. S., 137
Antrim, Joe, 120
Antrim, William, "Billy the Kid", 19, 120
Ascension, Mexico, 14
Atkinson, John, 38, 41
Bailey, J. C., 119, 128, 134
Barncastle, John D., 104
Barnes, Johnny, 54
Baxter, Dan, 137-138
Bean, Roy, 25, 32, 151
Bean, Samuel G., 25, 32
Behan, John Harris, 62, 128
Belmudes, 28-29, 164
Belt, D. L., "Doc", 107, 114, 130
Bencomo, Atanacio, 25, 164
Benson, Arizona, 78, 88, 105, 136, 156, 165
Bernal, Juan, 116
Biddle, Nicholas, 102
Bisbee, Arizona, 82, 127-130, 133
Black, J. F., 116
Black Range, 58, 79, 104
Black, Robert, "Arkansas,", 54
Blacker, A. (Judge), 41
Bledsoe, R., 130
Bond, Jim, 81, 86-88, 91, 95, 162, 165, 167, 177
Bon Ton Saloon, 127
Borajo, Antonio (Father), 37, 38
Bowe, Thomas, 28, 33
Bowman, Jim, "Cherokee", 60, 68, 145
Bright, Joseph, 39, 127
Bristol, Warren (Judge), 99, 103, 107, 113, 120
Broadway Restaurant, 94, 106
Brocius, William "Curly Bill", 54
Brown, George, 78-79, 88, 95, 105, 162, 165
Brown, Thomas, 143
Bryant, Sy, 128, 139
Bulzebuh Mine, 57
Burns, Edward, "Big Ed", 72, 73

Burns, James, 98-103, 106, 107, 110-112, 118, 150, 163, 165-166
Burro Mountains, 52, 65, 68, 98, 110
Caballero, Jose, 116
Cadena, Antonio, 40
Calhoun, R. N., 24
Campbell, I. F., 39
Campbell, J. W., 39
Candelario, Pedro, 41
Cantley, F. C., 131
Cardis, Louis, 37
Carlisle Mountains, 52
Carrolla, Jose M., "Portuguese Joe", 24, 31
Carson, Christopher, "Kit", 21
Cartwright, Frank, 116
Cauelario, Pedro, 40
Centennial Saloon, 88, 98, 99, 101, 173
Central City, New Mexico, 27, 28, 33, 57, 100-103, 110, 145, 174
Chandler's Milk Ranch, 55
Chato, 175
Chavez, Carlos, 131
Chihuahuan Desert, 21
Cherry Creek, Colorado, 12
Clancey, William, 127
Clanton, Billy, 54, 92, 167
Cleveland, George Washington, 126, 131, 133
Cleveland, Grover (President), 139
Clifton, Arizona, 116, 130
Comerford, J. E., 101
Comfort, R. E., 97
Cooke Springs, 77
Coomer, Dan, 52
Cooper, Price, 39
Copper Queen Mine, 127-128
Cortez, Placido, 26
Cottonwood Ranch, 115
Coyne, Tom, "Tomcat", 117
Cow Springs, 24, 32
Crane, James "Slim Jim", 54, 65

Crocker, Charles, 70, 80
Cubero, Mariano, 116
Cubero, Nester, 116
Daniels, Billy, 128, 130
Davenport, Millie, 145
Delaney, William, 128, 130, 133
Deming, Mary Anne, 70
Deming, New Mexico, 63, 70-71, 73-
    112, 117-165, 176, 177
Deno, Lottie (Charlotte Thurmond), 49,
    63, 106, 112
Dillard, William, 117
Dodge, Fred, 62, 128-129, 134, 161
Doña Ana County, New Mexico, 25,
    103-105, 114, 144, 163-164
Dowd, Dan, "Big Dan", 128, 130, 133-
    134
Dragoon Mountains, 92
Duck Creek, 126
Durand, Santiago, 39
Dwenger, William "Billy", 49-50, 68,
    97, 104
Dwenger, Dora, 49-50
Dwenger, H. F., 49-50
Earp, Virgil, 92-96
Earp, Wyatt, 5, 7-8, 16, 62, 79, 92-96,
    108-109, 167
Easton, David M., 104
Eaton, A. C., 125, 132
Eclipse Barroom, 136, 176
Edmunds Act, 140
Elephant Corral, 13, 94, 131
Ellis, Charles, 38
El Paso County, Texas, 35-43
El Paso Salt War, 4, 35, 44, 168
Ely, C. B., 102
Emmett, Dan, 8
Erskine, John, 114
Evans, Jessie, 11
Fambo, "Happy Bob", 54, 56
Ferguson, Robert, 132
Fleming, Jack, 138
Fleming, New Mexico, 138
Florida Mountains, 70, 79, 137, 141

Fort Bayard, New Mexico, 27-28, 33,
    58, 77, 114, 131, 164, 171
Fort Cummings, New Mexico, 57, 77-
    78, 82, 94-95, 136, 142, 165
Fort Griffin, Texas, 48-49, 63
Fort Selden, New Mexico, 10-11, 17,
    18
Fort Wayne, Indiana, 50
Fountain, Albert Jennings, 74, 99, 112,
    115-117
Franklin, Texas, 38, 44
Gage, New Mexico, 58, 124, 126, 131,
    132
Gaines, Louis, 58-59, 67, 173
Garcia, Juan, 28-29, 33, 50, 164
Garrett, Pat, 5, 15, 76, 104-105, 167
Garrison, U. C., 61
Georgetown, New Mexico, 49, 58, 60,
    67, 68
Gila River, 31, 116, 132
Gilmo, John W., 98, 101, 110, 133,
    150
Gilpin, G. D., "Doc", 121, 130, 144
Goldwater & Castaneda Store, 127
Goodfellow, George, M.D., 106, 130
Gordon, Carl, 62
Graham, William, 141-142, 147
Grant Hotel, 84, 86
Grant County Cattlemen's Association,
    144, 146
Grant County, New Mexico, 6, 12-19,
    24-32, 43, 48, 52-60, 75-80, 88,
    97, 104-117, 125
Grant County Townsite Company, 97,
    110
Graves, P. B., 56
Great Diamond Hoax, 53, 65
Grounds, William, "Billy the Kid", 54-
    55, 66
Hadden, R., 130
Hanover Mine, 49
Hanson, Joe, 114
Hardin, John Wesley, "Little
    Arkansas", 5-6, 15, 144
Harkey, Dee, 62, 141

Harlan, John Jefferson, "Off Wheeler",
    73
Harris, Len, 125
Harvey, H. H., 41
Hatch, Robert, "Bob", 92
Head, Harry, 54, 65
Heith, John, 128, 130
Henry, Joe, 138
Hickok, William Butler, "Wild Bill", 5,
    167, 168
Higbie, Rufus B., 97
Hill, Joe, 54
Hillsboro, New Mexico, 57, 104, 132,
    154
Hines, "Doc", 151
Hodgkins, Thomas, 132
Holguin, Gregorio, 40
Holliday, John Henry, "Doc", 16, 94-
    95, 108-109, 167
Horn, George, 119
Horse Springs, 127, 133
Howard, Charles (Judge), 36-41
Howard, James, "Tex", 128, 130
Howlett, Richard, 14, 28
Hubbard, R. B. (Governor of Texas),
    37, 42, 44
Hudson, Richard, "Dick", 95, 144
Hughes, Jim, "Sweetheart of the San
    Simon", 54, 65, 114, 117
Hughes, John, "Border Boss", 163
Hugo, Charley, 76, 165
Hume, James B., 125, 129, 133-134
Hunt, Zwing, 54-55
Hunter, James, 138
Irwin, Matt, 117
Johnson, F., 40
Jones, A. T. (Mrs.), 120
Jones, John B., 38, 40-46
Jornada del Muerto, 8-18, 103
Josanie, 141-142, 147
Joy, Christopher, "Kit", 126-127, 131-
    135
Kane, "Doc", 118-125
Kelly, Daniel, "York", 128-130, 133-
    134

Kerber, Charles, 37-46
Kendrick, W. T., 99
King, Sandy, "Red Curley", 54, 83-86,
    89-90, 95
Kingston, New Mexico, 104, 118
Kinney, John, 11, 37-46, 103, 114-118,
    121-122, 152-153
Kinney, Tom, 116-117
Kirker, James, 21
Krigbaum, James, 127-128
La Cienega de San Vicente (the
    marshes of St. Vicente), 21
Lafferr, Joseph N., 131, 135
Laird, Andrew B., 112-113, 146, 152-
    155
Lake Valley, New Mexico, 109, 114-
    117, 121, 143, 148
Las Cruces, New Mexico, 10-11, 32,
    74, 106, 114, 117, 153
Las Vegas, New Mexico, 48, 107
Lea, Adolph,, 10-13, 17, 103
Leadville, Colorado, 12
Leasburg, New Mexico, 10, 103
Lee, A. Mitchell, "Mitch", 126-127,
    131-132
Leland, Bill, (Butch Hill), 117
Leonard, Billy, 54, 65
Lincoln County, New Mexico, 31, 76,
    114
Lockhart, Willie, 143
Logne, H. A., 130
Longbaugh, Harry, "Sundance Kid", 8
Lordsburg, New Mexico, 53, 117, 132,
    134, 149, 153, 155-156, 159
Lowenstein, Moritz, 40
McBride, John, 38, 41
McComas, H. C., 99, 175
McClellan, William, "Billy", 98-103,
    106, 107, 110-111, 165
McDaniels, Jim, 11
McIntosh, Charles, 12, 18-19
McLaury, Frank, 54
McLaury, Tom, 54
McVeigh, William , 149
Maese, Leonardo, 116

Maricopa, Arizona, 76
Marriage, Ed, 129, 134
Martin, Jack, "King of the Jornada", 11
Martin, "Wild Bill", 24, 31
Martinez, Romulo, 62, 139, 140
Masterson, Bat, 16, 143, 156, 167
Mesilla, New Mexico, 10, 31, 36, 43, 74, 103, 114
Miller, J. P., 40
Miller, James, "Deacon Jim", 7, 163, 167
Mills, J. H., 47
Mimbres Junction, 70-71, 73
Mimbres River, 57-58
Minas Prietas, Sonora, 130
Mogollon Mountains, 17, 21
Montenegro, Gaspar, 116
Moore, G. W., 98-106, 110-111, 165
Mortimer, C. E., 38
Mollitor, F. W., 56, 58, 66
Munson, C. H., 101
Muse, H. E., 130
Musgrave, D. L., 151
Nelson, Bob, 24, 31, 58
Nolly, J. A., 127, 134
North, Thomas, 124
Nunez, Mariana, 40
Nutt Station, 95, 109, 117
Old Man Mine, 138
Orr, John, 24, 31
O'Connell, James, 138
O'Donnell, P. J., 145-146, 153
O'Tool, Barney, 58, 67, 173
Ownby, Anna, 84, 89
Ownby, Bramble B., 85
Pardu, Luben, 128
Parker, George, 60
Parlor Saloon, 138
Paschal, New Mexico, 98, 100-101, 110-111
Pattie, James, 21
Pattie, Sylvester, 21
Patton State Hospital, 157
Pedraza, Egenio, 116

Pennington, Edward, 70, 73, 80, 144, 158
Penrose, New Mexico, 138
Perkins, W. K., M. D., 125
Perry, John, 24
Phillips, William, "Hurricane Bill", 117
Pinos Altos, New Mexico, 27
Point of Rocks, New Mexico, 8, 10-13, 16-17
Posey, G. G., 99, 103
Prescott, Arizona, 22
Price, Anthony, "One Arm", 73-74
Price, J. E., 58
Proctor & Byron, 97
Pyramid Mountains, 54, 65
Rafferty, Patrick, 60
Ray, Charles, "Pony Diehl", "Pony Deal", 11, 54
Reese, Bob, 117
Reynolds, John, 128
Rincon, New Mexico, 74, 95, 114-116, 118, 121, 152
Ringo, John, 54, 168
Rio Grande River, 35, 42, 95, 114
Roberts, Annie, 127
Roberts, Charley, 144
Robidoux, Michel, 21
Robinson, Tom, 27, 33, 164
Rodriquez, Carpio, 53, 164
Roxy Jay Saloon, 54, 56
Rubio, Toribio G., 40
Runge, Louis, 143
Russell Gulch, Colorado, 12
Rutland, Jack, 84-85, 90
Sains, Doroteo "Tiger", 116
Salazar, Franscisco, 116
Sample, Owen W., "Red", 128, 130, 133, 134
San Antonio, Texas, 48-49
San Bernardino, California , 156-157, 159
San Francisco River, 127
Sanches, Victoriano, 118

Santa Fe Railroad, 36, 70, 108, 109, 114, 129
Santa Rita del Cobre, 21, 32, 106
Santa Rita Mountains, 27, 52
Scarborough, George A., 143-144, 146
Schaefer, George, "Sombrero Jack", 13
Scott, Thomas, 124
Selden, Henry R., 10
Selman, John, "Uncle John", 144, 146, 167
Separ, New Mexico, 85
Shakespeare, New Mexico, 53-58, 63-66, 83-86, 89-91, 96, 116, 155
Shannon, John, 118
Sheldon, Lionel (Governor), 104, 115, 121, 153
Sierra County, New Mexico, 19, 132, 143, 148, 154
Sierra, Margarito, 117
Sierra Mining Company, 116
Silver City, New Mexico, 4, 8-10, 12-14, 21-30, 35, 37-42, 47-52, 55-61, 70-71, 74-76, 88, 93-95, 97-98, 100, 102-107, 116, 119-120, 125-126, 129-130, 132, 137-138, 142-143, 145, 150, 155-156, 160, 170, 173
Silver City, Deming & Pacific Railroad, 119
Small, Charley, 150-151
Smith, "Bean Belly", 54
Smith, Charlie, "Hairlip Charlie", 139
Smith, James W., "Six-Shooter", 73-75, 80
Smith, Tom, 127
Socorro, New Mexico, 115, 126, 133, 144, 147
Southern Pacific Railroad, 70, 80, 124, 125, 127, 129, 132, 134, 142, 150, 158
Spear, George, 28
Spence, Pete, 92
Spencer, Charles, 131, 135
Stillman, Horace C., 128
Stilwell, Frank, 92

Stine, Edmund, 40
Stoudenmire, Dallas, 167
Sun, Charlie, 13
Swan, W. O., 132
Sycamore Creek, 24, 31
Tabler, Richard, "Three-Finger Dick", 118
Taggart, Frank, 126, 131-133
Tait, B. W., 120
Tappiner, John, 127
Tays, J. B., 38-41, 43-46
Telles, Jesús, 40
Telles, Salome, 40
Tettenborn, William, "Russian Bill", 54, 83-86, 89-90
Thorn, Miss, 120
Thurman, Dave, 154
Thurmond, Charlotte, see Lottie Deno
Thurmond, Frank, 49, 63, 99, 102, 106, 110, 112, 137-138, 146
Tombstone, Arizona, 48, 55, 62, 79, 92, 93, 128-130, 138-139, 150, 160
Topeka, Kansas, 36, 44
Tremont Hotel, 88
Tres Hermanas Mountains, 57, 66
Trinidad, New Mexico, 10
Tucker, C. A., "Italy", 138
Tucker, Dan, *passim*
Tucker, Maria, 147
Tucson, Arizona, 30, 48, 88, 91, 92, 106, 127, 151
Tutt, Dave, 168
Vail, Zack, 127
Van Patton, Eugene, 116
Ward, Don Jaun, 28, 39
Ward, Jerome L., 128-129, 135
Warden, John, 76
Warder's Café, 74
Ware, Nick, 131
Watts, John, 117
Webb, Abel, 13
Webster, Theopolis, 124, 132
Wells, Fargo & Company, 76, 100, 105, 125, 129, 142, 160

White, William, 94, 132
Whitehill, Harriet, 12
Whitehill, Harvey Howard, 4, 12-14,
    18-19, 25, 28, 30, 32, 49-52, 56,
    59, 61-73, 74-76, 90, 100-101,
    104, 107, 111, 117, 125-126, 131,
    143, 152-156, 172
Whitehill, Perrine P., 50, 104
Whitehill, Wayne, 12, 15, 29, 33, 87,
    111, 154, 156
Wickenburg, Arizona, 62
Williams, Charles, see Barney O'Tool
Williams, Charley, 55-59
Williams, J. 40
Williams, Willie, 137
Wilson, J. P., 76

Wilson, Steve, 131
Wolcott & Mills Saloon and Club
    House, 98
Woods, James D., 104, 107, 119, 125,
    130
Woods, John, 138
Woods, Ross, 54
Wright, J. M., 99, 101, 103
Young, Ewing, 21
Young, William, "Parson", "Silver
    Plate Dick", 49-50, 61, 64
Yavapai County Arizona, 62
Ysleta, Texas, 38-40
Yrigayen, Crescencio, 39
Yuma Territorial Prison, 130
Zuni Siding, 190

A retired Special Agent with the U.S. Treasury Department, and a former city detective, Bob Alexander is a thirty-five year law enforcement veteran. He currently teaches in the Criminal Justice program for Navarro College and is a Master certified Texas Peace Officer. Bob lives near Maypearl, Texas where he raises horses, and avidly pursues historic investigations into the escapades and exploits of Western frontier personalities.